Making good their escape from encirclement by the Axis, exhausted men and women of the Yugoslav Partisans trek through the woods near Miljevina in June 1943, after one of the toughest antiguerrilla campaigns of the war in the Balkans. More than 6,000 Partisans were killed in the four weeks of the German-led offensive.

PARTISANS AND GUERRILLAS

WORLD WAR II · TIME-LIFE BOOKS · ALEXANDRIA, VIRGINIA

BY RONALD H. BAILEY
AND THE EDITORS OF TIME-LIFE BOOKS

PARTISANS AND GUERRILLAS

Time-Life Books Inc.
is a wholly owned subsidiary of
TIME INCORPORATED

Founder: Henry R. Luce 1898-1967

Editor-in-Chief: Henry Anatole Grunwald
Chairman of the Board: Andrew Heiskell
President: James R. Shepley
Editorial Director: Ralph Graves
Vice Chairman: Arthur Temple

TIME-LIFE BOOKS INC.

Managing Editor: Jerry Korn
Executive Editor: David Maness
Assistant Managing Editors: Dale M. Brown
(planning), George Constable, George G. Daniels
(acting), Martin Mann, John Paul Porter
Art Director: Tom Suzuki
Chief of Research: David L. Harrison
Director of Photography: Robert G. Mason
Assistant Art Director: Arnold C. Holeywell
Assistant Chief of Research: Carolyn L. Sackett
Assistant Director of Photography: Dolores A. Littles

Chairman: Joan D. Manley
President: John D. McSweeney
Executive Vice Presidents: Carl G. Jaeger,
John Steven Maxwell, David J. Walsh
Vice Presidents: George Artandi (comptroller);
Stephen L. Bair (legal counsel); Peter G. Barnes;
Nicholas Benton (public relations);
John L. Canova; Beatrice T. Dobie (personnel);
Carol Flaumenhaft (consumer affairs);
Nicholas J. C. Ingleton (Asia); James L. Mercer
(Europe/South Pacific); Herbert Sorkin
(production); Paul R. Stewart (marketing)

WORLD WAR II

Editorial Staff for *Partisans and Guerrillas*
Editor: William K. Goolrick
Picture Editor/Designer: Raymond Ripper
Text Editor: Gerald Simons
Staff Writers: Brian McGinn, Tyler Mathisen,
Teresa M. C. R. Pruden, Henry Woodhead
Chief Researcher: Frances G. Youssef
Researchers: Marion F. Briggs, Josephine Burke,
Oobie Gleysteen, Chadwick Gregson, Helga Kohl
Art Assistant: Mary L. Orr
Editorial Assistant: Connie Strawbridge

Editorial Production
Production Editor: Douglas B. Graham
Operations Manager: Gennaro C. Esposito,
Gordon E. Buck (assistant)
Assistant Production Editor: Feliciano Madrid
Quality Control: Robert L. Young (director),
James J. Cox (assistant), Daniel J. McSweeney,
Michael G. Wight (associates)
Art Coordinator: Anne B. Landry
Copy Staff: Susan B. Galloway (chief), Victoria Lee,
Patricia Graber, Celia Beattie
Picture Department: Alvin L. Ferrell

Correspondents: Elisabeth Kraemer (Bonn);
Margot Hapgood, Dorothy Bacon, Lesley Coleman
(London); Susan Jonas, Lucy T. Voulgaris (New
York); Maria Vincenza Aloisi, Josephine du Brusle
(Paris); Ann Natanson (Rome). Valuable assistance
was also provided by: Dean Brelis, Mirca Gondicas
(Athens); Pavle Svabic (Belgrade); Martha Mader
(Bonn); Anne Angus, Karin B. Pearce (London);
Carolyn T. Chubet, Miriam Hsia, Christina
Lieberman (New York); Mimi Murphy (Rome);
Traudl Lessing (Vienna).

The Author: RONALD H. BAILEY is a freelance
author and journalist who was formerly a senior
editor of LIFE. He is the author of two volumes in
TIME-LIFE BOOKS' Human Behavior series, *Violence and Aggression* and *The Role of the Brain*,
and an earlier volume in the World War II series,
The Home Front: U.S.A. He has written a photography book, *The Photographic Illusion: Duane
Michals*, was a contributor to *The Unknown Leonardo*, a book about the inventive genius of
Leonardo da Vinci, and is now a contributing editor for *American Photographer* magazine. While at
LIFE, he edited a book of Larry Burrows' war photographs, *Larry Burrows: Compassionate Photographer*. He and his wife and four children live on a
farm in New York State.

The Consultants: COL. JOHN R. ELTING, USA
(Ret.), is a military historian and author of *The
Battle of Bunker's Hill, The Battles of Saratoga* and
Military History and Atlas of the Napoleonic Wars.
He edited *Military Uniforms in America: The Era
of the American Revolution, 1755-1795* and *Mili-
tary Uniforms in America: Years of Growth, 1796-
1851*, and was associate editor of *The West Point
Atlas of American Wars.*

JAMES BARROS teaches in the Department of Political Economy, Erindale College, University
of Toronto. He is the author of *The Corfu Incident of 1923: Mussolini and the League of Nations*
and *The League of Nations and the Great Powers: The Greek-Bulgarian Incident, 1925*, among
other books.

MICHAEL M. MILENKOVITCH, who was born in
Yugoslavia, received his B.A. in politics and jour-
nalism at Ohio Wesleyan University and his M.I.A.
and Ph.D. in international affairs and Soviet area
studies at Columbia University. He teaches in the
Political Science Department of Lehman College
of the City University of New York, and is the
author of *The View from Red Square* and *Milovan
Djilas: An Annotated Bibliography* and the co-
editor of *Milovan Djilas: Parts of a Lifetime.*

Library of Congress Cataloging in Publication Data

Bailey, Ronald H.
 Partisans and guerrillas.

 (World War II; v. 12)
 Bibliography: p.
 Includes index.
 1. World War, 1939-1945—Underground movements
—Balkan Peninsula. 2. Balkan Peninsula—History
—20th century. I. Time-Life Books. II. Title.
III. Series.
D802.B29B34   940.53'496   78-2949
ISBN 0-8094-2492-4
ISBN 0-8094-2491-6 lib. bdg.

For information about any Time-Life book, please write:

Reader Information
Time-Life Books
541 North Fairbanks Court
Chicago, Illinois 60611

CHAPTERS

PICTURE ESSAYS

CONTENTS

A ROYAL CAST OF CHARACTERS

Dressed in Albanian national costume, King Zog attempts a regal stance while being photographed with members of his family in the palmy days of his reign.

STORMY POLITICS OF THREE UNRULY REALMS

Long before World War II swept through Albania, Greece and Yugoslavia, violence and intrigue were a way of life there. For years, the Balkan countries had been racked by religious wars, boundary disputes, blood feuds, coups d'état and assassinations. The violence rose to a crescendo in 1914 when a Serbian shot the Austrian Duke Franz Ferdinand, igniting the First World War. And even in 1918, when the War ended, the Balkans remained in turmoil.

Yugoslavia was embroiled in internal disputes, which led to the murder of the Minister of the Interior in 1921 and the shooting of five deputies in Parliament in 1928. Appalled by this bloodshed, King Alexander I imposed a dictatorship on his realm, and in 1934 an agent of Croatian terrorists gunned him down. Because the heir to the throne, Peter, was only 11, Alexander's cousin Prince Paul took charge as regent. His pro-German policies stirred up more rebellion.

Albania was also plagued by unrest. Between July and December, 1921, the government changed hands five times. In 1928 a Moslem chieftain named Ahmed Bey Zogu declared himself King Zog I. But vendettas and murders were so common that the King feared for his life. He surrounded himself with guards and disarmed thousands of Albanian tribesmen; it was even said that his mother prepared his meals for fear he would be poisoned. Despite such precautions, he almost lost his life on a visit to Vienna in 1931, when he was forced with his guards to fight a gun duel with would-be assassins on the steps of the opera house.

The Greek monarchy was even more unstable than Albania's. King Alexander I—the only one of five Greek Kings who had not been overthrown or assassinated since 1829—suddenly died in 1920 after suffering the ignominy of being bitten by a monkey. For the next 15 years, Greece alternated between a republic and a monarchy. In 1935 exiled King George II, who had ruled briefly in the 1920s, regained his throne, but he proved to be weak and unpopular.

At the outset of World War II, all three countries—Albania, Yugoslavia and Greece—were disunited, unstable, headed by vulnerable regimes and ripe for Axis conquest.

The assassin of King Alexander I of Yugoslavia fights it out with French gendarmes beside the King's car in Marseilles, France, on October 9, 1934.

Hand on sword, King Alexander of Yugoslavia oversees a commemorative ceremony in Tzer honoring the Serbian soldiers who died in the First World War.

Shortly before abdicating in 1923, George II, Greece's powerless King, takes a ride in his touring car.

Premier John Metaxas, the dictator who ruled Greece from 1936 to 1941, delivers a speech.

Back in power, George II confers with his first Prime Minister, George Kondylis, in 1935.

A FLOUNDERING, FEEBLE MONARCH

When the war began, the nominal ruler of Greece was George II, but he had proved to be an unpopular King, largely because of his heritage. There was not a drop of Greek blood in his veins: George was the descendant of a Danish prince who had been foisted upon the Greeks in 1863 by the European powers after the country had been wrested from Turkish control.

To make matters worse, George insisted on acting like a foreigner. He had spent so much time in exile in England that he thought, talked and conducted himself like an Englishman. And in Greece he was insulated from most of his subjects by the entourage with which he surrounded himself.

The heir to the throne, Prince Paul (right) had no more understanding of his country than his brother: he spent most of his young manhood hundreds of miles away, living it up on the Riviera.

For a while, John Metaxas, King George's iron-fisted Prime Minister, kept the realm under control, but when he died suddenly in January of 1941, Greece was rudderless. Four months afterward, the hapless King George was driven from his throne by German invaders.

A lover of sports, cars and women, Paul I, the playboy crown prince of Greece, sails with a lady friend in the waters off Southampton, England, in 1929.

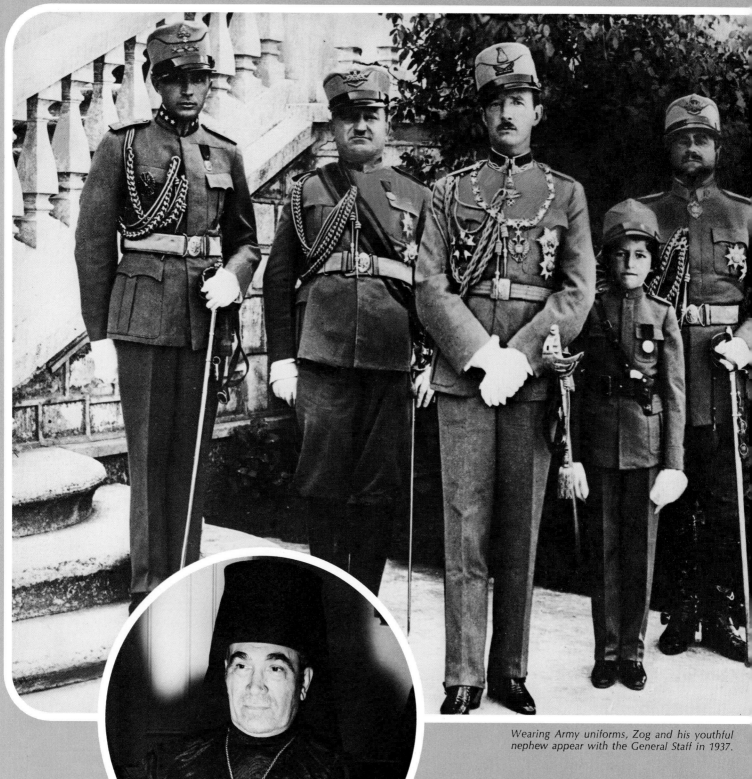

Wearing Army uniforms, Zog and his youthful nephew appear with the General Staff in 1937.

King Zog's fiercest opponent, Bishop Fan S. Noli, was a Harvard University graduate who became Albania's Premier in July 1924.

THE SPENDTHRIFT WAYS OF A SELF-MADE KING

Albania's King Zog was born of hill-tribe stock in 1895. He became Premier at the age of 27, and after overthrowing his arch-enemy Bishop Fan S. Noli *(left)*, assumed the Presidency at 30. At 33, he crowned himself King.

Once he reached the pinnacle of power,

Wearing a pained expression, King Zog is wed to Countess Geraldine Apponyi of Hungary in 1938.

however, Zog opted for a life of luxury instead of discharging his responsibilities. He squandered money on sumptuous carpets and swanky automobiles, and he kept a mistress. His household cost Albania half a million gold francs a year or 2.5 per cent of the country's total revenue. And when the Italians invaded Albania in 1939, he left the country, reportedly taking with him some four million dollars from the Albanian Treasury.

In the company of his beloved sisters, the King takes a breath of fresh air at his summer residence.

King Alexander, his wife and mother-in-law, Queen Marie of Rumania, go for a ride in a special rail car.

A TRIO OF UNSUITABLE RULERS

Between 1929 and 1941 Yugoslavia was ruled by three men in succession, none of whom was suited to reign.

King Alexander was a military man, with little enthusiasm for the monarchy. He detested the pomp and circumstance of his position, shied away from publicity and never allowed himself to be crowned. He lived in a spartan, simply furnished house in Belgrade and was so frugal that he had his old handkerchiefs mended. But Alexander permitted himself two extravaganc-es. He amassed a library of 20,000 books and acquired a stable of 23 Packard cars.

When Alexander died, his 11-year-old son Peter was too young to rule. Alexander's cousin Paul, whom the King had named regent in his will, assumed command, but he was a connoisseur of music, literature and painting, and he found Yugoslav politics unbearably dull. As regent he flitted back and forth to Germany for receptions with Hitler and lunches with Goebbels. In March 1941, Yugoslav officers overthrew his regency and put Peter on the throne. Three short weeks later, Peter himself was swept away—by the invading Germans.

On one of many trips to Germany, Prince Paul (left) chats with Luftwaffe Chief Hermann Göring.

Arriving in Belgrade for his father's funeral in 1934, the newly ascended King Peter II greets some of his generals while Prince Paul (center) stands nearby.

1

At 3 o'clock in the morning there was a knock on the door of John Metaxas, and the Greek Prime Minister stumbled sleepily downstairs in a dressing gown and slippers. Standing on his doorstep at that odd and ominous hour on October 28, 1940, was Emmanuel Grazzi, the Italian minister. Grazzi had a message to deliver from the Italian dictator, Benito Mussolini. It was blunt and menacing. The Italian Army wanted to occupy "a number of strategic points" in Greece "as a guarantee of Greece's neutrality." It was a trick borrowed from Hitler, who in 1940 had justified his aggression against neutral Denmark, Norway, Belgium, the Netherlands and Luxembourg on the ground that he was compelled to safeguard their neutrality. Arrogantly, Mussolini did not even bother to identify the points in Greece that needed protection, and he gave Metaxas just three hours to acquiesce.

A short, portly man of 69, Metaxas had the look of a complacent business executive. But beneath his insignificant appearance was the steel of a soldier—not to mention the character of a martinet. Metaxas had studied military science in Germany and, years before, had served as chief of the Greek General Staff. He had ruled Greece as its dictator since 1936; he had adopted the Fascist stiff-armed salute, had organized a national youth group, EON, which was an imitation of Hitler's and Mussolini's youth movements, had modeled his secret police after the Gestapo and had banned "subversive hymns to democracy"—such as the writings of some of his country's ancient philosophers and playwrights. He was no stranger to the uses of terror.

But he was, above all, a Greek, a fierce patriot who would make no compromise with threats from abroad—and he quickly made that clear to his Italian visitor. "Mr. Minister," Metaxas said, "I could not make a decision to sell my own house on a few hours' notice. How do you expect me to sell my country?"

With a crisp "No!" he rejected the ultimatum out of hand. Less than three hours later Italian troops crossed the Greek border, and the word *Ochi*—"No!"—became a battle cry in the streets of Athens. (Ochi Day, October 28, has been a Greek national holiday ever since.)

The kind of steely patriotism that moved Metaxas was a legacy shared by many of Greece's Balkan neighbors, and it had been tested often over the centuries. The mountainous

HITLER'S SOUTHERN FLANK

Balkan Peninsula, strategically located astride crossroads linking Europe, Asia and the Middle East, had attracted a long parade of aggressors: Romans, Huns, Slavs, Bulgars, Franks, Byzantines, Venetians, Hungarians, Crusaders, Austrians, Ottoman Turks, French. These invaders had little trouble conquering the Balkan countries, which were generally weak and divided by bitter ethnic and religious rivalries. But then, after surrender, real resistance traditionally began. The people would form small guerrilla bands and, skillfully using the rugged terrain to their advantage, harass the invaders with hit-and-run attacks.

The Balkan peoples in general and the Greeks, Serbs and Albanians in particular were experts at guerrilla warfare. The guerrillas of Greece and Serbia (which later became part of Yugoslavia) had repeatedly defeated the Turks in the 19th Century. And any new conqueror of those countries was certain to face a long, costly and frustrating war with "shadow armies"—the elusive, death-dealing guerrilla bands.

When Mussolini decided to add Greece to his empire, he already had a foothold next door. In April 1939 his army had quickly and easily occupied Greece's northwestern neighbor, Albania, the smallest of the Balkan countries.

Mussolini had next chosen Yugoslavia for conquest, but Hitler had emphatically vetoed that plan. In his own timetable for world conquest, the Führer required stability in the Balkans. In July of 1940 he had begun a year of preparation for his boldest venture, the invasion of the Soviet Union. It was essential that his armies' right flank be secure for the grandiose assault. Moreover, nothing must interrupt the steady flow of raw materials from the region: Balkan oil fueled his Luftwaffe and panzer divisions; Balkan chrome, manganese, copper, aluminum, lead, nickel and tin supplied his factories.

Germany's economic dominance of the area and its tacit threat of invasion all but assured Hitler that he would get what he wanted there. But to guarantee the submission of Rumania, Bulgaria and Yugoslavia, he proposed that they join the Tripartite Pact of the Berlin-Rome-Tokyo Axis, which would allow him to station German troops in those countries without a struggle. Rumania soon succumbed to German pressure and signed up as an Axis ally, and Hitler was confident that Bulgaria and Yugoslavia would follow

suit in spite of desperate British efforts to prevent it. For the moment at least, Hitler saw no reason to roil the Balkans by using military aggression there.

But Mussolini's ambitions were not to be contained. Since Hitler had denied him permission to grab Yugoslavia, he would take Greece instead—and he would do it without consulting Hitler. After all, the Führer never informed the Duce of his own invasion plans. "Hitler always confronts me with a *fait accompli*," Mussolini told Count Galeazzo Ciano, his foreign minister and son-in-law. "This time I am going to pay him back in his own coin."

Shortly after the invasion of Greece started, Mussolini broke the news to Hitler at a meeting in Florence. "Führer," he announced, "we are on the march." Hitler hid his anger, but he had no such reticence with his own generals. He told one of them that the Greek adventure was nothing but a *Schweinerei*—a swine's mess. It was that indeed: the British, under a 1939 treaty guaranteeing Greece's territorial integrity, were already beginning to send airplanes to Greece. Hitler knew he was doomed to become involved in what he had tried so hard to avoid—warfare in the Balkans.

In his determination to show Hitler that he could act on his own, Mussolini underestimated the Greeks and overestimated his own army. In Albania, his springboard for the invasion, he had assembled only nine divisions—some 100,000 troops. His own generals were doubters: they told him it would take an army more than twice that size to invade and occupy Greece. To compound his error, Mussolini was committing Italy to a second major battlefront while he was heavily engaged in East and North Africa.

Furthermore, the Duce gave his army only two weeks to get ready, picking October 28 for the invasion, to celebrate his successful march on Rome on that date in 1922. He felt sure his countrymen would be delighted by his new invasion. "I shall send in my resignation as an Italian," he told Ciano, "if anyone objects to our fighting the Greeks." He correctly predicted the reactions at least of those who would do the fighting: the Italian troops in Albania were as eager for the attack as Mussolini was. As the Army moved toward the Greek border, some soldiers brought along supplies of silk stockings and contraceptives.

The Italian invasion took the form of a three-pronged advance into Epirus and the Pindus Mountains of northwest

AN EASY FIRST STEP INTO THE BALKANS

Black-plumed Bersaglieri push their bicycles along the shoreline after landing at the port of Durazzo on the second day of the Italian invasion.

In the spring of 1939, after completing the conquest of Ethiopia, Italian dictator Benito Mussolini fixed his gaze on the tiny kingdom of Albania. Only 47 miles from the heel of the Italian boot, it was conveniently located for an attack on Greece and was already economically dominated by the Italians.

On the morning of April 7, 1939, the Duce sent an ultimatum to Albania's King Zog. When Zog refused to yield, four regiments of the Bersaglieri *(above),* an elite infantry division, several Air Force detachments and a naval squadron launched an attack against the Albanian port of Durazzo. The Albanians could not withstand the Italian onslaught and Zog, his Queen and their five-day-old son fled to Greece.

On the next day, Italian armored troops marched into Tirana, the capital. By April 12, Italian Foreign Minister Count Galeazzo Ciano *(right)* could write in his diary "Independent Albania is no more."

In Tirana, Foreign Minister Ciano (front, center) is saluted by a youth-corps member.

Greece. The northern prong was to seize the town of Florina and then push on toward Salonika, Greece's key port on the northern Aegean Sea. The southern prong would head down the coast of the Adriatic. The middle prong—consisting of two columns—was to proceed into the Pindus Mountains toward Metsovon, where an important pass controlled the main road leading southeast and east. From Metsovon the way would be open for the Italians, with their superior armor backed by overwhelming air power, to push down into central Greece.

But the Greeks were not nearly so helpless nor as ill-prepared as Mussolini had assumed. Metaxas was aware of the military build-up on his borders, and one of his accomplishments in his four years as dictator had been to strengthen his nation's defenses. In the tense months before the invasion, he had quietly begun mobilizing the Greek Army, calling up three divisions and part of a fourth so deceptively that even the Greek public had no clue to the size or nature of each call-up. By October he had more than two divisions on the Albanian front.

Once the attack began the Greeks had a second advantage over their better-armed invaders. They were defending their homeland. Not only did they have shorter lines of communication and supply, they had something to fight for and they knew the terrain.

Although normally split by political strife, the Greeks were united now as they never had been before. Fashionable ladies of Athens trekked to the mountains to organize hospitals. Peasants in villages near the front helped carry supplies. The Greek soldiers, defending their native mountains, could make the most out of narrow passes and jagged uplands where Italian tanks could not maneuver. As the three prongs of the Italian advance stabbed into their homeland, the Greeks carefully avoided frontal clashes in the valleys. While letting the Italians move forward with little resistance, they built up strength along the higher slopes of their mountain ranges.

Then, in the Pindus Mountains, about 15 miles from the vital pass at Metsovon, the middle prong of the Italian advance suddenly ran into trouble. The Italian spearhead was the 3rd (Julia) Alpine Division, a unit of 10,800 men named for the region they came from, the Julian Alps, and regarded as one of the best in the nation. As the 3rd went deeper into the mountains it met stiffening resistance. Its advance slowed—and stopped. On November 3 the division found itself under pressure on three sides from Greek forces. Then the Greek troops forced the Italians to give ground. The tide had turned.

The Greeks, pressing their classic mountain tactics in the days that followed, moved steadily forward along high-ridge lines, harassing the Julia Division as it retreated slowly along the valley roads below. Traveling in closely coordinated small units, the Greeks transported their light mountain guns and ammunition on the backs of sure-footed mules. Their food was supplied by local peasants. From time to time, Greek forces would descend in coordinated attacks, taking Italian units by surprise and forcing them to surrender. Finally the whole vaunted Julia Division broke and ran. It had lost, in dead, wounded and prisoners, fully one fifth of its strength.

By November 13 the Greeks had regained the territory taken by the Italians. The following day they seized the offensive and invaded Albania all along the northwestern front. Now the Italians were retreating so rapidly that cargo planes, sent to supply them by airdrops, showered bags of grain on the pursuing Greeks. On November 22 the Greeks captured Koritsa, an Italian base 20 miles inside the Albanian border, and pressed on again. By the end of the year, the Greeks were in control of more than one quarter of Albania, including the Adriatic port of Saranda, which the Italians had renamed Porto Edda in honor of Mussolini's daughter, Countess Ciano.

This dramatic success was a heady tonic for the Greeks. It seemed to be a classic instance of David smiting Goliath. Italy had 45 million people, more than five times the population of Greece, and it had far greater resources. In fact, the Greeks seemed more likely to be slowed by supply shortages than by the Italians. At one point the Greek counteroffensive stalled because there was no more ammunition; one unit was reported to have attacked an Italian outpost with clubbed rifles and rocks, capturing enough ammunition in the process to continue its advance into Albania. Many Greek soldiers were forced to live on little more than bread and olives; as a result, they lost so much weight that American correspondent Leland Stowe reported

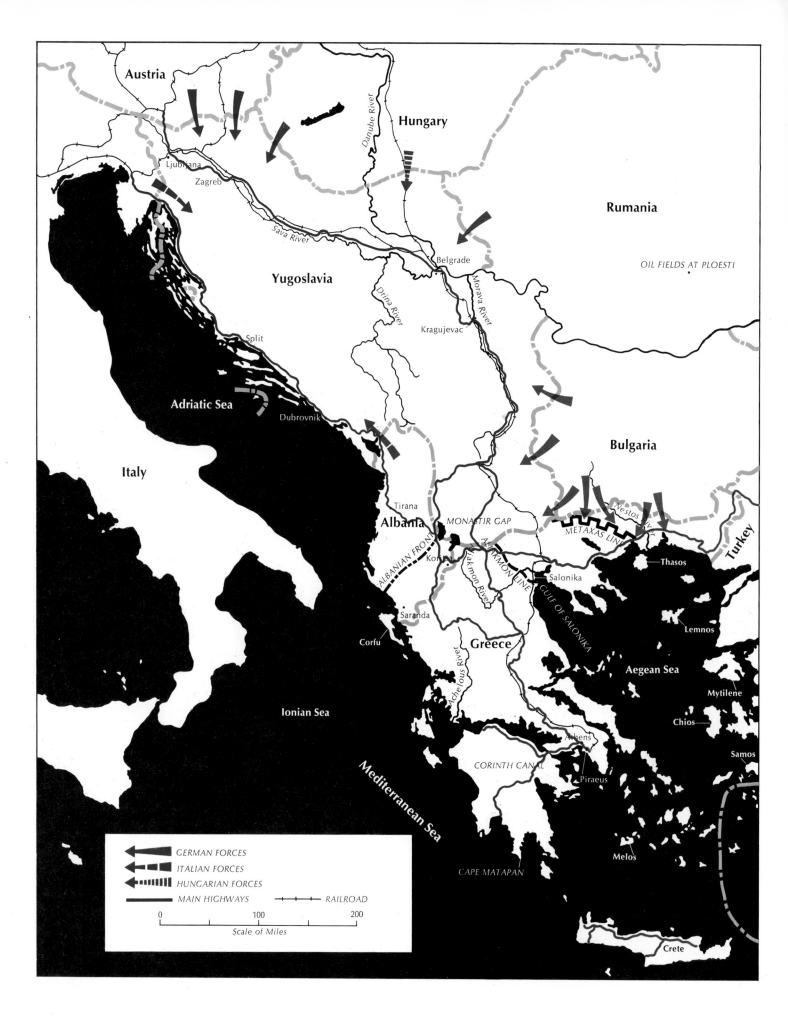

Austria

Hungary

Danube River

Rumania

OIL FIELDS AT PLOESTI

Ljubljana

Zagreb

Sava River

Yugoslavia

Belgrade

Drina River

Morava River

Kragujevac

Split

Adriatic Sea

Bulgaria

Dubrovnik

Italy

Tirana

Albania

MONASTIR GAP

Nestos River

METAXAS LINE

ALBANIAN FRONT

Korça

ALIAKMON LINE

Thasos

Salonika

GULF OF SALONIKA

Turkey

Saranda

Greece

Corfu

Achelous River

Aliakmon River

Ionian Sea

Lemnos

Aegean Sea

Mytilene

Chios

Athens

CORINTH CANAL

Samos

Piraeus

Melos

CAPE MATAPAN

Mediterranean Sea

⬅ GERMAN FORCES
⬅ ITALIAN FORCES
⬅ HUNGARIAN FORCES
━━ MAIN HIGHWAYS   ┼┼┼ RAILROAD

0   100   200
Scale of Miles

Crete

20

their uniforms "seemed about two sizes too big for them."

The David-Goliath legend was nurtured by stories of Greek derring-do, especially the exploits of the country's ragtag air force. At one point, in January 1941, the Greek air detachment at Koritsa in Albania consisted of just two pilots who flew a couple of outmoded Potez light bombers. In between missions the pilots were said to spend all of their time playing cards, interrupting their games only to tell each other the latest jokes about the Italians. The taller of the two, a lanky man with a black beard, was known as "The Dervish," for the elusive aerial maneuvers he performed in his lumbering Potez. On some missions he would take along the most insulting objects he could find to drop on the Italians after his bombs were expended—tin cans, old boots, chamber pots.

His contempt for the Italians was shared by most Greeks. In Athens an old Greek woman saw some Italian prisoners taken during the first four months of the war and said disdainfully, "I feel sorry for them. They are not warriors. They should carry mandolins instead of rifles."

In fact, the Italian troops were less to blame for their failures than were their generals. Italian journalist Mario Cervi, who served with the Italian Army in Greece and Albania, later wrote that the war was bungled from the outset. Before the invasion, for example, the Italian generals organized 250 Albanian saboteurs to infiltrate Greece; the Albanians pocketed their working capital and disappeared. Italian logistics were so poor that at one point no fewer than 30,000 transport animals and their drivers piled up at one port in Italy.

Mussolini made the campaign much more difficult by firing his distinguished chief of the General Staff, Marshal Pietro Badoglio, and awarding top commands to two incompetent generals. The first, General Visconti Prasca—a supposed expert on surprise attack who had written a book called *Lightning War*—permitted many of his tanks to bog down in the mountains instead of using them to exploit a short-lived breakthrough onto the plains to the west. Prasca's replacement, General Ubaldo Soddu, was dismissed after Mussolini discovered he was spending his spare time at the front composing music for commercial films. Considering all the mistakes that were made, said journalist Cervi—including the inadequacy of the invading force—"it

was not a battle between David and Goliath, but between two Davids, one of whom had right on his side."

Despite the inept Italian leadership and their own fighting spirit, the Greeks were finally forced to halt their offensive in Albania. They were stopped by logistical problems, compounded by one of the harshest winters in years. It was so cold on the mountain peaks—15° below zero—that rifle breeches froze shut, and so blustery that guns were blown over icy precipices. For warmth, numbers of Greeks dug large holes, covered themselves with blankets and slept in clumps. In blizzards "it was impossible to distinguish between friend and foe until the last moment," recalled a Greek infantryman, "and then the man who threw his hand grenade first was the winner."

Neither side had proper clothing or footwear, and frostbite soon became the most dreaded enemy. In mountain trenches thousands of men failed to realize they were freezing until they noticed that their feet were growing numb and swelling. Many victims had to be carried down on the backs of their comrades. Others hobbled painfully; by the time they reached a hospital, their feet often were two or three times larger than normal and had begun to turn black. Of the Greek war's estimated 110,000 dead and wounded, perhaps as many as one tenth suffered amputations as a result of frostbite.

From the warmth and comfort of his Palazzo Venezio, Mussolini announced that he was delighted with the toll taken by the cold. It snowed in Rome that Christmas, and he chose the occasion for a brief sermon: "This snow and cold are very good. In this way our good-for-nothing men and this mediocre race will be improved."

He was, nonetheless, growing increasingly impatient with the military stalemate that prevailed on the Albanian front through much of the winter. The Greeks, with their supply lines overextended and their troops exhausted, could advance no farther. The Italians, despite a gradual build-up to 28 divisions from the original nine, could not regain the offensive. Finally, early in March, as the snows began to melt in the valleys, Mussolini himself went to the front to "put an end to this passivity."

For the trip to Albania, the Duce piloted his own plane, wearing a flight suit over his beribboned uniform as Marshal

The attack on Greece and Yugoslavia got under way on the 6th of April, 1941, when German forces started to move across the borders at the points shown. After the Germans' initial assaults, Hungarian and Italian armies joined in the invasion. With Axis forces controlling both countries by late April, the stage was set for the formation of well-organized bands of guerrillas in Yugoslavia and Greece, who took to the mountains and began striking back at the invaders with deadly effect.

of the Italian Empire. At the front, he strutted to well-rehearsed demonstrations of support by his haggard troops and strolled among the wounded, bending down to say, "I am the Duce and I bring you the greetings of the Fatherland." When one soldier, his stomach torn open by a grenade, retorted, "Well, now, isn't that great," Mussolini moved quickly on.

On the morning of March 9, the Italians obliged their Duce with a final all-out offensive. To oversee it Mussolini climbed to an observation post high above a valley in the central sector of the Albanian front. In two hours some 100,000 rounds of artillery were fired. Then troops started forward along a 20-mile-wide front. Mussolini stayed at the post until late afternoon, long enough to see that his heralded offensive was failing. He left Albania 12 days later. "I am disgusted by this environment," he complained. "We have not advanced one step."

As Mussolini departed Albania, help was already being planned by Hitler. Back in November 1940, soon after the Italians invaded Greece, Hitler had decided to intervene with German troops. He was less interested in bailing out Mussolini than in ridding Greece of the threat of British air bases, from which RAF bombers could reach the Rumanian oil fields at Ploesti. Worse, British air power in the Balkans might jeopardize Operation *Barbarossa*, the invasion of Russia that was scheduled for May 1941.

Anxious though he was to avoid any delay in Operation *Barbarossa*, Hitler decided that he could afford to wait for the harsh Greek winter to end before sending his devastating panzer armies into Greece. While he waited, two events played into his hands: in January 1941, Metaxas died following a throat operation, leaving Greece without a strong leader; two months later Bulgaria signed the Tripartite Pact, clearing the way through that country for Greece-bound German troops based in Rumania. All the while, Hitler tried to fool the Greek government into thinking he was still

friendly. In Athens the wife of the German ambassador helped nurse Greeks wounded in the war against Italy. When the Greeks captured Koritsa, the German legation joined in the celebration by hoisting a Greek flag in honor of the occasion.

Whatever the effect of such activities on the Greek government, the British were well aware of Hitler's duplicity. In March, *Ultra*—the remarkable British counterintelligence operation that had broken the top-secret German military code—deciphered a directive from the Führer ordering his troops in Rumania to prepare for an invasion of Greece by moving south into Bulgaria. Although the necessity of keeping *Ultra's* success a secret prevented British Prime Minister Winston Churchill from sharing his knowledge with the Greeks, he did offer the aid of British ground troops.

The Greeks finally accepted the offer. But they guessed—correctly—that Churchill could not spare enough men from the campaign in North Africa to make a difference against a German invasion force. And they feared that the presence in Greece of a token British expeditionary force might only further enrage Hitler. The Greek government was so anxious to avoid provoking Hitler that as late as March, as British and Commonwealth troops were pouring into Greece, the government insisted that the commander, Lieut. General Sir Henry Maitland "Jumbo" Wilson, remain incognito as "Mr. Watt," even though the Germans were bound to recognize him by his conspicuous height and bulk. Meanwhile, German diplomats in Athens kept close tabs on incoming British forces. The German military attaché even went so far as to board one troop ship after it docked and chat with British soldiers while having a look around.

The British countered by attempting to knock out the radio transmitter that the German legation used for sending newly gathered intelligence back to Berlin. British agents managed to silence the transmitter briefly by overloading its power line. This expedient brought protests from the build-

Trudging through the snow in the winter of 1940, Greek troops search out Italians in the mountains of southern Albania. So severe was the weather that among the Italians alone it was said that 40 men froze to death daily.

Greek troops lead a train of pack mules along a hazardous mountain trail in northern Greece during the fighting against the invading Italians in 1940. In some mountain areas the terrain was so rough that mules lost their footing and fell into ravines, leaving the men to carry remaining supplies on their own backs.

23

ing's other occupants, including a dentist who was drilling a patient's tooth at the time.

While convoys were still ferrying British soldiers from Egypt to Greece late in March, an important naval battle was about to begin in the shipping lanes of the eastern Mediterranean. Since the previous November, when British carrier-based torpedo planes had crippled three battleships in the harbor of Taranto, Italy, the Italian fleet had done little but convoy ships to Libya. Now the Germans, promising help from the Luftwaffe, induced the Italians to intercept British troop convoys near southern Greece.

Admiral of the Fleet Sir Andrew B. Cunningham, commander of the British Mediterranean naval forces, learned of the new threat through *Ultra* and devised an elaborate two-step ruse to confuse the Italians. First, to keep *Ultra's* code cracking a secret from the Germans, he ordered a reconnaissance plane to fly close enough to the Italian fleet to be seen. This was designed to make the Italians think their fleet had been detected from the air. Then, on the afternoon of March 27, Cunningham made a show of sauntering ashore at his Egyptian base in Alexandria carrying his overnight bag and golf clubs. His arrival was sure to be noticed by the Japanese consul general, who kept his European Axis partners informed of the comings and goings of the British Navy. After dark, Cunningham hurried back to his flagship, H.M.S. *Warspite,* and steamed out of Alexandria in pursuit of the Italian fleet.

Cunningham's powerful force—three battleships, the aircraft carrier *Formidable,* four cruisers and 13 destroyers—caught up with the Italians the next day off Cape Matapan on the southern tip of Greece. The battle of Matapan was joined that night, and the British, with the help of two weapons the Italians lacked—radar and carrier-based planes—scored a decisive victory. The Italians, who received little of the air support Hitler had promised, lost three heavy cruisers, two destroyers and 2,400 men; the British lost one torpedo plane. After the battle the British rescued some 900 enemy sailors from the water. So one-sided was the British victory that Mussolini ordered his fleet confined to waters under firm Italian control.

The British had won naval domination of the seas around Greece. This was an absolute necessity: even as the Royal Navy carried troops from North Africa to Greece, British admirals were making contingency plans for their evacuation.

About the same time that the Italians were suffering their devastating defeat at Matapan, Hitler received some good news from Yugoslavia. On March 25, Yugoslavia's regent, Prince Paul, finally signed the Tripartite Pact. But that triumph was short-lived. Only 48 hours later a group of anti-German Army and Air Force officers staged a coup in Belgrade in protest of Paul's surrender to the Axis. The patriotic rebels sent Paul into exile and placed his 17-year-old cousin Peter on the throne, at the head of a new government that resolutely favored the Allies. Thus almost overnight, Yugoslavia became an enemy of Germany and Italy.

The Allies rejoiced. The presence of an anti-German government in Yugoslavia was considered vital by Churchill; he had been trying for months to prevent Prince Paul from signing the Tripartite Pact allying Yugoslavia with the Axis powers, and British military intelligence agencies had financed opponents of the regent.

For whatever help it received from outside the country, the coup was still an expression of Yugoslav nationalism. To royalists like Colonel Dragoljub (Drazha) Mihailovich, an Army staff officer and an advocate of guerrilla warfare, the uprising that put Peter on the throne was a heroic chapter in the long struggle against foreign aggressors. To the Communists and their leader Josip Broz, it meant a war that would give them the opportunity to mount a proletarian revolution. Broz was the party's secretary general, a mysterious figure known by some two dozen aliases, one of them Tito.

Yugoslav patriots of every political stripe forgot their bitter differences and surged through the streets of Belgrade shouting, "Better war than the pact!" They smashed the windows of the German Tourist Bureau, spat on a limousine

The submarine Papanicolis, one of four owned by Greece at the start of the War, cruises on the surface of the Adriatic Sea. Though she was 14 years old, the sub was fit enough to sink 27,000 tons of Italian shipping in one week.

carrying the German minister and cheered as an elderly Serbian peasant clambered out onto the marquee above a well-known clothing store. "At last we are all together," the old man yelled to the crowd. "We can face anything now, even death."

Word of the Yugoslav coup spread across Europe "like sunshine," reported the well-known British political writer Rebecca West. The news raised morale in Poland and France. In Greece, where the population expected German soldiers at any moment to move to the rescue of Italian troops pinned down in the mountains, Athenians cheered their new ally to the north. In London, which was still digging out from the wreckage of the blitz, Churchill announced to the world that Yugoslavia had "found its soul."

But in Yugoslavia the great hopes stirred by the coup soon faltered. The new government under young King Peter and the new Prime Minister, General Dushan Simovich, found itself confronted by the same insoluble problems that had forced Prince Paul to succumb to Hitler's pressures.

One of those problems was Yugoslavia's dependence on Germany as a source of manufactured goods and a market for its minerals and farm products. A second problem was Yugoslavia's lack of internal unity, which had plagued the nation since its creation after World War I. Its largest ethnic groups were the Serbs, Croats and Slovenes. The Serbs, an aggressive people who dominated Yugoslav political life, wanted to run a highly centralized government. The Croats, who looked down upon the Serbs as a crude backwoods people, preferred a loose federation of fairly autonomous provinces. The antagonism was intensified by religious differences; the Serbs were largely Eastern Orthodox and the Croats were Roman Catholic. To make matters even worse, there were the Macedonians, who wanted to form a nation of their own out of bits of Yugoslavia, Greece and Bulgaria, and scattered groups of Germans, Albanians, Italians, Hungarians, Rumanians and Turks, all seeking to preserve their own identity.

Yugoslavia's most immediate problem was military encirclement by the Axis. Of its four Balkan neighbors, only Greece was still free of Axis domination, and even now German troops were poised in Bulgaria to make quick work of Greece. Subservience to Germany had been Prince Paul's last forlorn hope of preserving Yugoslav independence. He

had taken this tack in spite of his strong ties to England. He was Oxford-educated and his sister-in-law was a member of the British royal house, but he had realized that Britain could not help him. For all Britain's and America's efforts to persuade him to resist Hitler, neither country had given him any hope for immediate military aid. "You big nations are hard," Paul told the American minister a week before the coup that deposed him. "You talk of our honor but you are far away."

Now, as King Peter and his generals grasped these grim realities in the waning days of March, they rapidly adopted the policies of the government that they had just overthrown. Anxious not to provoke Hitler, they assured the Germans that Yugoslavia would respect all existing treaties, including even the Tripartite Pact. They kept secret their military contacts with British and Greek officials, delayed ordering full-scale mobilization of the armed forces and even agreed to pay compensation for damage inflicted on German shops in Belgrade during the rowdy celebrations that followed the coup.

But there never was any chance of placating Hitler. On the very day of the coup, he had ordered his High Command to plan a full-scale invasion of Yugoslavia to coincide, if possible, with his thrust into Greece and to guard his invading army's right flank. Hitler also wanted to punish the Yugoslavs. "We will burn out for good the festering sore in the Balkans," Hitler told the Hungarian minister in Berlin. The Führer insisted that the invasion be carried out with unmerciful harshness in order to destroy Yugoslavia militarily and as a national entity. Ironically, the message outlining Hitler's invasion plans arrived in Rome during the night, and the chagrined bumbler who had stirred up the Balkan hornets in the first place, Benito Mussolini, had to be dragged out of bed to hear the contents.

The German General Staff planned the invasion with amazing speed, but there was a security leak, and the Yugoslav military attaché in Berlin, Colonel Vladimir Vauhnik, learned of the coming attack. He immediately notified his government. But Prime Minister Simovich thought that Vauhnik was being tricked, and he took no action. In his only positive move, designed to gain support for his fledgling government, Simovich had his minister sign a treaty of friendship and nonaggression with the Soviet Union on the night of April 5.

In Belgrade, April 6 dawned bright and sunny, bringing thousands into the streets very early in the morning. Some people were going to church or to market. Others, mainly Communists and their sympathizers, were assembling to demonstrate their support for the treaty that had just been signed with Russia.

The German planes appeared overhead shortly before 7 a.m. from the direction of Rumania and Austria. They came in waves of 30—the Messerschmitt-109s and Messerschmitt-110s, single- and twin-engine fighter planes, at 12,000 feet; the Dornier-17s and Heinkel bombers at 10,000 feet; the dreaded Stuka dive bombers at 2,000 feet and below. The first bombs fell on the royal palace, the War Ministry and other government buildings, including the National Library, where more than 1,300 medieval manuscripts—priceless relics of Serbian history—went up in flames. Soon the bombs were falling on hospitals, churches, schools and homes.

Belgrade had been destroyed 37 times by invading armies in its more than 2,000 years of existence, but never with such brutal efficiency as in this attack, which Hitler had bluntly code-named Operation *Punishment*. No one will ever know how many died—later estimates ranged from 4,000 to 20,000—but scenes of devastation were everywhere. Near the Church of the Ascension, where a wedding party had taken refuge in a crude bomb shelter—a trench edged by a couple of feet of earth—200 were killed by a direct hit. Where another shelter had been, American correspondent Leigh White found a bomb crater 30 feet across:

"Around its rim, in an almost symmetrical pattern, the naked bodies of some 30 or 40 people were strewn, like the petals of some evil flower."

One group of young Communists, who had been caught outside as they were getting ready for their demonstration, rushed to help put out a fire in a police warehouse. It happened that the warehouse contained books that had been banned and confiscated by the police. All the copies of a forbidden Soviet revolutionary novel, *How Steel Was Tempered,* were carried off by the young fire fighters, who later circulated them in the mountains to inspire the Communist Partisans in their guerrilla war against the Germans.

A Communist writer, Vladimir Dedijer, who would play an important role in the Partisan resistance, came upon an elderly woman—"with her hair all undone and a horror-stricken face"—crying her daughter's name. "When she came closer, I saw she was carrying something in her arms and smothering it with kisses. What she was carrying was the arm of her daughter, who had been torn to pieces by a bomb only a few moments before."

Early on that same morning, the German Twelfth Army launched ground attacks across the Bulgarian border into eastern Yugoslavia and northern Greece. A few days later, after building up strength and seizing a few bridgeheads, the German Second Army poured into northern Yugoslavia from bases in Austria and in German-allied Rumania and Hungary, followed by the Hungarian Third Army. Italians attacked from the west and the south. German strategy was to slice Yugoslavia into segments.

The Yugoslavs' prospects were bleak. When the invasion was launched, they had only 700,000 men under arms, and

In Vienna on March 25, 1941, Yugoslavia's Prime Minister Dragisha Cvetkovich (seated, left) signs the Tripartite Pact allying his country with Germany and Italy. Signing for the Axis powers are German Foreign Minister Joachim von Ribbentrop (seated, center) and Italian Foreign Minister Galeazzo Ciano.

In the heart of heavily bombed Belgrade, a German motorcycle unit patrols a street against a background of piled rubble and gutted ruins. German air raids killed between 4,000 and 20,000 people, laid waste to large sections of the city and started fires that could be seen from the Rumanian border 37 miles away.

more than 400,000 of them were ill-trained recent inductees. The Army's weapons were obsolete. Its transport consisted mostly of ox carts (American correspondent Robert St. John counted no fewer than 1,500 on one road after the German attack). It took the Yugoslavs an entire day to move troops and supplies a distance that the Germans could cover in an hour. Worst of all, the Yugoslav government decided to stretch the Army thinly along nearly 1,900 miles of border instead of withdrawing southward to better defensive terrain, as several generals had recommended.

In any case, the Yugoslavs stood no chance against invasion from all sides. German panzers quickly pierced Yugoslav defenses, and the saturation bombing of Belgrade, which had wiped out the nerve center of Yugoslavia's primitive military communications network, quickly threw the country's forces into hopeless confusion by severing telephone and telegraph connections. The Yugoslavs were, said American correspondent White, "like blind men fighting an enemy whose whereabouts they could never ascertain."

Both of the country's major cities were in German hands within a week. Zagreb, the capital of Croatia, fell to tanks of the 14th Panzer Division, which had raced almost 100 miles in one day through the crumbling Yugoslav defenses and entered the city to the cheers of pro-German Croats. Belgrade was captured by an enterprising SS officer named Klingenberg, who, after finding the Danube bridges destroyed, managed to get his small patrol across the river in captured rubber rafts.

On April 17—just 11 days after the invasion—the remnants of the Yugoslav General Staff and Cabinet signed an armistice agreement. The rest of the government, including the teen-age King Peter, had already fled south by plane to Greece. Lesser officers and other soldiers escaped into the woods or mountains. These little bands of diehard patriots were overlooked by the Germans in the lightning speed of their conquest.

Only 151 Germans died during the 12 days of combat, and the ease of victory caused Hitler to underestimate the fighting spirit of the Yugoslavs, a mistake that soon would come back to haunt him.

The rapid collapse of Yugoslavia had a crucial bearing on the campaign in Greece. Before the Germans swept simultaneously into Greece and Yugoslavia on April 6, the Greeks

and their British allies had based the deployment of their troops on the forlorn hope that the Yugoslavs somehow would slow down the invaders.

The defense of Greece consisted of three separate positions (map, page 20). In the northwest the bulk of the Greek Army—some 14 divisions—was still engaged with the Italians along the Albanian front. In the northeast nearly 70,000 Greek troops manned the Metaxas Line, a series of concrete pillboxes and fieldworks that stretched in a 130-mile arc from the mouth of the Nestos River to the juncture of Greece's borders with Yugoslavia and Bulgaria. Some 60 miles behind the Metaxas Line, British General Jumbo Wilson deployed the vanguard of his British and Commonwealth troops along the Aliakmon Line running through mountainous terrain between the Gulf of Salonika and the Yugoslav border.

Wilson realized at the outset that all of these defenses were precarious. A German flanking attack could easily turn the Metaxas Line. Wilson urged the Greeks to fall back on his shorter Aliakmon Line, but they demurred, reluctant to give up their Aegean port, Salonika. Wilson also knew that German panzers might well break through the Monastir Gap near the Yugoslav border and race behind his own Aliakmon Line, cutting off the British from the Greek Army fighting the Italians on the Albanian front. He hoped for reinforcements, but at the last minute he learned that a division and a brigade promised him by his government had been tied down in North Africa by a German offensive. Wilson had to make do with a bad situation and such troops as were now available to him.

The forces at his disposal included the 1st British Armored Brigade Group and the Anzac Corps, composed of the New Zealand Division and the 6th Australian Division. In addition, three Greek divisions were attached to Wilson's command. One of the Greek divisions—supposedly a motorized unit—consisted of about 2,000 untrained men and a dismaying collection of old trucks, motorcycles and small civilian cars. The mere survival of Wilson's command was, as a British general later put it, "a gamble in which the dice were loaded against us from the start."

Wilson's worst fears were confirmed in the first 72 hours of the offensive. The Germans quickly enveloped the Metaxas Line. While three infantry divisions hit the line head

on, a panzer division crossed the southeastern corner of Yugoslavia, sliced southward behind the line and roared into Salonika on the 9th of April, thereby cutting off northeastern Greece and forcing the Greek defenders to surrender. At the same time, other panzer units to the west raced through the Monastir Gap into Greece, cutting off the main Greek Army.

Less than a week after the Germans struck, General Wilson was forced to begin a series of withdrawals. On April 10 he started to pull back his line southward toward Mount Olympus, pivoting it to meet the German threat to his left flank. But despite mountainous terrain considered impassable to tanks, the panzers quickly broke through, bumping along the area's only railroad track, crossing a hazardous river and following rough trails through the Mount Olympus area. On April 16 the British began a hasty but orderly withdrawal across the Plain of Thessaly, south of Larissa.

The long retreating column immediately became a shooting gallery for the Luftwaffe. At the start of the invasion, the British Air Force in Greece had been outnumbered 10 to 1, and by this time few fighter planes were left to oppose the dive-bombing Stukas. And after the Stukas came the strafing Messerschmitts. "From dawn to dusk," wrote Lieutenant Robert Crisp, a British tank commander, "there was never a period of more than half an hour when there was not an enemy plane overhead. It was the unrelenting pressure of noise and the threat of destruction in every hour which accentuated the psychological consequences of continuous retreat, and turned so many men into nervous wrecks who leapt from their driving seats and trucks at the first distant hum—often without stopping their vehicles—and ran from the roads." After each raid the British evacuation route was blocked by burning vehicles. "Groups of men moved up and down the road," Lieutenant Crisp wrote, "heaving battered trucks and lorries into wayside ditches to keep the way out clear."

Crisp had lost his tank in the early days of fighting in the north; like many other outmoded British armored vehicles it broke a track, and he had to find transportation for the retreat south. Along the congested roadside Crisp and his crew came upon an abandoned three-ton truck with three bullet holes in the radiator. To their delight it turned out to

With a gigantic explosion, the bridge over
the Corinth Canal (top), separating the
Peloponnesus from the mainland of Greece,
collapses into the water. Demolition charges
were fixed on the bridge shortly before
German paratroopers were dropped to save
the structure. The British claimed to have
detonated the explosives by firing rifles at them
from a distance of several hundred yards.

GLOOMY END TO A FUTILE BRITISH EXPEDITION

In headlong retreat, truckloads of British troops move toward the coast for evacuation by boat.

As a Greek youth watches, British soldiers destroy equipment that might be of use to Germans.

Few soldiers in the war had a more thankless task than the British, New Zealand and Australian troops who were sent to help defend Greece in 1941. Less than three divisions were dispatched from North Africa in March to keep the British promise to assist the Mediterranean nation in the event of attack. From its inception, however, the operation was doomed to failure. The British could spare "only handfuls" of troops to fight in Greece. Even Prime Minister Winston Churchill admitted that the operation "looked a rather bleak military adventure dictated by noblesse oblige." His pessimism proved tragically correct.

Almost from the moment of their arrival, the soldiers were involved in a fighting withdrawal down the Greek peninsula. During the two-week retreat Luftwaffe harassment was so intense that frequently the Allies could move only at night. Stukas swarmed so close above, said one New Zealander, that "they're 'round your head like hornets." Roads were clogged with staff cars, trucks, ambulances and Bren gun carriers. Disabled vehicles were shoved into ditches, with their engines smashed and tires slashed to prevent the enemy from using them. On the sides of the roads, troops moved at a snail's pace, gradually discarding burdensome items—bedding, clothing, cans of food, even weapons.

Arriving at the coast the weary troops huddled under the protective cover of olive trees to avoid air attack and await evacuation by boat to Crete or North Africa. On the night of April 24, the first evacuees clambered aboard landing craft that ferried them to British destroyers, cruisers, transports and hospital ships waiting offshore. Virtually everything that could float was pressed into service. Four British airmen, two Greeks and two nuns made the journey from Athens to Alexandria—600 miles—in a motorboat. In the next four nights, nearly three quarters of the 58,000 men sent to defend Greece were successfully evacuated, the only real success of an otherwise disastrous campaign.

Weary British troops, evacuated from Greece, doze in close quarters on a ship. Too uncomfortable to sleep, one soldier rests his head in his hand.

be a New Zealand officers-mess truck loaded with puddings, cakes, cases of fruit and jam, and crates of beer and whiskey. All it needed to make it run was water—and this was supplied from a four-gallon can by a crewman named Plews who straddled the hood and, according to Crisp, maintained "an irregular but sufficient trickle" as the truck moved along the road. "Whenever the water tin emptied we stopped to refill it from the streams and pools," wrote Crisp. "In those circumstances it only needed a couple of raw mouthfuls to get us going, and we rolled down to Lamia singing bawdy songs and making rude gestures at the Luftwaffe overhead."

The pressure on the withdrawal was so intense that on the 19th of April the Greek government agreed the British should go ahead with the plans for full-scale evacuation that had been mapped out before the fighting began. The evacuation was hastened by two events that revealed the hopelessness of the Greek cause. On April 18, Greek Prime Minister Alexander Koryzis learned that his Cabinet was rife with defeatism and even treason. A special order granting Easter pay to the Greek troops had been mysteriously amended by the Minister of War so that it read "pay and leave." Taking advantage of the order, many Greek soldiers went on leave in the midst of the fighting. The revelation of these scandalous facts so distressed Koryzis that he returned to his home and—clutching an icon of the Virgin Mary in one hand and a revolver in the other—committed suicide. Newspapers in Athens reported the cause of his death as "heart failure."

Three days later, on April 21, Wilson's last hope for reinforcement, the 300,000-man Greek Army in Albania, completely disintegrated. Belatedly, those troops had been ordered south to protect Wilson's left flank. But the Greeks were exhausted after nearly six months of fighting and disheartened at the prospect of abandoning hard-won Albanian territory. In their retreat south, they were harried from the rear by Italians and cut off from the east by Germans. A few gallant units fought a pitched battle with a regiment of the SS Adolf Hitler Division at Metsovon, near the scene of the Greeks' first success against the Italians in November. But they were soon encircled and overwhelmed.

To save his men from dying pointlessly, the Greek corps commander, General George Tsolakoglou, surrendered the troops along the Albanian border. For this act the Germans rewarded Tsolakoglou nine days later by making him chief of their puppet government of Greece. Mussolini was furious. He felt that the Greeks should have surrendered to the Italians, and he complained to Hitler. Under Hitler's orders, the armistice terms, which had been generous to the Greeks, had to be redrafted and the signing of the agreement ceremonially reenacted with full Italian participation two days later on April 23.

Meanwhile, to buy time for their evacuation, the British prepared for one last stand along the approaches to Athens and southern Greece. For their delaying action, they selected a site near Thermopylae, the pass made famous in 480 B.C. by a Greek army's suicidal stand against the Persians. Before reaching the site, however, some of the soldiers halted by the roadside, and the engineers smoothed a nearby field with their combat shovels. Then, while Lieutenant Stephanos Zotos, a young Greek temporarily attached to a unit of Royal Engineers, watched in astonishment, "twenty-two men came on the field, wearing white shorts and their colorful shirts. A referee appeared, holding the prescribed whistle." And a soccer match that had been scheduled for that day went on as planned.

"The game was reaching the end of the first half-time," Lieutenant Zotos wrote, "when a dozen Stukas appeared over our heads and started strafing a convoy moving along the road, only a few yards away from the field. Nobody moved and the game continued as the players dribbled, passed and kicked the ball with unrelenting zest. Lieutenant Smith looked at the sky where the enemy planes might reappear at any moment, and I heard him whisper, 'I don't understand why the umpire does not stop the match.'

"There was nothing else that could interrupt the game. Only the whistle of the referee could halt what British tradition dictated."

After the game was over, the players joined the rest of the retreating column while the rear guard of Aussies and New Zealanders hastily occupied defensive positions at Thermopylae. The Germans attacked on the 24th of April. Their head-on assault into British artillery fire cost them 15 tanks. In the meantime, emulating the classic flanking maneuver of the old Persian invaders, the 141st German Mountain Regiment began scaling the heights overlooking the pass. The defenders held out until late that night. Then, their delaying action accomplished, they fell back in the direction of the evacuation beaches.

Two days later, the British foiled a further German attempt to cut off their route to the beaches. The Germans dropped two battalions of paratroopers on either side of the Corinth Canal, which separates the Greek mainland from the Peloponnesian peninsula. Their aim was to prevent demolition of the bridge over the canal so that oncoming panzers could rush across it and catch the British. But the British had already fixed explosive charges in place on the span when the paratroopers landed, though they had not had time to wire them. As Germans clambered over the bridge looking for the explosives, two British officers took aim with their rifles from several hundred yards away and fired. The last of several shots detonated the explosives and the bridge collapsed into the canal 150 feet below. The retreat continued.

North of Athens, 4,000 British troops were temporarily trapped by the airborne assault on the bridge. But at two beaches near Athens and four in the southern Peloponnesus, the evacuation continued over a period of five moonless nights. On the day before a given unit was to depart, it would distribute to Greek civilians its remaining food and supplies (including 50 cases of gin, which later served one hospital as an antiseptic after denatured alcohol ran out). Then the troops headed for dispersal areas where they got rid of their vehicles (8,000 were destroyed or abandoned) and hid in olive groves until the ships came. The ships arrived at night—a motley but efficient flotilla of British and Greek vessels that included eight cruisers, 19 destroyers, 19 transports and assault vessels, and scores of smaller craft. After loading, the ships usually embarked by 3 a.m. They were well on their way when the sun rose; with it came the Luftwaffe, which inexplicably never bothered the evacuation fleet during the night.

Though the almost total lack of British air cover made the operation far riskier than the epic embarkation at Dunkirk the previous year, the evacuation was an extraordinary success. Some 43,000 British troops, along with about 7,000 Yugoslav, Greek and other civilian refugees, reached Egypt or Crete, the big Greek island 60 miles southeast of the Peloponnesus. The number would have been even higher had not two exhausted commanders lost their nerve—with tragic results.

On the night of April 28 a British flotilla of two cruisers and nine destroyers hove to near Kalamata on the southwest coast to rescue some 7,000 troops under attack by the vanguard of the pursuing 5th Panzer Division. The jittery captain in command of the flotilla overestimated the fierceness of the fighting ashore and ordered his ships back to sea after picking up only 332 soldiers. Though the troops left on the beach might have held out until rescue ships appeared again the following night, their despairing commander surrendered in the morning.

The conquest of Greece by the Germans was drawing to a close. Early on Sunday, April 27—exactly three weeks after Hitler launched his invasion of Yugoslavia and Greece—German motorcycle troops roared into Athens, followed by clanking tanks. "At nine o'clock," wrote Kaity Argyropoulo, a Greek diplomat's wife, "the familiar city sounds, so trivial and yet significant to our trained ears, abruptly ceased. The roads of the town suddenly emptied. And in the tense, abnormal silence that quickly ensued, I heard in the far distance the rumble of tanks. It was the end!"

She went to her window and, looking toward the lofty Acropolis, "I saw the swastika flag rise over its northern parapet." She closed her shutters, "and as irrepressible tears rolled down my cheeks, I sensed the fathomless sob of a nation that had lost its liberty."

In the days that followed, the people of Athens heard and retold several different stories about the raising of the German flag. According to one account, a Greek soldier refused German orders to lower his country's blue-and-white flag and then threw himself over the parapet to his death a hundred feet below. Another story held that the soldier took down the Greek flag and wrapped himself in it before he jumped. It made no difference which, if any, version was true. The Greek people believed in the storied soldier's martyrdom, and it helped them to bear their hardships during the harrowing years of resistance and guerrilla warfare that followed.

THE BUMPIEST BLITZKRIEG

Their turrets loaded down with fuel cans, a column of German panzers charges across the Bulgarian border into Greece along a winding road in the mountains.

OBSTACLES ON THE ROAD TO ATHENS

When the Germans invaded Greece in April 1941, they were eager to get the operation over with as quickly as possible, in order not to upset the timetable for their invasion of Russia, scheduled to occur two months later. To subdue the ancient Balkan land, Field Marshal Wilhelm List was assigned an overwhelming force of approximately 13 divisions, which included two panzer divisions, two mountain divisions and the Führer's own bodyguard outfit, the SS Adolf Hitler Division.

The Germans had applied the techniques of the blitzkrieg—lightning war—with great success in Poland, the Lowlands and France in the previous 18 months. But Hitler's legions had never tackled a country as rugged and forbidding as Greece, with its barren mountain ranges, narrow passes and deep gorges. The transportation network was primitive: a single railway connected northern Greece with Athens, many roads were no better than paths and even the main highways were too narrow in places for vehicles to pass each other.

To make matters worse, spring came late to the Balkans in 1941; snowdrifts still blocked the mountain passes in April and heavy rains washed out the dirt roads in the valleys.

Once the invasion was launched, German infantrymen soon discovered that intelligence had underestimated the strength of the Metaxas Line fortifications along Greece's Bulgarian border. Some of the stoutly built strong points withstood repeated dive-bombing attacks, artillery bombardment and infantry assaults.

The Germans were forced to improvise and find ways to defeat both the enemy and the terrain. They brought up special smoke-making equipment to blind and virtually suffocate the Greek defenders of the impregnable Kelkayia fort in the Metaxas Line. Combat engineers carved passageways out of mountainsides and widened road bends with explosives to allow vehicles and artillery to pass. They constructed bridges and resurfaced or repaired roads. Yet in spite of such impediments, it took the Germans only 21 days to reach Athens.

Anchored solidly in rocky hillsides, stubbornly defended concrete bunkers of the Metaxas Line withstood the impact of 2,200-pound Luftwaffe bombs.

Antitank barriers made from logs and iron bars stretch along the Metaxas Line, which forced panzers to seek alternate routes of attack.

In a narrow, roadless pass near Mount Olympus, a German vehicle comes momentarily to a halt astride a railroad track that the driver is using as a highway.

Blocked by a road demolition, German soldiers struggle to heave a motorcycle up a steep slope and thus to help keep up the momentum of their offensive.

German motorcyclists bump slowly along a stretch of hurriedly constructed corduroy road, made of roughhewn logs laid side by side by combat engineers.

SS troops of the Adolf Hitler Division serve as human brakes as their personnel carrier, which ran off the roadway, teeters on the edge of a rocky incline.

German artillerymen fire 150mm guns at enemy units in rugged Greek mountains. Wicker cylinders (foreground) protected artillery shells during shipment.

THE FINAL RACE TO VICTORY

The Germans drove on relentlessly, with regimental commanders frequently riding in the lead to spur their men. The fast-moving motorized and mountain divisions soon outran their supply lines, and many units had to fight on empty stomachs.

When the advance appeared to falter, unit commanders pressed their men all the harder. In a mountain pass near Kastoria, after huge demolition charges had hurled boulders into the air and killed three men, the leading unit of one SS battalion was pinned down by Greek machine guns. In a desperate attempt to get his troops moving again, the frustrated battalion commander pulled the pin from a hand grenade and rolled it right up behind the last man. With this added incentive, the soldiers began to inch forward.

The main Greek army, worn out after

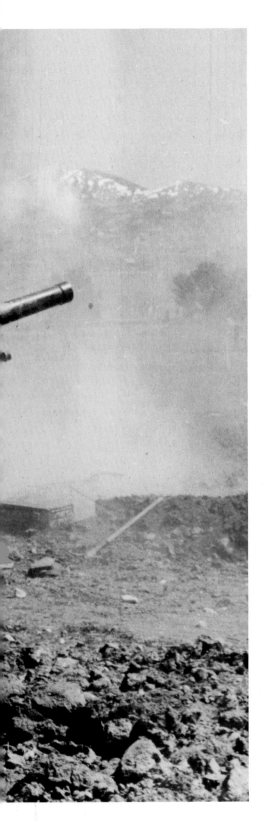

German Stuka bombers wing their way over the mountains to attack Greece's outgunned defenders.

Pursuing British units at Thermopylae, German cavalry troops cross a bridge just built by engineers.

half a year of fighting in Albania, surrendered to the Germans on the 21st of April. But the Germans still had to contend with the British who had come to the aid of the Greeks. The withdrawing British troops demolished bridges, blasted craters up to 100 feet wide in the roads and fought skillful rear-guard actions in the narrow mountain passes at Olympus and Thermopylae.

But the German spearheads pushed forward as tanks made frontal assaults on British positions and mountain troops scaled the surrounding peaks and enveloped the defensive positions on the flanks.

As the British fell back to the south, German mountain troops climbed to the top of Mount Olympus, legendary home of the Greek gods, and raised the swastika on April 16. After the British pulled back from their position at Thermopylae on the 24th of April, advance units of two German divisions raced to Athens. They arrived in the capital within five minutes of each other on April 27.

Standing on the Acropolis, the Parthenon behind them, German troops raise their country's flag. The man at far right fires a pistol to signify the German take-over.

2

After the German conquest of Yugoslavia and Greece, there remained one major threat to Hitler's southern flank—the British-occupied island of Crete. The largest of the Greek islands, Crete lay about 200 miles south of Athens, within bombing range of the mainland of Greece and the vital oil fields in Rumania, source of much of the fuel for Germany's war machine. The British had established airfields on Crete the previous year, and the island's importance as an Allied base had escalated when the defeated British expeditionary force took refuge there after the evacuation of Greece in April of 1941.

Even before the Germans had finished driving the British out of Greece, one of Hitler's favorite generals had come up with a bold plan for pushing them out of Crete as well. The scheme was so novel, ambitious and daring it had no precedent in military history. Crete was to be seized from the air by Hitler's new parachute troops, known as *Fallschirmjäger*, "hunters from the sky."

The author of the plan was General Kurt Student, an austere 51-year-old former fighter pilot who commanded German airborne operations. Student had no trouble persuading his own boss, air force commander Hermann Göring, that the airborne invasion would work. Göring quickly recognized it as an opportunity for dramatically refurbishing the image of his Luftwaffe after its recent failure to win the air war over Great Britain. He arranged for Student to meet with Hitler on April 21 at the Führer's mobile headquarters, a train hidden in a tunnel in eastern Austria, from which the dictator was personally overseeing the completion of the Greek campaign.

At first Hitler was cool to Student's proposal. "It sounds all right," he said, "but I don't think it's practicable." Hitler was preoccupied with the upcoming invasion of Russia, now scheduled for the 22nd of June. That operation had already been delayed for six weeks by the necessity of intervening in Yugoslavia and Greece, and Hitler wanted no further diversions from what he envisioned as his supreme military endeavor.

But as Student sketched in the advantages of his scheme, it became more and more appealing to the Führer. Crete was ideal for an airborne assault. Only 160 miles long and up to 40 miles wide, it was within easy range of German-occupied Greece but could not be easily reinforced by the

HUNTERS FROM THE SKY

British from the sea. Moreover, the island could serve as a springboard for a series of similar assaults across the eastern Mediterranean. Prime targets were the British colony of Cyprus and the Allied lifeline in the Middle East, the Suez Canal.

Hitler was intrigued by the prospect of employing Germany's elite parachutists on a grand scale. Thus far, the *Fallschirmjäger* had been used only sparingly in the invasions of Holland, Belgium and Norway. Even those small airdrops had proved remarkably effective, inspiring paralyzing fears and rumors among the enemy. The Dutch, for example, had insisted that German paratroopers descended upon them diabolically disguised as nuns, monks and streetcar conductors. Such scare stories pleased Hitler, as did his apocalyptic vision of blitzkrieg from the sky. "That is how the wars of the future will be fought," he had once predicted, "the sky black with bombers, and from them, leaping into the smoke, the parachuting storm troopers, each one grasping a submachine gun."

By the end of his session with Student, Hitler was so enthusiastic he was even suggesting tactics for the seizure of Crete. He told Student that the paratroopers should be dropped in packages, "simultaneously at many places," to confound the enemy. This approach, which fitted perfectly with Student's own intentions, contradicted the cardinal rule of traditional German military doctrine: keep the troops concentrated.

Preparations for Operation *Mercury,* Hitler's code name for the project, began at the end of April when the conquest of Greece by German ground forces was completed. Near Athens, Greek labor gangs were put to work carving out nine hastily improvised airfields. From there the 7th Paratroop Division would launch a combined glider-and-parachute assault on the three airstrips strung along the northern coast of Crete. Once the *Fallschirmjäger* were in control, waves of transport planes carrying foot soldiers of the 5th Mountain Division would land. After that, two seaborne flotillas would bring in the reinforcements and the heavy weapons.

The 5th Mountain Division was already in Greece, where it had distinguished itself by storming the heavily fortified Metaxas Line on the Bulgarian border. But the paratroopers had to be rushed in from their bases in Germany. And their equipment had to be brought down from northern France, where it had been neatly packed in parachute containers for the airborne invasion of England that never materialized. The paratroopers were transported to Greece by train and truck, and in the strictest secrecy, traveling only at night. They were kept ignorant of their destination, ordered to remove their unit badges—an eagle plunging through a wreath of oak and laurel leaves—and forbidden to sing their boisterous paratrooper songs.

In spite of the secrecy, the British already knew about Operation *Mercury.* The propagandist Lord Haw-Haw had been referring to Crete for several weeks as "the island of doomed men" in his nightly broadcasts to Britain. More credible reports had come from intercepts of top-secret German military radio traffic in Greece, which had been deciphered by the British code-breaking system *Ultra.* So many details of the planned assault had been divined—including the scheduled date, May 15—that Churchill could later write: "At no moment in the war was our Intelligence so truly and precisely informed."

Churchill viewed Crete as "a fine opportunity for killing the parachute troops," and he ordered that the island "must be stubbornly defended." His personal choice to lead that defense was an old friend from New Zealand, Major-General Bernard Freyberg, a 51-year-old oak of a man whose troops affectionately called him "Tiny." Freyberg was a much-decorated, oft-wounded hero of World War I, and Churchill liked to recall the day back in the 1920s when he asked his friend to show him his war wounds. "He stripped himself, and I counted twenty-seven separate scars and gashes." Churchill dubbed him "Salamander" because he had "thrived in the fire" of the First World War and had been "literally shot to pieces without being affected physically or in spirit."

Freyberg was so immune to fear that he once told a reporter, "I think there must be something wrong with my glands." All the same, he despaired of his new assignment in Crete. He had come there directly from Greece, where he had led his New Zealand division in the futile effort to stem the German invasion, and he wanted nothing more than to return to Egypt with his own unit and reorganize its shattered remnants. Moreover, the defenses of Crete were in appalling disarray. He was the island's seventh commander in seven months. Although Churchill had constantly harped on the need for stiffening the garrisons there, Britain's commitments in the Middle East were so widespread that little had been done to beef up the forces on the island. Freyberg took a good look and on May 1 cabled the Middle East Commander-in-Chief, General Sir Archibald Wavell: "Forces at my disposal are totally inadequate to meet attack envisaged."

Actually, Freyberg had at his disposal a potentially formidable garrison. He was in command of more than 40,000 men, almost twice as many as were to be included in the German invading force, which would total approximately 23,000 troops. But 11,000 of his men were inadequately trained Greeks and Cretans, and two thirds of the remaining British, Australians and New Zealanders had been dumped on Crete after the demoralizing defeat on the Greek mainland. Many of them were service troops—cooks, clerks and truck drivers—separated from their units and living at large in the hills and olive groves.

Freyberg also had to cope with an acute shortage of supplies. Some soldiers had escaped with nothing more than a blanket and a rifle. To make matters worse, the Greeks were armed with five different kinds of rifles, no two of which used the same type of ammunition. There were not enough tanks, mortars, grenades, artillery shells, entrenching tools or barbed wire. The field guns lacked proper

sights, and some gunners had attached wooden sights to them with chewing gum.

The most serious problem was the shortage of airplanes. At the beginning of May, there were only 36 British fighters on Crete's three airstrips. Ground troops quipped that RAF no longer stood for Royal Air Force, but for "Rare as Fairies." By the eve of the German assault, as a result of frequent Luftwaffe raids, there were only half a dozen serviceable RAF fighters on Crete; so few that to avoid a needless sacrifice they were flown back to Egypt.

The geography of the island helped the Germans to impose a daylight blockade against British attempts to reinforce Crete from the sea. As Freyberg put it, the island "faced the wrong way," and he wished that he could "spin it around." Both the principal port at Heraklion and the fueling base at Suda Bay were situated on the north coast, facing the Luftwaffe bases 200 miles away in Greece, but more than 400 miles from British supply bases to the south in Egypt. Forced to run the aerial blockade north of the island, the British Navy set out from Egypt with 27,000 tons of munitions during the first three weeks of May. Under heavy air attack, the Navy succeeded in landing only one ninth of these supplies, including 16 light tanks and nine heavy Matilda infantry tanks.

For all their handicaps, however, the defenders did possess one tremendous advantage. Thanks to *Ultra,* they knew how, where and approximately when the German assault

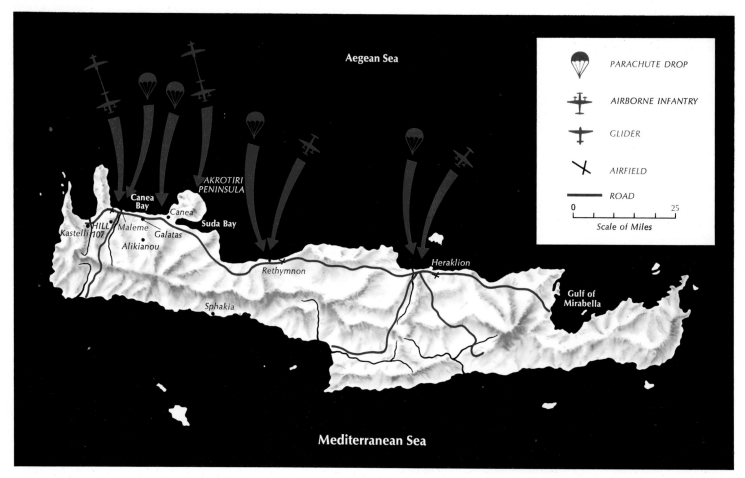

was coming, and they were able to deploy their forces accordingly. Their defenses were concentrated around the enemy's main targets, the three airstrips and their adjoining ports, along a 70-mile stretch of road on Crete's narrow northern coastal plain. From west to east, these targets were Maleme—with the port of Suda Bay—Rethymnon and Heraklion (map, left). Within a few days Freyberg was more sanguine about British chances than he had been when he first arrived, and on the 5th of May he cabled Churchill, who had begun to fret about the situation on Crete: "Cannot understand nervousness; am not in the least anxious about airborne attack; have made my dispositions and feel can cope adequately with the troops at my disposal." But Freyberg was alarmed by the possibility of an attack from the sea. He therefore requested assistance from the Royal Navy and told the Prime Minister: "Provided Navy can help, trust all will be well."

The German airborne armada appeared over the windless Aegean Sea south of Greece early on Tuesday, May 20. It was five days late—transporting more than a million gallons of aviation fuel to the Greek airfields had proved to be more difficult than the Germans had anticipated—but when it finally came into view nothing could diminish its lumbering majesty. There were so many planes—493 of the three-engine Junkers-52 transports, known as "Aunties" because they were slow but reliable—that they actually blotted out the rising sun.

In the vanguard came towplanes pulling some 70 steel, wood and canvas gliders. The plan called for the gliders to be cast off about six miles from the primary target, the Maleme airstrip in western Crete. Each glider carried 11 fully equipped men, including the pilot, who was expected to fight alongside the airborne troops. Some of the pilots were recently mobilized civilian glider enthusiasts. One had been driving a taxi in Vienna just three weeks before.

The rest of the Aunties carried parachute troops. There were 12 of them to a plane, and as the minutes passed, they grew more and more anxious. Aboard one of the Ju-52s, a battalion commander named Baron von der Heydte kept checking his watch. It was to be von der Heydte's first combat jump. A thoughtful former student of law and philosophy, he described the experience in a postwar memoir, *Daedalus Returned:* "Slowly, infinitely slowly, like the last drops wrung from a drying well, the minutes passed. There is nothing so awful, so exhausting as this waiting for the moment of a jump. . . . When there is no going back, most men experience a strange sinking feeling, as if their stomachs had remained on the ground."

Now the young German warriors were 400 feet over Crete, their planes flying as slowly as they possibly could without stalling. The order rang out: Ready to jump! As von der Heydte stood poised at the door, "the slipstream clutched at my cheeks and I felt as though they were fluttering like small flags in the wind." Below the aircraft, southeast of the Maleme airstrip, he could see the village of Alikianou where the shadows of the planes "swept like ghostly hands over the sun-drenched white houses while behind the village there gleamed a large mirror—the reservoir—with single-colored parachutes like autumn leaves drifting down toward it.

"Then came the command to jump—*Raus!* I pushed with my hands and feet, throwing my arms forward as if trying to clutch the black cross on the wing. And then the slipstream caught me, and I was swirling through space with the air roaring in my ears. A sudden jerk on the webbing, a pressure on the chest that knocked the breath out of my lungs, and then—I looked up and saw, spread above me, the wide-open hood of my parachute. In relation to this giant umbrella I felt small and insignificant."

It was 7:30 a.m. and on the ground many of the defenders in the target area between the Maleme airstrip and Suda Bay were still at breakfast. Earlier they had undergone what the New Zealanders referred to as the morning "hate"—the daily bombing and strafing attack by the Luftwaffe just after dawn. As usual, the dive-bombing Stukas held the greatest terror. Many of the planes had sirens fixed to the bottom of their fuselages—and the sirens screamed and whined so eerily, according to one defender, that they "gave you a sick feeling in the stomach and loosened the joints of the knees." Following a pause, the Stukas had intensified their attack, dropping earsplitting 500- and 1,000-pounders. Then came silence, and through the pall of dust and smoke the defenders suddenly caught a glimpse of the gliders. Fifteen minutes later—"flowering like bubbles from a child's pipe," said one of the New Zealanders, "but infinitely more sinister"—the parachutes of the sky hunters filled the air.

Eyewitnesses were so impressed that years afterward they would claim they had seen the parachutes descending in a dazzling bouquet of colors—red, green, yellow, violet. In fact, they came in only two varieties: mottled green for the enlisted men, white for the officers. The supply containers, however, were marked by canisters of color-coded smoke for easy identification. The smoke may have confused the observers on the ground.

An even more startling effect was noted by the men of the 5th New Zealand Brigade dug in east of the Maleme airstrip. They were sure they heard the blare of a bugle, and they were right. One of the first Germans to jump was Ernst Springer, a huntsman from Upper Silesia, and as soon as he landed Springer pulled out his hunting horn and blew a signal for the attack.

It took the paratroopers five seconds or so to float to earth after their chutes opened, and in the agonizing interval they were easy marks for the defenders. One New Zealander, opening fire on them from a well-camouflaged slit trench, thought it akin to shooting ducks.

Two miles farther east of the airstrip, where the pilots of the German transports grossly misjudged the drop zone, an entire battalion of paratroopers plopped practically in the laps of the New Zealanders entrenched in an olive grove. During those first chaotic minutes, Lieut. Colonel D. F. Leckie, commanding the 23rd New Zealand Battalion, killed five paratroopers from the comfort of his own headquarters. His adjutant, a shipping clerk in peacetime, shot two more without even getting up from his packing-case desk. That day, the German battalion lost 400 of its 600 men. The roster of one of its companies, found in the pocket of a dead German officer, showed 126 names; within three hours 112 of the men listed there were dead.

Many Germans who reached earth safely found themselves caught up in a nightmare of confusion and faulty planning. Careless airdrops separated the men from their weapons. Defenders were dug in everywhere in three times the numbers the Germans had anticipated. The Cretan civilians, who intelligence reports had predicted would be docile or even friendly, menaced the Germans from behind windows, rocks and trees, wielding the same kind of knives and shotguns that they had employed against their Turkish oppressors three decades before.

Weeks of aerial reconnaissance had failed to reveal the extent of the intricate British camouflage system. So clever was the camouflage that even the defenders were sometimes fooled; a few days before the attack, one unit had started digging a latrine near Maleme only to discover that a mortar position was just 10 yards away.

In some cases, the German aerial reconnaissance was at fault. A detachment of paratroopers, landing on the coast between Maleme and Suda Bay, mistakenly attacked a field hospital. Though clearly marked from the air by red crosses,

A fake antiaircraft gun stands in a field on Crete, part of an effort to deceive German aerial reconnaissance. The British were anxious to hide the inadequacy of their defenses—they had only 32 heavy and 36 light antiaircraft guns for the entire island—but the ruse did not prevent the Germans from bombing the island's airfields and other military installations at will.

the hospital was identified on German maps as merely a "tented encampment." The paratroopers suddenly found themselves with wounded patients on their hands, including a German pilot shot down earlier over Crete who greeted them with a Nazi salute. Soon a German officer arrived, pulled out a camera and began clicking pictures of the pajama-clad prisoners. The pictures were never developed: a few minutes later, a New Zealand sniper secreted in an olive grove about 400 yards away shot the officer through the head.

In the confusion of those early hours, the paratroopers got less help from the Luftwaffe than they had expected. Fighter pilots circling overhead could not distinguish friend from foe in the hundreds of small encounters being fought below them in the olive groves, terraced hillsides and village streets.

One encounter involved New Zealand Colonel Howard K. Kippenberger, whose brigade was defending an area known as Prison Valley, southwest of Canea. "As I panted through the gap in the cactus hedge, there was a startling burst of fire fairly in my face, cutting cactus on either side of me," Kippenberger said later. "I jumped sideways, twisted

my ankle, and rolled down the bank. After whimpering a little, I crawled up the track and into the house, and saw my man through the window. Then I hopped out again, hopped around the back and, in what seemed to me a nice bit of minor tactics, stalked him round the side of the house and shot him cleanly through the head at ten yards. The silly fellow was still watching the gap in the hedge and evidently had not noticed me crawl into the house."

All of the problems that plagued the paratroopers around Maleme—misjudged drops, inadequate intelligence, lack of air support—were repeated later in the day when airborne assaults were launched against the airstrips farther to the east at Rethymnon and Heraklion. The attacks there were delayed more than an hour because the transport planes, returning from Maleme to the Greek airfields to pick up the next wave of paratroopers, sank up to their axles in the soft sand of the runways, throwing up clouds of dust more than half a mile high. As a result of the delay, pilots failed to catch up with their formations and to coordinate their approaches to the jump zones. And the fighters and bombers, unaware of the delay, delivered their softening-up attack prematurely.

Over the target area, British gunners had a field day firing at the slow Junkers transports. At Heraklion, 15 transports were shot down. A gunner later recalled the planes bursting into flames and the paratroopers inside "feverishly leaping out like plums spilled from a burst paper bag." As each parachute opened, the silk exploded into flames. The ordeal continued on the ground. When some paratroopers took refuge in a field of three-foot-high barley and began sniping at the defenders, the British flushed them out by setting fire to the barley. In just one hour at Heraklion, a German battalion lost 300 men and 12 officers.

By the end of the first day, the German attack was in jeopardy all along the northern coast of Crete—from Heraklion on the east to Maleme on the west. Some 10,000 Germans had descended on the island by parachute and glider, and nowhere had they achieved their first-day goals—the capture of the three airstrips and Heraklion, Rethymnon and Canea. About 40 per cent of the assault force were dead, wounded or prisoners.

The full dimensions of the German failure—though not

Former World Heavyweight Boxing Champion Max Schmeling leaps out of a plane during a parachute exercise in preparation for the German paratroop invasion of Crete in May of 1941. For his part in the battle, Schmeling was decorated with the Iron Cross, First Class, by Reich Marshal Hermann Göring. The Reich Marshal was furious when he later learned he had been misinformed about the boxer's performance—Schmeling had been knocked out of action by dysentery for most of the campaign.

the extent of the losses—became known that night to General Freyberg through a chance discovery. At Freyberg's headquarters in a quarry tunnel near Canea, Lieutenant Geoffrey Cox, editor of a military newspaper for the New Zealanders, was browsing through a pile of captured enemy documents when he discovered the complete operations order for the regiment that landed around Maleme. With the help of a pocket dictionary he had used as a journalist in Vienna before the War, Cox roughed out a translation. Then, by the light of a hurricane lamp in Freyberg's cave, he read it aloud to the general. The document revealed in detail the original strength, direction and objectives of the initial German attacks. From this intelligence, it was clear that most of the parachute troops had already been dropped on Crete.

Except for this fortuitous discovery, however, Freyberg was dangerously uninformed about the actual course of the first day's action. Most of the British radio sets had been abandoned in Greece. Commanders had to depend mainly on the telephone. Now bombs and paratroopers had cut most of the telephone cables, and the defenders had to resort to the risky method of entrusting their messages to runners. One runner was sent from Rethymnon to Suda Bay, a distance of 45 miles. Harassed by snipers and twice forced to slip through enemy lines, he showed up at his destination six days late.

The most dangerous gap in Freyberg's information was the threat developing that first night just east of the Maleme airstrip. There, in a dry riverbed, survivors of the German glider landings and parachute drops were building up a potentially dangerous concentration. Freyberg was not aware of the threat, nor did he appreciate the importance of the airstrip. Had he realized its value, he might have taken the airfield and prevented the Germans from using it for reinforcements.

For a time, the commander of the German airborne forces, General Student, was also in the dark as to what was happening. Sitting on the second floor of the Hotel Grande Bretagne in Athens, which only a few weeks before had served as British headquarters, Student anxiously awaited news that would confirm his faith in the *Fallschirmjäger* and the bold plan he had sold Hitler. It was a plan, von

der Heydte observed later, that "had become a part of him. . . . He believed in it and lived for it and in it."

When the first reports started coming in shortly before midnight, the news was bad. Many of Student's old associates in the field, including the division commander and the regimental commander at Maleme, lay dead or wounded. The overall commander of the operation, General Alexander Löhr, was asking whether preliminary arrangements should be made for breaking off Operation *Mercury*. Hitler was reported to be attributing the first day's failures to a severe head wound Student had suffered in Holland the previous year.

But Student was a gambler who was able, in von der Heydte's words, "to appreciate the enemy's situation accurately even when actual information about the enemy is wrong." Intuitively, he reasoned that the main thrust of the German attack should be directed toward the tiny airstrip at Maleme. Though Student remembered the runways there as looking no longer than three tennis courts from the air—and though control of the airstrip was still in dispute—he decided to "stake everything on one card." He would land at Maleme all of the transport planes carrying the 5th Mountain Division. The main defenses of the island at Suda Bay, Rethymnon and Heraklion "would have to be rolled up from the west," as he put it.

Student issued the necessary orders and then, belatedly hedging his bet, sent a flying officer to scout the situation at Maleme. Just after dawn, the pilot landed a Junkers-52 at Maleme despite heavy British fire. The fact that he could land at all—and take off a little while later—hinted at the dramatic change that had taken place around the airstrip during the night. The New Zealanders of the 22nd Battalion had abandoned the southern cornerstone of the airstrip's defenses, Hill 107, and the weary German paratroopers, scarcely able to believe their luck, had simply trudged up the hill without a struggle.

For the 22nd's commander, Lieut. Colonel L. W. Andrew, the withdrawal from Hill 107 capped nearly 24 hours of terrible frustration. Andrew was a determined and brave man. When a bomb fragment struck him in the temple at Maleme, he had simply pulled out the metal slivers and kept going. But he had been bedeviled all day and night at Maleme by the lack of radio communications. He had lost touch with his three forward companies and consequently had been unable to counterattack effectively during the first day while the paratroopers were still disorganized and vulnerable. After midnight, believing that his command post on Hill 107 was being surrounded, he pulled back. He had no way of knowing that the enemy was outnumbered, short of ammunition and exhausted.

The Germans were so tired, in fact, that scattered groups of men from the 22nd Battalion were able to pull back through German positions without interference. As the New Zealanders—with their boots slung around their necks to keep from making noise—crept past the Germans, they could hear the parachutists snoring. "If the enemy had made an all-out effort in counterattack that night, or on the morning of the 21st," General Student said later, the "very tired remnants could have been wiped out."

On the afternoon of the 21st—the second day of the assault on Crete—Student started landing the 5th Mountain Division at Maleme. At 4 p.m. Junkers transports carrying a full battalion of mountain troops appeared overhead. Three at a time, the planes began to set down—only to run into British shellfire.

From a distance of about 6,000 yards, the New Zealanders had nine field guns trained on the landing area. Their shells wrecked some transports and forced others to overshoot the airstrip; still others crash-landed on the beach at the far end of the strip or in the vineyards beside it.

Aboard one of the transports was a German war correspondent, Kurt Meyer, who later gave this description of the landing: "Brown fountains of earth leap up and shower the machines which have already landed with earth, smoke and dust. The pilot grits his teeth. Cost what it may

he has got to get down. Suddenly there leaps up below us a vineyard. We strike the ground and bounce. Then one wing grinds into the sand and tears the back of the machine half round to the left. Men, packs, boxes, ammunition are flung forward. We lose the power over our own bodies. At last we come to a standstill, the machine standing half on its head."

Despite the difficulties, 63 planes landed that evening. Many disgorged their mountain troops while still moving. They quickly linked up with the paratroopers dug in to the west and south of the airstrip, then used abandoned British armored vehicles to bulldoze aside the wrecked planes on the airfield to make room for the arrival of reinforcements. The Germans now had a secure foothold at Maleme, and with rising confidence they awaited the arrival of the seaborne force due to land before dark on the beaches west of the airstrip.

But the German flotilla was late. In striking contrast to the modern air armada that had invaded Crete, this force presented an archaic appearance as it crept across the Aegean Sea from Greece. It consisted mostly of 25 two-masted wooden motorboats called caïques, which had been commandeered from Greek fishermen. The boats were heavily laden with 2,300 mountain troops and an arsenal of weapons and matériel that could not be carried by plane—artillery, tanks, horses.

It was already dark when the flotilla came within sight of Crete. With the Luftwaffe grounded for the night, the slow-moving vessels were vulnerable to the powerful warships of the British Mediterranean fleet operating under the cover of darkness. Shortly before midnight, an enemy squadron of three cruisers and four destroyers intercepted the flotilla, their searchlights stabbing at the helpless ca-

Struggling German troops, using a large truck, wrestle a wrecked British plane off the runway at Maleme, on the island of Crete, after capturing the strategic airfield. Prior to the German attack on May 20, 1941, all airworthy British aircraft were flown to Egypt, leaving the Luftwaffe unopposed in the skies overhead.

ïques, as one German soldier later remembered it, "like fingers of death." The Italian light destroyer *Lupo,* escorting the flotilla, valiantly tried to divert the British, but its little cannon was as useless as a popgun.

The first British salvos struck a caïque laden with ammunition. It exploded and others started to burn. British destroyers began ramming the caïques squarely amidships, slicing them in half, and soon the water was strewn with struggling mountain soldiers. In two hours, the German flotilla lost nearly half its ships and more than 300 men. The survivors turned back to Greece—as did a larger convoy of caïques with 4,000 men aboard, which ran into another squadron of British marauders before it could land at Heraklion in the east later that morning.

From his headquarters ashore, General Freyberg could see the reddening sky above the burning Maleme-bound German fleet. He was in the process of preparing a counterattack against the build-up of mountain troops at Maleme. Freyberg could have called on the 7,000 trained infantrymen in the area around his Canea headquarters, but he still did not realize the airstrip had assumed pivotal importance. As a result, only two battalions—fewer than 2,000 men— were committed to the counterattack, which was launched four hours behind schedule. Even so, one battalion of New Zealanders managed to fight its way more than three miles along the coast to the edge of the airstrip before dawn. They could see the German transports landing on the airstrip with fresh reinforcements of mountain troops. But when daylight came the Luftwaffe arrived and started attacking in force. The battalion was obliged to withdraw.

Meanwhile, the other battalion had set out for the high ground to the south of the airstrip. This battalion was made up of Maoris, the Polynesian aborigines of New Zealand. When the Maoris attacked the Germans in a valley east of Maleme, "there rose from their throats a deep shout 'Ah! Ah! Ah!' as they advanced firing," said one of their New Zealand officers. "Then the cartridges in their magazines being exhausted, they broke into a run with bayonets leveled and their shouts rising as they went. . . . Men went down but they still charged."

Eventually, as the Luftwaffe pressed its attack, even the Maoris were forced to pull back under the relentless pounding of the planes. But they came back proudly, flashing the thumbs-up signal, two of their members carrying a pot of stew slung across a rifle.

The counterattack had failed, and all afternoon on May 22, the third day of the attack on Crete, the Junkers transports continued to land at Maleme. Swarming in through the shellfire at the rate of one every three minutes, the planes brought in some 2,000 additional mountain troops.

That evening, the commander of the 5th Mountain Division, Major General Julius Ringel, arrived to take charge of his men. A shrewd tactician known to them as "Papa Julius," Ringel was noted for his motto "Sweat saves blood." He put it into practice immediately by sending the main body of his troops south into the rugged foothills—"over land," he said, "that the devil created in anger." The Germans had neglected to provide summer uniforms for the paratroopers and the mountaineers. Sweating in more than 100° F. heat, the men swung east toward the southern flank of Freyberg's New Zealanders.

On the following morning, Ringel sent a smaller detachment along the coast west of the airstrip on a special reconnaissance mission. Since the first day of the attack, one unit, consisting of 75 paratroopers, had not been heard from. They had landed on the outskirts of Kastelli, a tiny fishing port 15 miles to the west of the Maleme airstrip, and that was the last anyone knew of them. Ringel was determined to find out what had happened. After searching all day, the detachment stumbled across the unburied corpses of the paratroopers. Some of the men had been knifed or clubbed and the mountaineers immediately concluded that their bodies had been mutilated after death by Cretan civilians. The word "atrocities" filtered back to headquarters.

Actually, the paratroopers had fallen in fair combat to a hastily organized regiment of 1,000 Cretan irregulars led by a New Zealand major, T. G. Bedding. Because the regiment was equipped with fewer than 600 rifles and had had only three weeks of training, Bedding's preattack orders had been to put up merely a token resistance. But the fishermen and farmers were heirs to a centuries-old tradition of guerrilla valor. They had donned their national costume of breeches, boots and scarlet sashes, and armed themselves with axes, curved Syrian knives and rusty flintlocks

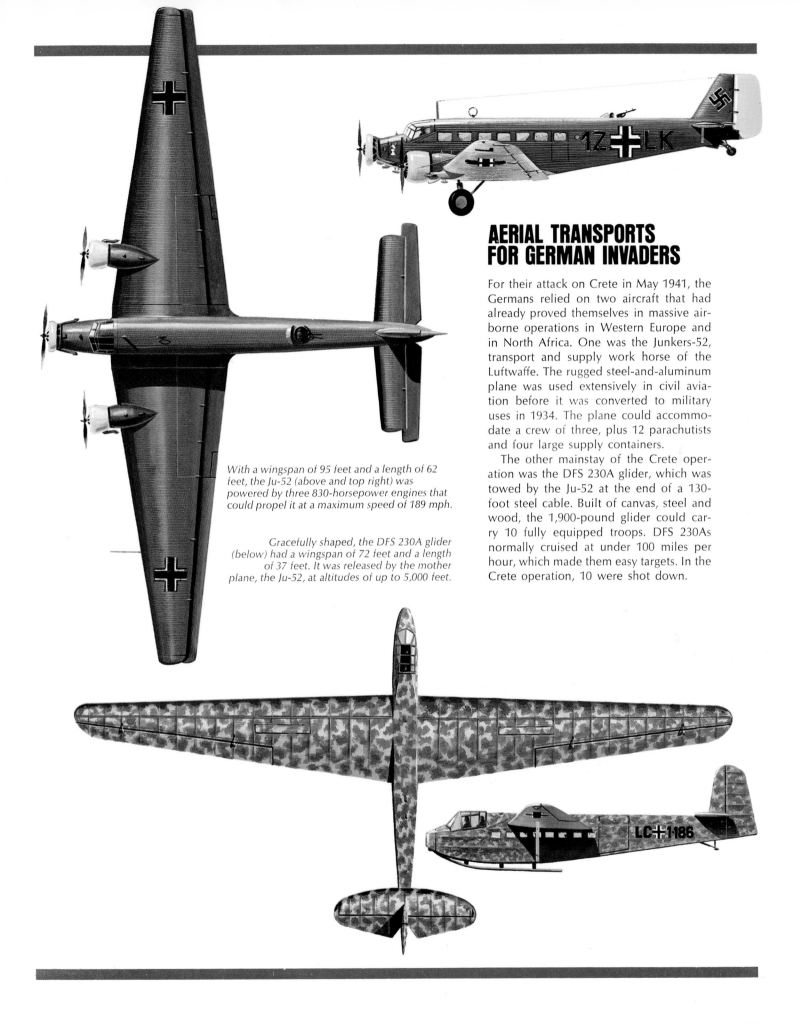

AERIAL TRANSPORTS FOR GERMAN INVADERS

For their attack on Crete in May 1941, the Germans relied on two aircraft that had already proved themselves in massive airborne operations in Western Europe and in North Africa. One was the Junkers-52, transport and supply work horse of the Luftwaffe. The rugged steel-and-aluminum plane was used extensively in civil aviation before it was converted to military uses in 1934. The plane could accommodate a crew of three, plus 12 parachutists and four large supply containers.

The other mainstay of the Crete operation was the DFS 230A glider, which was towed by the Ju-52 at the end of a 130-foot steel cable. Built of canvas, steel and wood, the 1,900-pound glider could carry 10 fully equipped troops. DFS 230As normally cruised at under 100 miles per hour, which made them easy targets. In the Crete operation, 10 were shot down.

With a wingspan of 95 feet and a length of 62 feet, the Ju-52 (above and top right) was powered by three 830-horsepower engines that could propel it at a maximum speed of 189 mph.

Gracefully shaped, the DFS 230A glider (below) had a wingspan of 72 feet and a length of 37 feet. It was released by the mother plane, the Ju-52, at altitudes of up to 5,000 feet.

that had been used against the Turks in the 19th Century.

Within an hour of the parachute attack on Kastelli, two thirds of the invaders had been killed and the rest were being overrun by Cretans chanting an old Greek war cry. When these Germans surrendered, Major Bedding locked them in the town jail for their own safekeeping, "as a good many of the inhabitants were gunning for them."

After the German mountain troops discovered the "atrocities," however, a Stuka bombing attack was called in on Kastelli. A direct hit on the jail freed the German prisoners, and they joined with the mountain troops in finally subduing the Cretan irregulars. In reprisal for the alleged atrocities, 200 village men were lined up in the square and shot to death.

The situation on Crete was now deteriorating so rapidly for the Allies that General Freyberg concluded that "this place has become no fit abode for important people." The Greek monarch, King George II, was one such person. He had taken refuge on the island on the 24th of April, when the Germans were closing in on Athens. All of a sudden it became imperative to evacuate the King to Egypt. The King had left his house near Canea as soon as German paratroopers began dropping around him on the first day of the attack. Accompanied by a British military escort, he now had to make an arduous, three-day journey over the White Mountains by foot and mule in order to reach a prearranged evacuation point on the southern coast of the island. He slogged over snow-capped peaks and slept on the ground, resplendent in his royal gold-braided uniform. "His Majesty treated it like an outing," said the British military attaché, Colonel J. S. Blunt, after the King was picked up by a destroyer.

In the meantime, a showdown was impending between the attacking German forces and the island's defenders. The British garrisons at Rethymnon and Heraklion in the east were still holding their own against the paratroopers, but Maleme was irretrievably lost. Freyberg's New Zealanders were now approximately eight miles to the east of the Maleme airstrip, defending a line running north and south through the heights near the hilltop village of Galatas. They were under such intense pressure from the Luftwaffe, which could send in as many as 400 fighters daily, that movement during the day was almost impossible. Meanwhile, fresh mountain troops, pouring into Maleme and marching east, had linked up with a parachute regiment that the defenders had effectively contained in Prison Valley, southwest of Galatas, since the first day of the attack. The stage was set for perhaps the most stirring battle of the entire struggle for Crete.

All day on May 25 the Germans attacked Galatas. The 10th New Zealand Brigade—an improvised unit including gunners, truck drivers, cooks and even band musicians—suffered heavy casualties. The brigade had only two trucks, and they were incessantly busy taking men to the dressing station—"in loads like butchers' meat," as the brigade commander, Colonel Kippenberger, described it.

Even so, the New Zealand brigade put up a furious fight. Kippenberger, a 44-year-old former lawyer, provided much of the inspiration. He repeatedly ventured up front, at one point rallying a group of stragglers who were stumbling back from the line by walking among the men and shouting, "Stand for New Zealand!"

But by evening Galatas was reported "stiff with Jerries," and Kippenberger made his decision: the village had to be retaken "or everything would crumble away." At twilight he assembled 200 infantrymen, many of them volunteers, and two light tanks of the British 3rd Hussars under the command of Lieutenant Roy Farran. Two crew members in one of the tanks were wounded, so Farran gave two New Zealand engineers a quick lesson in running a tank. "Of course," he told them, "you seldom come out of one of these things alive."

Kippenberger launched his counterattack with the tanks in the lead: "The infantry followed up at a walk, then broke into a run, started shouting—and, running and shouting, disappeared into the village. Instantly there was the most startling clamour, audible all over the field. Scores of automatics and rifles were being fired at once, the crunch of grenades, screams and yells—the uproar swelled and sank, swelled again to a horrifying crescendo. Some women and children came scurrying down the road; one old woman frantic with fear clung desperately to me. The firing slackened, became a brisk clatter, steadily becoming more distant and stopped."

Inside the village, the counterattackers had caught hun-

A HOSPITAL WHERE GERMANS AND BRITISH WORKED SIDE BY SIDE

For all the ferocity of the fighting on Crete, the opposing German and British forces often showed a surprisingly chivalrous compassion and concern for each other.

The British looked after wounded German airmen in their already crowded 7th General Hospital west of Canea, while the Germans tended to British casualties at a dressing station in a gully to the south. During a tour of the station, Baron von der Heydte, a battalion commander of the German airborne troops, made a point of visiting an English soldier. "I knelt beside him and brushed his blonde hair back from his forehead. 'The war is over for me, sir,' he said. 'I hope it will be for you, too, in the not-so-distant future.'"

Perhaps the most remarkable example of German and British harmony occurred at Knossos, where the British had built a hospital and a radio station. When the Germans fired on the radio station, the British protested because of the hospital's proximity. The Germans agreed to cease fire if the radio station was dismantled. The British complied with this request, and the hospital was converted into a joint facility, staffed by both German and British medical personnel.

The spirit of cooperation was extended to the grave when von der Heydte established a common cemetery for British and German soldiers off the road from Alikianou to Canea. The Baron invited captured British officers to the consecration ceremony and exchanged quiet greetings with them at the cemetery. "At that moment," he later wrote, "we did not consider ourselves enemies, but friends who had been defeated by the same harsh fate."

Next to a wrecked plane, a German pilot is treated for a broken leg by British medics.

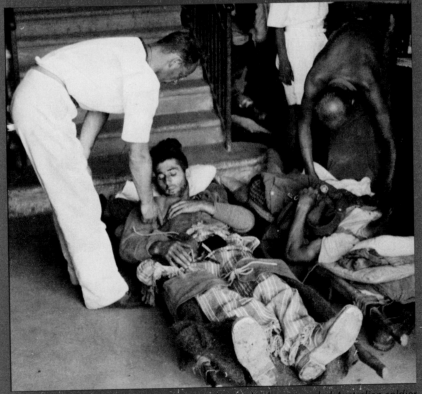
At a medical station at Suda Bay, a German doctor checks a wounded Australian soldier.

dreds of mountain troops by surprise. The New Zealanders stalked through cottages and back alleys, routing the Germans with grenades and bayonets. Both of the light tanks were hit, and on the main street Lieutenant Farran lay wounded in the gutter cheering on the infantry, "Good show, New Zealand, jolly good show!"

The Germans soon retreated from Galatas. But despite the success of the counterattack, the New Zealanders were ordered to pull back toward Suda Bay—there were not enough reserves to consolidate the victory on either flank of the village. Galatas was abandoned and that night, in the eerie silence, a young Cretan girl who had been hiding in the ruins walked among the fallen—friend and enemy—covering bodies with old carpets and offering goat's milk to those who were still alive.

The gallant assault on Galatas was the kind of counterattack that might have saved Maleme a few days before, but it had come too late. The German force in the west now numbered 8,000 men. Freyberg's forces, although still numerically superior, were exhausted and running out of ammunition and supplies. As a fighting force they were finished. On the 26th of May, Freyberg sent a cable to his Middle East commander in Cairo: "I regret to have to report that in my opinion the troops under my command here at Suda Bay have reached the limit of endurance. . . . From a military point of view our position is hopeless." The next

Stretching across the scorched landscape of Crete, a serpentine column of British, New Zealand and Australian soldiers grimly makes its way to the island's southern coast, where British ships were waiting to evacuate the men to Egypt. Of the 32,000 British troops on Crete, only 18,000 made it to Egypt. The others were either killed or captured by the Germans.

day he received permission from London to retreat more than 30 miles south over the mountains to the little fishing village of Sphakia on the southern coast. From there, his forces were to be evacuated to Egypt.

For the second time in a month, a large British force was headed toward the sea to be rescued by the Royal Navy. Thousands of soldiers streamed down a winding road that ended abruptly in a 500-foot-high cliff overlooking the tiny beach at Sphakia. Weary, thirsty and so hungry that some of the troops ate raw chicken, the retreating force had become, in Freyberg's words, "a disorganized rabble making its way doggedly and painfully to the south."

Even so, their morale was unbroken. Accompanying the troops, New Zealand war artist Captain Peter McIntyre kept hearing a song "humming through my head. Gradually I became more conscious of it. I could swear I had heard snatches of it whistled from the columns in the valley. The song of the retreat, 'Waltzing Matilda'—ridiculous in a way and quite inappropriate but somehow expressive of the hopes of these men, hopes of seeing Australian homes or New Zealand homes again. The Aussie hat lying by the broken truck sent it through my mind again. 'You'll come a-waltzing, Matilda, with me.' "

At first, the Germans did not pursue the retreating British. They thought that the enemy force had moved east to link up with the British garrison at Rethymnon. Luftwaffe planes might have spotted the Aussies and New Zealanders, but none came—German fighters and bombers were already being diverted from Crete to prepare for the invasion of Russia.

After a late start, the Germans reached Rethymnon on May 30. Instead of the main enemy force, they found there an Aussie colonel carrying a white towel tied to a stick. He was Colonel T. C. Campbell, whose defenders had counterattacked the paratroopers at the airfield east of Rethymnon repeatedly in the past 10 days, killing 700 and capturing 500. Freyberg's attempts to notify him of the evacuation had failed, and when Campbell heard tanks approaching he had only one day's rations left—and concluded that there

was no alternative but to surrender his 900-man garrison.

The British garrison at Heraklion, 30 miles farther east, had better luck. It had received the evacuation orders, and during the night of May 28 a convoy of two cruisers and six destroyers took aboard some 4,000 men. Some of the wounded had to be left behind.

Within hours of the evacuation at Heraklion, however, German bombers caught up with the convoy. In the attack that followed, two British destroyers were sunk, two cruisers badly damaged and 800 men were killed, wounded or captured. When the convoy finally reached port in Egypt on the night of May 29, a piper from the Black Watch Regiment stood high on the bridge of a crippled cruiser, mournfully playing a regimental march, "Hielan Laddie."

The Royal Navy had suffered frightful losses since the battle for Crete began. The toll included 1,800 men dead, two cruisers and seven destroyers sunk, and 20 other vessels damaged—including three battleships and the aircraft carrier *Formidable*.

For four nights the Royal Navy attempted to evacuate the more than 12,000 troops at Sphakia, but the Luftwaffe attacks were so intense that on June 1 the effort had to be abandoned. As a result, 5,000 men were left stranded in Crete; among them were units who had fought the toughest rear-guard battles. Not all surrendered: six months later some 500 would still be at large in the mountains, fighting alongside Cretan guerrillas.

The cost of the Cretan campaign in British, New Zealand and Australian troops was high—4,000 dead, 12,000 taken prisoner. But the Germans also lost 4,000 men. So heavy were their losses that they were forced to reappraise the whole concept of airborne warfare.

In August, the Führer presented the Knight's Cross to his airborne commander, General Student, and then, casually over herbal tea, told him, "the day of the parachutist is over. The parachute arm is a surprise weapon and without the element of surprise there can be no future for airborne forces." Henceforth, Student's beloved hunters from the sky would fight mostly as earth-bound infantry.

A COSTLY AIRBORNE CONQUEST

Under a trail of smoke, German parachutists float to the ground during the invasion of Crete. The flaming airplane is one of 151 Junkers-52s lost in the battle.

"THE TOUGHEST FIGHTERS IN THE GERMAN ARMY"

General Kurt Student, architect of the invasion of Crete, ponders strategy aboard an airplane bound for the island on the sixth day of fighting.

During preparations for the airborne invasion of Crete by 10,000 parachutists and glider-borne troops in May 1941, General Kurt Student, mastermind of the operation, expected nothing less than a "swift and decisive success." German intelligence estimated that fewer than 15,000 British troops held the island (the actual number was almost 42,000). Many of the defenders were known to be battle-weary evacuees of the recent fighting in Greece. Furthermore, intelligence believed that the Greek soldiers under British command "wouldn't fight any more" and that the "demoralized" Tommies would easily be overwhelmed. But just to make sure the British would remain demoralized, the VIII Luftwaffe Corps, with more than 500 fighters and bombers, softened them up by strafing and bombing their positions for three weeks.

A smashing victory seemed all the more certain because the invasion was to be spearheaded by the cream of the German armed forces. Adolf Hitler had not hesitated to declare at one time to Albert Speer, one of his top aides, that "the paratroopers are the toughest fighters in the German army, tougher even than the Waffen S.S."

Confident though they were of victory, the Germans nevertheless left nothing to chance. Each jumper carried half a dozen grenades, a submachine gun and a long knife. His personal equipment consisted of spare socks and pants, a blanket, a small cookstove and two days' rations, including a chocolate bar, one-inch cubes of bread, three ounces of toilet paper and a phonetic phrase book with such handy commands for captured British troops as, "If yu lei yu will be schott." To combat fatigue, some of the paratroopers also carried hypodermic syringes and a stimulant made of caffeine-sodium salicylate.

Sewn into each pack were the "Ten Commandments of the Parachutist," a blend of German mysticism and tactical principles. The 10th Commandment exhorted the paratrooper to "be as nimble as a greyhound, as tough as leather, as hard as Krupp steel, and so you shall be the German warrior incarnate."

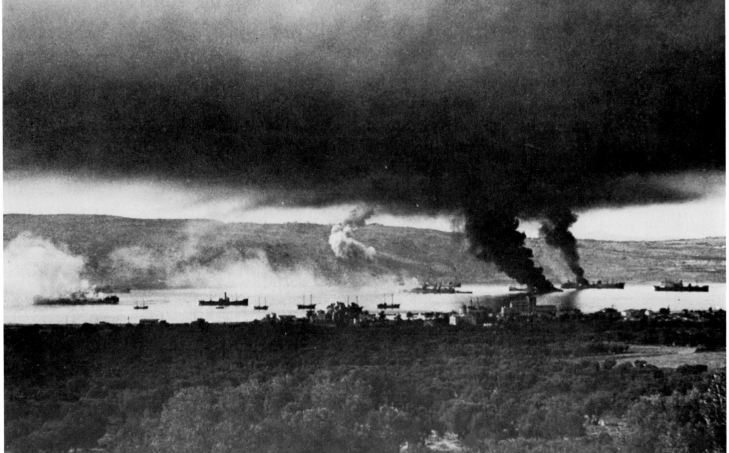

Stuka dive bombers (top) fly over Crete. Their prime targets were ships in Suda Bay, two of which (bottom) are shown damaged and casting palls of smoke.

BEHIND THE SCENES OF A COMPLEX ASSAULT

Mounting the invasion of an island as big as Crete proved to be an enormous and complex logistical undertaking. From the start, the operation was beset by organization and supply problems that caused two postponements.

The 7th Airborne Division, which was to bear the brunt of the attack, had to be rushed by rail and truck from bases in Germany to bivouacs near seven staging fields in southern Greece. A supporting division was stranded near Bucharest for lack of transportation and had to be replaced at the last moment by the 5th Mountain Division, which was based in Greece.

Supply problems were staggering. Packers stuffed more than 20,000 parachutes —the men carried two for safety. Each airborne division required 150 to 200 tons of weapons and ammunition. Since drinking water on Crete was scarce during the summer, several hundred thousand bottles of mineral water had to be collected from plants in Athens and the port of Piraeus.

The staging airstrips were in bad shape, and German engineers and construction crews, using Greek laborers, worked feverishly to improve the fields or build new ones. On Melos Island a landing strip was built in three days. Before takeoff at almost all of the fields, local fire brigades were brought in to hose down the runways in an attempt to combat dust; nevertheless, some airplane motors clogged. Visibility was poor, upsetting schedules.

In spite of the problems, the paratroopers themselves were in high spirits as they winged their way toward Crete in the early morning hours of May 20, 1941. On one of the planes, they broke into the boisterous "Song of the Paratroops": "Fly on this day against the enemy! Into the planes, into the planes! Comrade, there is no going back!" Yet in little more than an hour—the time it took to fly from Greece to Crete—the high hopes of the paratroopers and their commanders would be shattered by a surprisingly tough British foe.

At dust-clouded Tanagra airfield north of Athens, Ju-52s wait for clearance to take off for Crete.

Rip cords clenched between their teeth, paratroopers board a Ju-52.

Seen from a German glider, Ju-52s skim across the Aegean to Crete.

On D-day, scores of German paratroopers descend on Crete

Partially covered by his canopy, a dead parachutist lies sprawled by a tree.

64

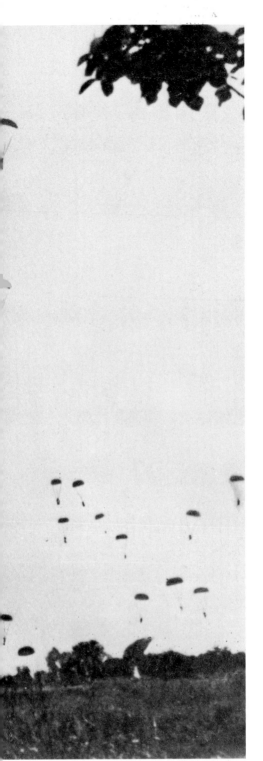

after being dropped from low-flying Junkers.

Crash-landed near Maleme, a Ju-52 sits wrecked in a field as two soldiers pass by in a motorcycle.

Machine guns at the ready, German airborne troops scramble away from their damaged glider.

DEATH IN VINEYARDS AND BARLEY FIELDS

For the German paratroopers, the invasion of Crete turned into an unmitigated horror. As soon as the doors of the lumbering Ju-52 transports were opened, the men were stunned by intense British ack-ack fire that was bursting around them. Leaping out of the planes, they were caught in a cross fire of machine-gun and rifle bullets. Planes and gliders were blasted out of the air. Parachutists were easy targets for snipers perched in trees.

"The sloping fields of the vineyards were littered with bodies, many of them still in their harnesses with the parachutes tugging gently at them in every mild puff of breeze and getting no response," one New Zealander later recalled. "Among the olives, corpses hung from branches or lay at the foot of the gnarled trees, motionless on the trampled young barley. Only here and there a discarded overall like the discarded shell of some strange insect showed that its owner had got away."

On the day before D-day, some German soldiers coax a reluctant mule aboard a caïque. At sea, the motorized sailboats were navigated by pocket compass.

Packed shoulder to shoulder on a ramshackle caïque, mountain troops sail toward Crete. Many of the boats broke down en route and had to be towed.

Their boat destroyed, survivors await rescue on a raft as others cling to the sides.

A PATCHWORK FLEET ON AN ILL-FATED MISSION

On Crete the embattled German troops who had survived the airdrops anxiously awaited the 2,331 men of the 5th Mountain Division and the supplies they were to bring by sea. But the makeshift fleet of some 24 dilapidated Greek motorized sailboats, or caïques, that were to carry the troops could only do four knots on calm seas. And they were perfect targets.

On the second night of battle, May 21, some German paratroopers climbed a hill and gazed out to sea. "What we saw from there was like a giant firework display," one wrote later. "Rockets and flares were shooting into the night sky, searchlights probed the darkness, and the red glow of a fire was spreading across the horizon."

The paratroopers watched for 20 minutes and then, shocked and depressed, returned to their headquarters. "It was only too easy to guess what had happened," an officer noted. "The British Mediterranean Fleet had intercepted our light squadron and, there was no doubting, destroyed it."

Colonel Hans Brauer, German commander at Heraklion, gives an order to a parachutist. Brauer's troops suffered 200 casualties before ground actions began.

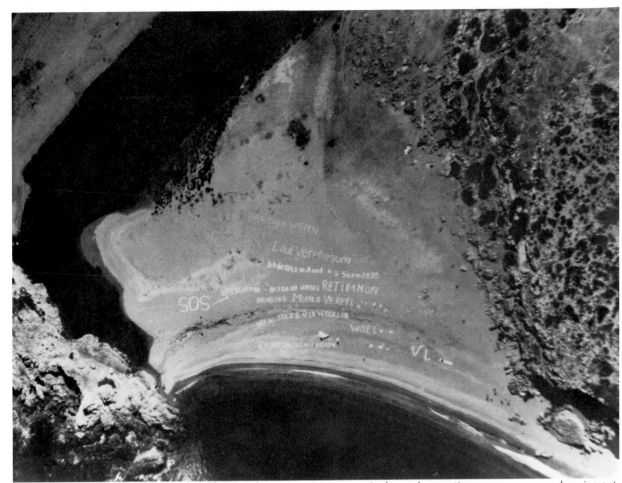

Their radio damaged, German troops at Rethymnon leave an urgent message in the sand requesting more weapons and equipment.

A German soldier recovers weapons from an airdrop container.

COSTLY BLUNDERS AND INGENIOUS SOLUTIONS

For 13 days after they landed, the German paratroopers were involved in furious close-quarter combat. One of the roughest actions took place at the town of Rethymnon, prized for its airstrip. Just about everything went wrong.

The company that was to lead the attack on the airfield was virtually wiped out in the landing and on the ground. Many of the men were killed as they scrambled to weapons containers. German planes, unable to distinguish friend from foe, killed 16 of their own men. To add to the problems, troops were running out of ammunition—and their radio equipment was destroyed by artillery fire.

Isolated from other units, the only hope that the beleaguered troops at Rethymnon had left was to attract the attention of the Luftwaffe. A radio operator hit on the idea of laying out a call for help on the sand of a nearby cove. The three-foot-high letters were constructed from white stones and shells. From an aerial photo *(above)*, the German command learned of the men's predicament and dropped badly needed supplies and munitions to them.

Paratroopers guard British prisoners on Crete in May 1941. Though overpowered, the British fought "like bulldogs," said a German general.

Paratroopers stand guard on the parapet of a prison near Galatas that was captured at the end of May.

Flag in place, Germans occupy a strategic hill.

An action photograph shows a German soldier with a flamethrower dashing off to attack a British tank.

"THE GRAVE OF GERMAN PARACHUTISTS"

The turning point in the battle for Crete occurred after the remainder of the 5th Mountain Division arrived at the Maleme airfield from Greece, along with crucial supplies. Now the Germans had enough men to smash the British on May 26 at Galatas, the last major defensive strong point west of Crete's capital, Canea, and the nearby port of Suda.

Following the ferocious day and night struggle at Galatas, "the rising sun shone on a gruesome picture of the nocturnal battle," reported a German officer who was present. "Friend and foe were lying in the streets, on the heights and in the gardens, countless weapons and equipment covered the streets and demolished tanks were standing alongside the road."

It took the Germans only six more days to complete their conquest of Crete. But the price was high—4,000 men dead, another 2,594 wounded. When General Student visited his men after the fighting at Canea, "there was no evidence in his features that he was joyful over the victory—his victory—and proud at the success of his daring scheme," said a battalion commander. Wrote Student bitterly: "Crete was the grave of the German parachutists."

In the final fighting, paratroopers advance under fire to assault a British position near Heraklion.

Residents of Crete who gave assistance to the British undergo interrogation by a German paratrooper.

After the defeat of Heraklion, victorious but exhausted airborne troops are led into the shell-pocked town by its mayor, wearing the white skimmer at center.

3

By late spring of 1941, Hitler had good reason to think that Yugoslavia was finished. Its generals had capitulated, its young King had fled into exile and its people seemed thoroughly cowed by the Wehrmacht. Accordingly, the Führer chopped the country into weak ministates, then shared the chore of controlling them with three Axis partners—Italy, Bulgaria and Hungary—and a handful of local puppets. So eager was he to get on with Operation *Barbarossa,* his invasion of the Soviet Union, that he left in Yugoslavia only four weak divisions, composed mostly of men considered too old for active combat.

Hitler had hardly turned his back on Yugoslavia when the country erupted in a spontaneous revolt. Singly and in small groups, sometimes armed only with clubs and knives, Yugoslavs killed German guards, ambushed patrols and confiscated their weapons. Armed bands attacked truck convoys, and blew up bridges and rail junctions. But these forays were haphazard at best, and the rebels realized that they had to organize.

The Chetniks were the first—and, for a short while, the only—organized guerrilla force to take the field. They took their name from *cheta,* the 19th Century guerrilla band that had harassed the Turkish occupation forces and, with the assistance of the Serbian Army, had driven out the conquerors. The modern Chetniks were predominantly Serbs. Like their predecessors, they wore tall sheepskin caps adorned with a skull-and-crossbones emblem. They let their hair grow long and cultivated beards, in keeping with the custom that called for male communicants of the Serbian Orthodox Church to refrain from shaving and cutting their hair for 40 days following the death of a loved one. As they saw it, they were now mourning their country's lost freedom, and they vowed to remain unshaven and untrimmed until the day of liberation.

The Chetniks were led by Army Colonel Drazha Mihailovich, a thoughtful, distinguished Serbian career officer who had refused to surrender when Yugoslavia capitulated in April. Politically, Mihailovich was a royalist, determined to preserve the monarchy and also the Serbs' traditional dominance in the Yugoslav government. Rallying some 30 officers and enlisted men, Mihailovich made his way into the hills and forests of western Serbia. Having fought there as a young lieutenant in the First World War, he knew that

CHETNIKS AND PARTISANS

the rugged terrain was ideal for hit-and-run guerrilla tactics. Furthermore, the area was close to rail lines and other military targets in the Western Morava valley. Here, on a sheep-grazing plateau known as Ravna Gora, he began building and training a guerrilla army of former soldiers and local peasants.

Mihailovich and his men had been inflamed by Hitler's brutality toward the Yugoslavs and particularly toward the seven million Serbs, the nation's most militant nationalists. Immediately after occupying Yugoslavia, the Germans had deported 200,000 prisoners of war—all of them Serbs. And now, thousands upon thousands of Serbs were being massacred by Germany's puppet regimes, and thousands more were being executed by the Germans in reprisal for German troops killed by the guerrillas.

Mihailovich proceeded slowly in his vengeance. He decided to build up and conserve the strength of the Chetniks and to undertake only small, low-risk operations that would harass the Germans without provoking massive counterattacks or terrible reprisals against the civilian population. He would not mount his full-scale uprising until the German forces had been so weakened by attrition that the Chetniks, with assistance from the Allies, could throw out the conquerors. This cautious strategy coincided with broadcasts that were made that summer by the government-in-exile in London, which called the present uprising premature and urged all Yugoslavs to bear their ordeal quietly until Allied help could arrive.

Though Mihailovich's strategy was basically sound, it had a detrimental effect on his men. Lacking a sense of urgency, the Chetniks took a casual approach to guerrilla operations. The *vojvodas*—leaders of Mihailovich's scattered bands—were building up their own little fiefdoms, with the result that they sometimes refused to obey orders from headquarters. Inevitably, the rank-and-file Chetniks gave their loyalty to their *vojvodas* rather than to Mihailovich, and military discipline as a whole was slack.

In spite of these limitations, the Chetniks' operations in the summer of 1941 attracted widespread attention. Confused reports smuggled out of Yugoslavia to the Allies made the name Chetnik synonymous with resistance to the Axis powers. By September, Mihailovich had managed to establish direct contact with the British, using an improvised radio transmitter powered by 500 flashlight batteries. His sketchy communiqués on Serbian resistance—widely respected as being the first organized guerrilla activity anywhere on the European continent—fired the imagination of a world that had begun to believe Hitler was invincible. The messages also brought Mihailovich official recognition from his government-in-exile, which named him commander of the Yugoslav Army in the Homeland.

But it soon emerged that Mihailovich had guerrilla rivals. His radio reports made no mention of them, and the Allies learned only a little about them from Yugoslav refugees and British intelligence contacts. The British did find out that those other guerrillas were Communists and that they were called Partisans (Tito explained that the name was derived from *partidas,* Spanish for the guerrilla bands that had harassed Napoleon during his invasions of Spain and Russia in the early 19th Century). But that was the extent of their information about them. In September of 1941, no one in the West even knew the name of the Partisan leader.

That mysterious Communist already had plenty of names; he had used more than two dozen aliases before adopting his current one, Tito. And he had needed every one of those aliases—as well as a great deal of luck, stamina and drive—to survive the many close calls that marked his astonishing career.

He was born Josip Broz into a Croatian-Slovene peasant family and worked as a factory laborer in his early jobs. In the First World War, when Croatia was still part of the Austro-Hungarian empire, he served in the Imperial Army as a noncommissioned officer and was captured in action against the Russians. While working on the Trans-Siberian Railroad as a prisoner of war, he cast his lot with the Bolsheviks. He was a dedicated Communist when he returned to his native Croatia in 1920, and his political faith was subsequently hardened by years in Yugoslav prisons for illegal Communist activities. His energy, decisiveness and commanding manner won him the respect of Communist bureaucrats. It was later said that the name Tito was inspired by his take-charge style; in issuing orders in Serbo-Croatian he would say "you do this" *(ti)*, "you do that" *(to)*.

During the 1920s and 1930s, the Yugoslav Communist Party dwindled under steady police pressure. In 1939, after

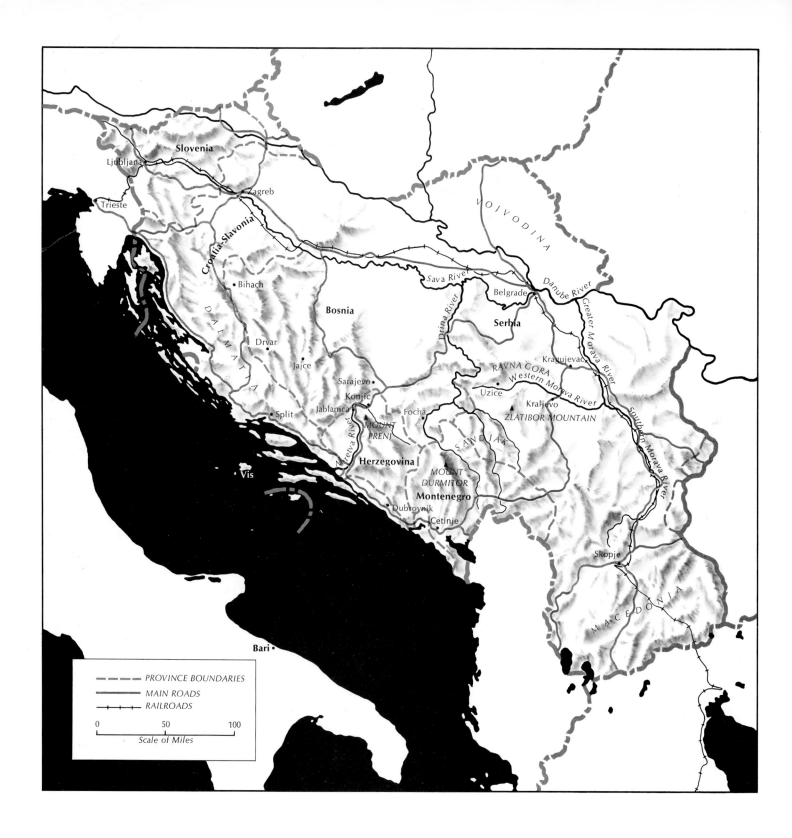

Yugoslavia's rugged terrain was tactically ideal for guerrilla warfare. It abounded in excellent mountain hideouts and forced the Axis occupation troops to depend on tenuous lines of supply. There were few major highways and railroads, and bridges over rivers and gorges were vulnerable to sabotage. But the terrain also worked against the guerrilla bands. It divided the country into historically defined but hotly contested areas (broken lines), preserving old ethnic and religious hostilities and thus preventing the development of a unified resistance against the occupation.

76

the leader of the Yugoslav Communist Party had been liquidated in Stalin's great purge, Tito was appointed secretary general of the party and charged with rebuilding it.

In the first year of his stewardship, Tito boosted party membership from 3,000 to 12,000. His recruits included many students at the University of Belgrade and a large number of women. Most of the students came from peasant families, and their knowledge of the mountainous countryside—where to hide out, whom to trust or distrust—would prove an invaluable asset in guerrilla operations. Tito also had a hard core of battle-tested "Españoles," party members who had fought with the International Brigades in the Spanish Civil War. Once in the field, the Partisans welcomed new volunteers of every political persuasion and from every ethnic and religious background. But all of Tito's key personnel were party members, and he knew he could count on their strict obedience and absolute loyalty to his revolutionary objectives.

Tito's long-range goal was to transform Yugoslavia into a Communist nation, but his short-range tactics were dictated by the needs of the Soviet Union, which he called "our dear socialist fatherland, our hope and beacon." The Communists had been late in joining the resistance because Tito had had orders to shun the War as a family feud between those imperialist nations Germany and Great Britain. But all that changed in June 1941, when Germany violated the nonaggression pact it had signed with the Soviet Union two years before and invaded Russia. It immediately became Tito's Communist duty to attack the German occupation with vigor, thereby diverting German troops from the Russian front and denying Germany raw materials from the Balkans. Unlike Mihailovich, Tito was prepared to suffer heavy losses to achieve his ends.

By late September of 1941, the battle lines in Yugoslavia converged in Serbia, the hotbed of resistance. The Chetniks and the Partisans—respectively numbering more than 5,000 and 13,000—had seized control of nearly two thirds of the countryside, and the Germans were bringing in reinforcements to put down the insurrection. The headquarters for the two guerrilla organizations were situated only 25 miles apart, Mihailovich's in peasant cottages on the Ravna Gora, Tito's in the thriving market town of Uzice, which the Partisans had occupied after an imperiled German garrison had hastily withdrawn. Tito, who had a taste for unproletarian luxury, had tried at first to run his guerrilla campaigns from a fashionable villa in a Belgrade suburb. He had to be extremely careful because the residence of the German military commander in Belgrade was only a few hundred yards away. Tito's bathroom was equipped with an escape door, hidden in the cupboard behind the washbasin, that led to a secret place under the roof where he kept two revolvers and 16 hand grenades.

In September, when it became unsafe for him to remain in Belgrade, Tito slipped out of the city and joined his Partisans in western Serbia. At Uzice the Partisans replaced the local government with their own "Uzice Republic," tried and executed collaborators, and began publishing a party newspaper, *The Struggle*.

The Partisans made good use of materials and equipment the Germans had left behind, including nearly 300 tons of tobacco, 23 truckloads of cigarette paper, the machinery for a rifle factory and 70 million dinars (more than one million dollars). Gratefully removing the money, the Partisans set up a rifle factory in an underground shelter and began turning out 400 weapons a day. And using the tobacco and paper, they began producing their own brand of cigarettes—Red Star.

The Partisans recruited with ingenuity and zeal. One reckless group even went looking for volunteers in a German-occupied town. They slipped into the fire station, commandeered the firemen's uniforms and band instruments and then paraded through the streets past unsuspecting German soldiers. On the way out of town, they struck up the "Partisan March" and for their daring won a few new comrades.

Their standard recruiting methods were less flamboyant and more productive. To compete with the Chetniks' patent appeal to fellow Serbs, the Partisans stressed their own aggressive patriotism and anti-Fascism. When reverent peasants expressed fears of Communist atheism, the recruiters drew parallels between the social teachings of Marx and of Jesus, whom they called the first Communist. For citizens who showed interest in Communist theory, they held indoctrination classes. When they captured a town, they not only set up a new government but also destroyed archives, to make it more difficult to restore the old system. They left no doubt in the Chetniks' minds that they were building politically for the postwar future.

The deep differences between the Partisans and Chetniks led to a few skirmishes. But both organizations were small, short of arms, supplies and experience, and they could ill afford fratricidal hostilities in the face of increasing German strength. They therefore managed to suppress their enmity and to coexist fairly well, at least temporarily. Mihailovich reluctantly joined forces with Tito in several forays against German-held towns. The two leaders even met in September 1941 to discuss ways to cooperate more effectively, and a second meeting was scheduled for late October.

But before the second meeting took place, there occurred two events that ruptured relations between the two groups. First, in late September the British landed a liaison officer, Captain D. T. "Bill" Hudson, by submarine on the Yugoslav coast. His mission was to clarify the still-murky situation for his government and to offer some encouragement to Mihailovich, whom the British considered the leader of the whole Yugoslav resistance. Hudson, who had worked as a mining engineer in Serbia before the War, made his way through Partisan-held territory to Mihailovich's headquarters on the Ravna Gora plateau. He assured Mihailovich of British aid, and his pledge raised the Chetnik leader's confidence and reduced his need for distasteful compromises with the Communists.

The last real chance for effective cooperation between the two guerrilla forces disappeared when word of two German reprisals against the Serbs reached Mihailovich. The Germans had received orders from Hitler himself to increase to 100 the number of Yugoslav civilians to be shot for every soldier killed by the guerrillas. On October 20 the Germans descended on the Serbian town of Kraljevo, recently the target of a joint Chetnik-Partisan raid that killed about 30 German troops. According to official German reports, their troops put to death about 1,700 of the inhabitants; the Yugoslavs claimed that nearly 6,000 people were slain. On the next day, the Germans also wreaked havoc on

the town of Kragujevac, near the site of a Partisan raid that had killed 10 German soldiers and wounded 20. By the Germans' reckoning 2,300 townsmen were executed. The Yugoslavs said the number was 7,000.

To guarantee that the tale of horror would be spread, the Germans spared a few hundred townsmen. Approximately 600 more were kept at the killing ground for four days to bury the dead. They did a poor job, digging graves so shallow that for a long time afterward homeless dogs unearthed the bodies and ate them.

The bloodbaths confirmed Mihailovich's worst fears for the Serbs' survival. He blamed himself for departing from his original cautious strategy and joining the Partisan attack that inspired the German atrocity at Kraljevo. And he had no intention of cooperating with the Partisans in another operation that would result in the deaths of more Serbs than Germans.

For his part, Tito had no particular desire to coordinate his operations with those of Mihailovich. But the Moscow party line called for cooperation between independent guerrilla forces, and Tito obeyed orders. In advance of the scheduled second meeting with the Chetnik leader, he prepared and sent to Chetnik headquarters a detailed plan for a unified Partisan-Chetnik command. Mihailovich gave the proposal scant consideration.

The two leaders met on October 26 in a peasant's house in the village of Brajichi, not far from Chetnik headquarters on the Ravna Gora. Mihailovich and his bearded advisers sat on one side of a large table, Tito and his clean-shaven staff on the other side. Behind the two groups stood the bodyguards of the leaders.

Mihailovich and Tito presented a striking contrast in leadership styles. Mihailovich was essentially a bureaucrat rather than a field commander, an introvert who was slight of stature and wore steel-rimmed glasses. "He struck me," Tito said later, "as a nice, pleasant-mannered sort of man—a typical regular officer."

Tito, on the other hand, was a man of action. He was sturdily built, fastidious in his dress, but unpolished and aggressive in manner. He had spent a crucial portion of his life in the Soviet Union and had brought home a Russian wife. The thing about him that struck Mihailovich was his accent: it was Croatian and Mihailovich had never heard

anything quite like it. The Chetnik leader suspected that Tito was Russian.

The atmosphere at the meeting was tense, even hostile. Mihailovich added to the strain by playing a joke on Tito: he offered him a glass of a local concoction known as "Sumadija tea," which was not tea at all but warmed and sweetened plum brandy. Tito took a long sip and began coughing violently. While Tito wiped the drink off his immaculate uniform, Mihailovich burst into laughter.

The two leaders managed to come to agreement only on secondary issues. They agreed to share the arms output from the Partisans' rifle factory in Uzice and to divide any supplies sent to Mihailovich by the British. But Tito wanted the two movements to form a joint command—Moscow's orders called for a popular front—and Mihailovich was firmly opposed to such a step, feeling that Tito's kind of guerrilla warfare would be suicidal for the Serbs.

The negotiations broke down on this central issue, and the breach between the Partisans and the Chetniks proved to be irreparable. The day after next, the 28th of October, brought the first of a number of vicious skirmishes between Chetnik and Partisan units. It was uncertain who started the clashes; each side blamed the other. But there was no question that the particular attack that triggered an all-out civil war was initiated by the Chetniks. On the night of November 1, a large Chetnik force tried for a quick knockout blow by assaulting Partisan headquarters at Uzice. The Partisans were not surprised by the attack, but they were outraged—and their fury was intensified when they discovered that they were being assaulted by rifles from their own factory in Uzice.

The Partisans counterattacked and, following two weeks of fighting, surrounded Mihailovich's headquarters on the Ravna Gora plateau. They laid siege and waited for further orders from Tito in Uzice. Tito's next move was decided by a radio broadcast from Moscow in which the Russians, unwilling to jeopardize relations with the Western Allies, echoed the British view that Mihailovich was the sole leader of the Yugoslav resistance. The Partisan veteran Vladimir Dedijer wrote in his diary that "Tito stood still, aghast. I had never seen him so surprised."

But Tito realized that he had to play along with Moscow's

wishes. He quickly called off the attack on Mihailovich's headquarters, explaining to his comrades, "We must be careful not to cause difficulties in the foreign relations of the Soviet Union."

Despite further attempts at negotiations, the Partisans and the Chetniks were embarked upon a fratricidal war. Still, there was the common enemy to fight and, for the time being at least, driving out the Germans and Italians took precedence. In late September, the Germans launched an offensive to clear the countryside of guerrillas and protect the rail line that carried supplies south to their bases in Greece. They brought in heavy reinforcements, including a full division from the Russian front, and attacked along a 125-mile line with tanks and bomber support—some 50,000 well-equipped Germans against less than 20,000 tatterdemalion guerrillas.

The Chetniks were the first to recoil under the attack. Mihailovich was desperate for arms and ammunition. The Chetniks received one parachute drop of supplies from the British on November 9. But after that Captain Hudson radioed his government to stop sending arms until the civil warfare in Yugoslavia had ceased. Depressed by the shortage of weapons and ammunition, by successful Partisan attacks and by continuing reprisals against Serbian civilians, Mihailovich allowed himself to be persuaded by the Germans to meet secretly with their representatives on November 11. The Chetnik leader told the Germans that he was agreeable to a short truce: if they ceased attacking Chetniks, he would stop sabotaging their communication lines. He also asked the Germans for ammunition, saying he needed it that very night. Instead, the Germans demanded his unconditional surrender, and Mihailovich had no option but to go on fighting them.

The German offensive quickly put both guerrilla forces to rout. Two German divisions advanced on Partisan headquarters in Uzice, and Tito, declining to fight a suicidal battle, ordered his men to evacuate the town.

Unit by unit, the Partisans started to retreat across the Zlatibor Mountain into the Sandjak, a wild, mountainous region on the border of Serbia and eastern Bosnia. They carried with them—on horseback, by oxcart and truck—an enormous burden of ideological and fiscal baggage: their printing press, 5,000 unbound copies of Stalin's *History of the Communist Party of the Soviet Union,* which Tito himself had translated into Serbo-Croatian, and a couple of dozen chests of silver that weighed nearly 100 pounds each. Near the Serbian border, Partisans buried 20 of the chests beside a stream, then resumed their journey with the remaining chests. (The buried treasure remained concealed until 1943, when a flood unearthed it, enriching the area's peasants.) "We had a patriarchal, fetishistic attitude toward silver," one of Tito's associates wrote later. "We always dragged several cases around with us in the belief that we might need it in some critical situation."

Tito was among the last Partisans to flee Uzice, and twice he almost became a casualty. At the edge of town, he was strafed by German planes. Later, he was pursued so closely by German soldiers that he could hear them shouting. One week after the Partisans' flight from Uzice, German units drove the Chetniks from their Ravna Gora headquarters. Like Tito, Mihailovich had a close call. Finding himself in a house surrounded by enemy troops, he jumped out of a window and hid in a small trench covered with leaves and shrubbery until the Germans left. The escapes of Mihailovich and Tito so enraged the Germans that they put a price of 100,000 reichsmarks in gold—approximately $40,000—on each of their heads.

By the end of 1941, the revolt in Serbia had been crushed. To seal their victory and to prevent another uprising, the Germans (and their Bulgarian allies) went from village to village, shooting hostages and burning the homes of peasants who had given refuge to the guerrillas.

The costly defeat had a profound effect on Mihailovich. It convinced him that the Chetniks should go underground and remain there until the Allies arrived to liberate Yugoslavia. Reflecting later on his flight from the Germans, he declared, "When it was over and, with God's help, I was preserved to continue the struggle, I resolved that I would never again bring such misery on the country unless it could result in total liberation. When the day comes for us to rise, we will rise." But for all practical purposes, his hopes for continuing the struggle at a future date were foreclosed by his misguided efforts to save lives after the rout.

Mihailovich disbanded his main force and led a skeleton staff of Chetniks into hiding in the Serbian wilderness.

While several units continued their resistance independently, most of his guerrillas returned to their villages and resumed their regular lives.

Others, with Mihailovich's approval, enlisted in the home militia of General Milan Nedich, the puppet Prime Minister whom the Germans had installed to help them restore order in Serbia. Mihailovich was no admirer of Nedich, but he now perceived Tito and the Communists as the real enemy. Besides, in his hopeful scenario for a future uprising, he saw several advantages in melding his men into Nedich's home guard. From their new vantage point, they could supply him with valuable information about German troop movements. They could also carry on the civil war against the Partisans without fear of interdiction by the Germans. And, when the time came to rise against the Germans, they would be well equipped for the attack with German weapons and ammunition. All this was in line with a venerable Balkan strategy known as the "uses of the enemy," a policy of temporary accommodation with the conqueror for long-term gain. Mihailovich did not think of this new policy as collaboration, and he sincerely believed that it would work.

These radical moves by Mihailovich were unknown to the British, for Captain Hudson had been inspecting Tito's operations when the German offensive struck. After Hudson caught up with Mihailovich, the Chetnik leader was so furious over the halting of British supply consignments that he refused to let the captain break radio silence and get in touch with headquarters. Thus Hudson spent a few months as an outcast, denied contact with either Mihailovich or his own government. In Cairo he was listed as "missing, presumed dead." Meanwhile, Mihailovich was benefiting handsomely from the blackout on information from Yugoslavia. His government-in-exile in London promoted him to the rank of brigadier general in December, and a month later he was promoted again—to minister of the Yugoslav Army, Navy and Air Force.

While Mihailovich staked his future on the "uses of the enemy" strategy, Tito was thriving on adversity. The Partisan leader had learned not to be deterred by the Germans' reprisals; hard experience had taught him that their terror tactics only brought him new recruits—vengeful people who had lost homes and loved ones and hence had nothing more to lose by joining the resistance. And the German victory in Serbia had taught Tito that he needed to develop a special kind of guerrilla force to meet the challenge of Germany's powerful and well-trained conventional army.

The guerrilla's stock in trade—hit-and-run attacks on a small scale—would not suffice. Nor could Tito hope that he would be able to match the overwhelming numbers and firepower of the German forces in pitched battles. What he needed was a large force that combined both the mobility of small bands of guerrillas and the striking power of larger, well-organized units.

Tito set about to create such a force.

In the last days of 1941, he led his supporters from the Sandjak region northwest into Bosnia. On the way he gathered volunteers from Montenegro and, with the survivors of his defeat in Serbia, formed the First Proletarian Brigade. Composed of about 1,200 men and women, it was organized along regular-army lines but trained in specialized guerrilla tactics, such as mine laying and sabotaging communications. This force was to remain in the field constantly, ready to strike on short notice and move on. These were Tito's shock troops. He also saw them as the nucleus of a Communist army of liberation—a force that would be tru-

On an inspection tour British liaison officer D. T. "Bill" Hudson, standing with his hands behind his back and flanked by two OSS representatives, is greeted by a Chetnik major (left) and some guerrilla supporters. During his two and a half years in Yugoslavia, Hudson once lived for nearly four months on a diet of potatoes. His arduous tour of duty won him the Distinguished Service Order as well as a promotion from captain to colonel.

RELENTLESS PURSUERS OF AN ELUSIVE ENEMY

Advancing behind a Renault R-35 two-man light tank, German troops counterattack after a sudden Partisan raid on a forward position. To guard against such surprise attacks, the Germans constructed a network of small, heavily armed strong points about six miles apart and used armored cars and trains to patrol the roads and rail lines between these forts.

In spite of nearly insuperable handicaps, the German occupation troops managed to press their war on the Yugoslav guerrillas with increasing effectiveness. By late June, 1941, the crack combat units that had conquered the country had been pulled out for the invasion of the Soviet Union and replaced by four divisions, all under-strength and composed mainly of older garrison troops. This force lacked the training and equipment to stem the rising tide of hit-and-run attacks on German supply lines and installations.

Month after month, the Germans chased the Partisans from one area to another but could not force them to fight a decisive battle. The frustrated German units often lashed out at the only targets available—villagers on whom the Partisans depended for food, intelligence and new recruits.

By June 1943, the Germans were employing guerrilla-like tactics of their own to counter the guerrillas. They brought in combat-seasoned troops from other fronts and adopted the Partisans' most successful weapons: surprise and mobility. Avoiding ambushes along roads and railways, elite mountain troops advanced through rugged terrain to attack the guerrillas in their hideouts. Fast-moving ranger units called Jagd-kommando, whose troops often disguised themselves as peasants, scouted for guerrilla bases and hospitals in the most inaccessible areas. German security police and SS units, under Himmler's direct control, carried out operations against the guerrillas with particular brutality.

If pursued on a larger scale, these tactics might have contained the Partisans. But the Germans, locked in bitter fighting on far-flung fronts, could never spare enough first-rate troops to beat the guerrillas at their own game.

Pointing toward a suspected Partisan position, a German officer dispatches a patrol to probe wooded upland terrain in Bosnia in 1943.

Hot on the trail of a guerrilla band, German security police find a just-abandoned campsite in Slovenia. In their haste, the guerrillas left behind a tent, blankets and cooking utensils.

SS troops mow down fugitives in Serbia in 1942. Thousands of innocent civilians were killed by the Germans, who looked upon them as "bandits" or "Communist suspects."

ly national in character, transcending the ethnic and religious strife that until now had kept Yugoslavia a mere collection of provinces.

Tito found a fruitful field for operations in Bosnia, a province torn by unceasing strife among Catholics, members of the Eastern Orthodox Church and Moslems, the descendants of Slavs who had converted during the Turkish occupation. Bosnia, along with parts of the former provinces of Croatia and Herzegovina, had been put together by Hitler to form the so-called Independent State of Croatia, with a highly mixed population of 6.5 million. As its leader, the Germans had installed a vicious, home-grown Fascist named Ante Pavelich, a long-time advocate of Croatian independence and the founder of a pro-Catholic terrorist organization known as Ustashi, or Rebels. Even from his exile in Italy during the 1930s, Pavelich had managed to direct his Ustashi in a campaign to break up the recently founded nation of Yugoslavia—a campaign that had culminated in 1934 in the assassination of King Alexander, the father of the current King, young Peter.

As Hitler's puppet, Pavelich set about eliminating what he called "alien elements"—Serbs, Jews and Gypsies. The Serbs comprised approximately 30 per cent of the state of Croatia's population and nearly all were members of the Eastern Orthodox Church. Pavelich's formula for dealing with the Serbs was simple and brutal: one third were to be expelled to Serbia, one third converted to Catholicism and one third exterminated.

Ustashi storm troopers descended upon the Serbs with knife, gun and bludgeon. They tortured, plundered, raped, killed. In their campaign to obliterate the Serbs, they were aided by many Moslems, old enemies of the Serbs.

The Ustashi were also abetted by some Catholic clergymen in Croatia. Some of the leading churchmen denounced Pavelich's butchery, but others resigned themselves to his gunpoint conversions on the grounds that at least the obnoxious practice saved lives. A few radical Catholic priests heartily endorsed the massacres; one said, "Until now we have worked for the Catholic faith with missal and crucifix. Now the time has come for us to go to work with rifle and revolver." The Germans, who shared local occupation duties with the Italians, were first embarrassed and then sick-

ened by the Ustashi's indiscriminate bestiality. Their commanders threatened to replace Pavelich if he did not stop the wholesale killings. But he took the precaution of having his likely successor murdered, and the Germans, unable to find a suitable substitute, let the matter drop.

The Ustashi massacres went on and on. By the time the killing was finally brought to an end, the Ustashi had taken an incredible toll of Serbs—variously estimated at from 350,000 to 750,000.

As Tito expected, the Serbs who survived were ready to fight beside anyone who might destroy their persecutors. Fleeing into the mountains and forests of Bosnia, many Serbs joined Tito's Partisans. Others were driven into Partisan ranks when the Germans started a new offensive against the guerrillas in January 1942. Some of the Serbs gained their revenge by joining Chetnik bands still in the field. When Tito entered the southeastern Bosnian town of Focha in late January, a Chetnik unit had preceded him; the vengeful Chetniks had left the banks and backwaters of the Drina River littered with the corpses of Moslems, many of them with their throats slit.

Tito now established his headquarters in Focha. Though he had weathered the latest German assaults, he was desperate for arms and supplies. He appealed by radio to the Soviet Union for aid and said that the supplies should be airdropped on a plateau near Mount Durmitor, 30 miles southeast of Focha. In February he received a radio signal from "Grandpa"—the code name for his contact in Moscow—suggesting that Soviet planes might soon arrive.

Every night a crew of Partisans based in a village four miles away trudged out through the snow to the drop zone. There they waited until sunrise, ready to set four piles of straw on fire as a beacon. On the night of March 27 the roar of motors overhead sent their hopes soaring. But the planes turned out to be British aircraft, scattering leaflets commemorating the first anniversary of Yugoslavia's anti-German coup of 1941.

Finally on the 29th of March—after 37 nights of waiting in bitter cold for the Soviet supplies that never came—the Partisan crew was called back from Mount Durmitor. "Grandpa" had radioed Tito from Moscow: "All possible efforts are being made to help you in armament. But the technical difficulties are enormous. You should, alas, not

Guarded by Partisans, a column of weary German prisoners winds its way through the dirt streets of Uzice, Yugoslavia, in October of 1941. The highly mobile Partisans were so short on transportation, food and facilities for caring for prisoners that when they abandoned Uzice the following month, they released 250 Germans. But as the fighting became more bitter, prisoners and wounded were frequently executed on the spot.

count on our mastering them in the near future." At the time, the Russians were desperately fighting the German invaders and they could not spare supplies or the planes to deliver them. But Tito correctly suspected that the "technical difficulties" were in large part politically motivated. Britain and the United States were still championing the Chetnik leader Mihailovich, and the Russians—critically dependent upon Western aid—still refused to jeopardize relations with their Allies.

In April 1942 the Partisans were suddenly beset from almost every side when Germany and its Axis partners launched yet another offensive in Bosnia, Herzegovina and Montenegro. The Partisans had increased their strength to three Proletarian Brigades, but they now faced a formidable array of enemies: Germans, Italians, Ustashi, the Croatian National Guard and—collaborating militarily with the Axis for the first time—local Chetnik units.

This powerful offensive drove the Partisans from their headquarters at Focha. Early in May, Tito moved south to Montenegro with two of his brigades to assume personal command of his beleaguered detachments there. Montenegro—"Black Mountain"—was a forbidding place. For centuries in this land of precipitous slopes and steep ravines violence had been taken for granted. Montenegrins, warriors almost by vocation, were the only large group of people on the Balkan Peninsula who had successfully resisted the Ottoman Turks. The martial tradition persisted, and in the 20th Century Montenegrins still habitually carried guns. When the Yugoslav Army capitulated to the Axis, the Montenegrins hid their weapons from the Italian occupation troops, intending to use them later. One group even managed to bury an entire battery of field guns.

When the Italians tried in July 1941 to set up a separate state there, the Montenegrins rose up. They succeeded in seizing most of the countryside before the Italians rushed in reinforcements from Albania and pushed them back. As in other provinces, the local Partisan and Chetnik units at first fought side by side against the common enemy. In Montenegro, however, the local Partisans went to violent

extremes that quickly alienated potential recruits. They tried to install a "Soviet republic" by force, and they staged indiscriminate executions and hurled the bodies into ravines. For this practice the Montenegrin Chetniks pinned a macabre nickname on their Partisan rivals: "Pitmen."

By the time Tito arrived in Montenegro in mid-May, 1942, the local Partisans and Chetniks were locked in a virulent civil war. Milovan Djilas, one of Tito's top associates and himself a Montenegrin, wrote sardonically of one clash: "For hours both armies clambered up rocky ravines to escape annihilation or to destroy a little group of their countrymen, often neighbors, on some jutting peak six thousand feet high, in a starving, bleeding, captive land. It came to mind that this is what had become of all our theories and visions of the workers' and peasants' struggle against the bourgeosie."

With help from the Chetniks, the Italians began to push the local Partisans northwest from Montenegro toward Bosnia. Like other groups of Chetniks in Bosnia, the Montenegrin brands had resorted to the "uses of the enemy" strategy—the policy of expediency aimed at subverting the enemy. In return for Italian arms, supplies and money, they agreed to stop harassing Italian garrisons and communications and to fight the Partisans. The leaders had concluded the deals without consulting Mihailovich, who was in Serbia at the time.

Mihailovich and his fugitive headquarters arrived in Montenegro in early June, about two weeks after Tito, and in various meetings with the leaders of independent local Chetnik bands he learned the details of their accommodation with the Italians. He disapproved of the agreements that they had reached, some of which would later be labeled treasonous by the Partisans. But Mihailovich did not want to interfere, and even if he had, he lacked the power to stop the Montenegrin Chetniks from collaborating with the Italians.

Whatever the reasons for Mihailovich's inconsistency, the result was a considerable strengthening of his tactical position. He now had nominal authority over thousands of Italian-armed Chetniks in the area. Moreover, the British resumed token airdrops and continued to credit him with the whole of Yugoslav resistance. He had once more been promoted by his government-in-exile, this time to Chief of Staff of the Supreme Command. Mihailovich was now a legend. In the U.S. he was pictured on the cover of TIME and described in *The New York Times Magazine* as the commander in Serbia of "one vast battlefield"—this at a time when the Chetniks in Serbia were virtually inactive against the Axis occupation.

In the meantime, Tito and his Partisans were struggling through their worst crisis since their defeat in Serbia. In June the Partisans in Montenegro were forced by enemy action to retreat northward from Montenegro into Bosnia, where Tito incorporated them into his main force, which now numbered five brigades, or about 6,000 guerrillas in all. But it was impossible to feed so many Partisans in the barren mountains of Bosnia, where the peasants themselves could barely eke out a living. For weeks the Partisans lived on unsalted boiled mutton from the sheep herds they kept with them on the march. Their unbalanced diet, nearly devoid of vegetables or fruits, weakened them, and many came down with scurvy. To make up for the vitamin deficiency, they ate young beech leaves and pressed the juice out of beech bark and drank it.

Militarily, the Partisans' plight was precarious. They were surrounded by the enemy and were so short on ammunition that the well-armed local Chetniks jeeringly referred to them as "five bulleteers." Nor was help yet in sight from the Russians. As for the British, they had given no sign of ever sending aid to the Communist Partisans. By now the British had learned that someone named Tito was the Partisan leader, but they still knew very little about him. In fact, so little was known, it was rumored in the West that Tito was a woman and alternatively that his name was an acronym for a syndicate—the letters standing for *Taina* (Secret) International Terrorist Organization.

Undismayed by his bleak prospects, Tito on June 19 made a bold decision—one that would mark a historic turning point for Yugoslavia. He decided that his five Proletarian Brigades would take the offensive. They would fight their way out of the Axis encirclement and march 200 miles northwest into the very heart of Pavelich's Independent State of Croatia. The audacity of the plan was clear proof of Tito's evolving genius as a guerrilla strategist. As he later explained, "Every defeat had at once to be made up for by a

A CROATIAN SADIST AT THE HELM

A statue of Yugoslavia's King Peter is toppled by Croats.

After conquering Yugoslavia in April 1941, the Axis set up a puppet regime in its western region. Called the Independent State of Croatia, the new entity was carved out of an area teeming with Nazi and Fascist sympathizers and put under German-Italian control. The nominal ruler was King Victor Emmanuel's nephew, the Duke of Spoleto. But the Duke preferred the high life of Rome and never set foot in Croatia.

The real ruler was Ante Pavelich, a zealous Croatian nationalist and fanatical hater of Serbs who had been in political exile in Italy. Pavelich led a terrorist group called the Ustashi in a brutal campaign against Jews and Serbs in Croatia.

"A good Ustashi," he told his men, "is he who can use his knife to cut a child from the womb of its mother." According to an Italian correspondent, Pavelich once put a wicker basket on his desk—filled with 40 pounds of eyes gouged from victims of the Ustashi.

Croatian leader Ante Pavelich meets Italy's Fascist dictator Benito Mussolini in Rome.

victory—anywhere—so that morale did not suffer. For this reason even our worst defeats, even the big enemy offensives, had no effect on the morale of our men, for we ourselves at once went over to the offensive, choosing the place where the enemy least expected it."

Tito began his epic march on June 23, breaking through the encircling enemy and heading northwest. The Partisan leader and his staff had shrewdly chosen a route that followed the border line between the Italian and German zones of occupation. This caused the enemy commanders no little confusion over which army should deal with the Partisans. As a result of the delays, the Partisans' chief opponents on the march were the Croatian state's Axis collaborators, the fanatic Ustashi and the weak Croatian National Guard. The National Guardsmen were so ineffectual that the Ustashi contemptuously called them the "Partisan supply unit," meaning, as Tito himself explained, "we catch them and take all their clothes and weapons, then send them home naked to be re-outfitted and captured again."

The Partisans' journey soon settled into a pattern of slow marching and fierce fighting, with stopovers of a few days in the occasional towns or villages they liberated along the way. They passed through some areas where the destruction wrought by the Ustashi left them nothing to fight over or to liberate. Of one ravaged valley, Dedijer wrote, "It looked as if a magician's hand had stopped all life. The houses were all razed; nothing but rusted nails, grass and weeds. Everywhere fruits were ripening, but there was no trace of a human being."

The five Partisan brigades rarely traveled as an integral force; most of the time, detachments were patrolling or striking at targets located a good distance away from the route of march. But even so, the main body—guerrillas and their herds and pack animals—formed a column two miles long. The men in the main force were responsible for carrying seriously wounded comrades, whose numbers rose well into the hundreds as the fighting march wore on. The Partisans could not leave their wounded behind. They had learned this lesson during the retreat from Uzice when the Germans caught up with a field hospital that lagged behind the main body of Partisans. Many of the 60 or so wounded had lost arms or legs. When they attempted to scramble

away, the Germans ran tanks back and forth over them.

The Partisans themselves frequently showed no mercy to enemy wounded. Official German reports said that when Tito's units raided Axis hospitals to get medical supplies, "the sick and wounded would be slain in their beds."

To avoid detection by German planes and pursuit by German tanks, the Partisans often marched by night and slept by day under the best cover they could find. Wherever they camped, the leaders maintained strict party discipline. Each unit assembled daily for indoctrination by its political commissar and for a session of self-criticism on its tactics. To maintain the good will of the local peasants, looting was forbidden, and some offenders who had stolen as little as a pair of shoes or a jug of milk from a peasant were summarily shot. Relations between the male and female guerrillas were carefully policed, a difficult task since nearly one fifth of the Partisans were women. Sexual relations were banned, and when any man and woman broke the ban, one of them was sent to a different unit. Persistent offenders reportedly were shot.

This puritanical code did not prevent Tito and several of his top aides from taking Partisan mistresses. The leaders did try to be discreet, but somehow they were found out. The guerrillas relished a story about Tito and his temperamental mistress, Zdenka, who resented having to conceal her role by posing as his secretary. Tito, unnerved by one of Zdenka's temper tantrums, put the problem to his personal bodyguard, a tough veteran of the Spanish Civil War: "Tell me, Comrade Djuro, what am I to do with her?" The bodyguard slyly reminded Tito of his own orders regarding chronic sexual offenders: "I would have her shot, Comrade Tito!"

In each town they liberated, the Partisans set up a rudi-

Outfitted with rifles and Partisan uniforms, teen-age boys serve as messengers for Tito's Second Proletarian Brigade. The youths—some as young as 12—played a crucial role as couriers between Partisan units. To deliver their communications, they exposed themselves to hunger, severe weather and possible capture. "Our boys," said Tito, "grew up into heroes such as we have seldom had throughout the history of our nations."

mentary municipal government under a local People's Liberation Committee. They started a postal service, printing a red star over the stamps of the Croatian state. They organized schools and health services. They also established "people's courts" and kept them busy meting out punishment to the Ustashi and their collaborators.

In one town hundreds of peasant women whose families had been slaughtered by the Croatian state's puppet regime came to witness the execution of 50 convicted prisoners. Their eyes were full of hatred, and one woman performed a bizarre act of vengeance. "When the first volley of bullets was fired," Dedijer wrote, she advanced on the dead victims. "She ran at their still warm bodies, jumping over them, with eyes closed, groaning. Her long white skirt became red with blood, but she continued trampling the bodies under her feet, groaning more and more. At last she was taken away from the corpses, her eyes still closed, grey hair wet with sweat, the muscles on her face loosened, as though with some kind of inner relaxation."

Chaplains accompanied the Partisans. In each town and village they found a backlog of religious duties to perform, for the Ustashi had killed or driven away all of the local Orthodox priests. The churches that had been left largely intact were befouled and desecrated; they had to be cleansed and reconsecrated. There were babies to be baptized—216 of them in just one village. Father Vlado Zechevich, a former Chetnik commander who had joined the Partisans in Serbia, pitched in to help the chaplains even though he no longer was a believer. He dutifully covered his uniform and revolver with a priest's vestment and performed as many as 100 baptisms a day.

The Partisans' labors in the towns did not distract them from military matters. They set up a courier service. Almost all of the couriers selected were young girls who quickly proved their courage, carrying messages through the mountains and sometimes through enemy lines, on foot or horseback, by bicycle or motorcycle. The Partisans organized local units to defend their revamped villages and towns and gathered food for the next leg of their march. They recruit-ed vigorously, though it was hardly necessary. As soon as they reached a town or village, volunteers out for revenge flocked into their ranks.

During the first few days of November, Tito and his Proletarian Brigades closed in on the final objective of the long march: Bihach, an important town of some 12,000 people, strategically located only 70 miles south of Zagreb. The Ustashi fought savagely for two days to hold the town, but in the end the Partisans drove them out.

The great victory came on November 5, and it was a fitting capstone to the remarkable achievements of Tito's five months on the road. He had started the march with five brigades totaling about 6,000 guerrillas and with no territory firmly under his control. He now claimed a National Liberation Army of 150,000 guerrillas (it was only 45,000, according to German intelligence); he had liberated about one sixth of Yugoslavia and was holding it with his own network of municipal governments and local Partisan units.

Now was the time, Tito radioed Moscow, to set up something like a national government. He did just that. In Bihach he convened a meeting of 54 delegates from his People's Liberation committees. To mollify the Russians, who insisted that the Partisans maintain the fiction of a broadly based, democratic popular front, Tito staged his meeting with consummate care. It was held in a convent decorated with large drawings of Stalin, Churchill and Roosevelt. The delegates elected a body innocuously titled the Anti-Fascist Council of National Liberation of Yugoslavia, which then approved a distinctly noncontroversial platform endorsing individual rights, private property and free elections after the War. As its president, the council selected Ivan Ribar, a flexible Yugoslav politician who 20 years before had presided over the National Constituent Assembly when it outlawed the Communist Party.

More than ever, Tito's guerrilla war—a war fought alone, without help from the Russians or the British—had become political as well as military. His meeting at Bihach served as a warning, at home and abroad, that the Partisans were now a force to be reckoned with.

COMRADES-IN-ARMS

Traveling through fields to avoid German road patrols, a well-armed brigade marches behind a mounted officer as Partisans set out at dusk on a sabotage mission.

A NATIONWIDE UPRISING OF "BANDITS"

For two months after the Germans overran Yugoslavia in April of 1941, the people in the capital city of Belgrade seemed apathetic toward the German occupation forces. Then, in June, bands of young Communists suddenly attacked more than a hundred newsstands, snatched up bundles of pro-German newspapers, doused them with gasoline and set them afire before disappearing into the crowds on the streets.

By July the urban Partisans—as these Communist guerrillas were called—were aiming at more ambitious targets: a German military garage was blown up, German soldiers were attacked during the night on unlighted streets, gasoline dumps were set on fire, trucks were sabotaged, telephone lines were severed.

The city-based Communists were responding to a call to arms issued by their party leader, Tito, who in turn was responding to a call from Moscow to help relieve the pressure on the Red Army following the German invasion of the Soviet Union.

In order to build a broad-based movement and to get away from the cities, where the German troops were concentrated, Tito sent his most capable organizers into the countryside. There they could rally the peasants and establish Partisan units with minimum risk of being detected and arrested by the Germans.

The rural Partisans adopted a simple supply method suggested by Tito himself. "If you need something," he said, "go out on the road and get it from the Germans." In separate actions they captured four tanks and used them in an assault at Kraljevo in October 1941. According to a Partisan leader, they even managed to seize three light bombers the following year and fly them on a bombing run against the enemy.

As the Partisans increased in numbers and strength, they became such an effective fighting force that German troops withdrew from entire areas and posted warnings where the guerrillas were known to be hiding—*Achtung! Banditengebiet* (Beware! Bandit Territory).

In the town of Cacak, a commissar, or political leader, of the local Partisan detachment exhorts a rapt group of fighters and citizens in October 1941.

A determined-looking woman Partisan shoulders an Italian rifle. During the war, 100,000 women served with the Partisans and an estimated 25,000 died.

Standing at attention, the soldiers of the 1st Croatian Battalion present a formidable appearance as they wait to receive their unit banner in May of 1942.

Dazed and wounded Partisans rest at Milinklade in June 1943 after a nine-hour bombing attack.

HONED ON HARDSHIPS, AN ARMY TAKES SHAPE

The scattered detachments and brigades of Partisans were formally organized into the National Liberation Army of Yugoslavia in November 1942. The men were outfitted in captured German and Italian uniforms, stripped of all detested insignias, and each unit proudly carried its own flag.

But despite their military appearances, the Partisan units bore little resemblance to conventional military formations. When Heinrich Himmler, head of the SS, scoffed at them as "a thousand vagabonds who have been herded together to suddenly become a brigade," he was not far off the mark. Some had received a few weeks of training, but most acquired their combat skills in action. They lacked heavy artillery, and their only protection from enemy air attacks lay in night movements and operations conducted when German bombers were grounded by bad weather.

The Partisans compensated for their deficiencies by their mobility and elusiveness. They traveled light, hit the enemy and quickly disappeared. They could evacuate any position in 15 minutes and were constantly on the move. During brief rest stops, they often were afraid to lie down for fear their exhaustion would not allow them to get up again.

On a narrow Dalmatian road, winding over a hill beside the Adriatic, an Italian truck comes under fire as a Partisan hiding in the rocks (foreground) watches.

CRIPPLING THE VITAL TRANSPORTATION SYSTEM

The 6,000 miles of Yugoslav railway lines and the roads and telephone wires that ran alongside them were favorite targets for the Partisans' attacks. The Germans, hampered by the scarcity of trucks and fuel and by the primitive roads, used the railways both to carry supplies for their armies in Italy and Greece and to transport their occupation troops around the countryside.

The Partisans tore up miles of track, destroyed rail stations and demolished viaducts that carried lines across mountain gorges. By late 1942 one Partisan demolition expert had wrecked 70 trains by using captured enemy bombs as mines and had gained for himself the sobriquet "Ilija the Thundermaker."

Since Yugoslavia's mountainous terrain limited the range of radio transmissions, the Germans had to rely on telephone and telegraph wires for much of their communications. The Partisans cut down the poles

and took the wire to prevent the enemy from using it again. And when the Germans sent men to repair the lines, Partisan snipers picked them off.

On the rock-covered roads, the Partisans scattered steel spikes to puncture tires and strewed deceptive concrete-encased mines that looked like stones. They sprang from ambushes in narrow mountain passes and along tortuous coastal roadways to pounce on enemy troops and vehicles and to scavenge weapons and ammunition for Partisan recruits.

A German truck goes up in flames in Belgrade. Many enemy vehicles were destroyed by Partisans who dropped delayed-action fire bombs in gas tanks.

Aided by local peasants, Partisan saboteurs pry up a stretch of railroad track near Sarajevo in 1943.

Partisan fighters ride atop a light Italian tank, one of 15 seized near the Neretva River in February 1943. Captured tanks were used in attacks on Germans.

Butchering a pack pony, Partisans prepare to eat the tough meat raw. At the time, the guerrillas were on a mountain, encircled by 12 enemy divisions.

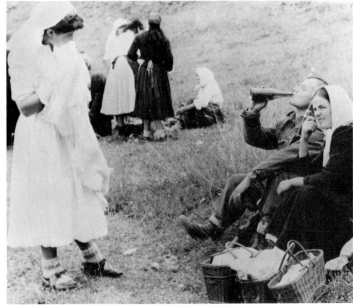

A Partisan fighter pauses to enjoy a meal supplied by peasant women.

Guided by Partisan smoke signals, an RAF Halifax readies to drop supplies.

Wounded Partisans take a momentary rest break during their flight from the Germans in 1943.

Moving the wounded to protected hideouts, Partisans in Slovenia use ox-drawn carts as ambulances.

AID FOR THE WOUNDED, RITES FOR THE DEAD

The Partisans suffered many casualties during the war: more than 300,000 were killed and over 400,000 were wounded. To care for the wounded, they built a network of small, carefully concealed hospitals in remote forest and mountain areas. Conditions were primitive at best; operations were often performed without anesthetics, and hacksaws were frequently used for amputations. There were not many surgeons and they moved from one hospital to another. In order to obtain drugs and medicines, raids were mounted against enemy hospitals and pharmacies.

A candle in his hand, the father of a division

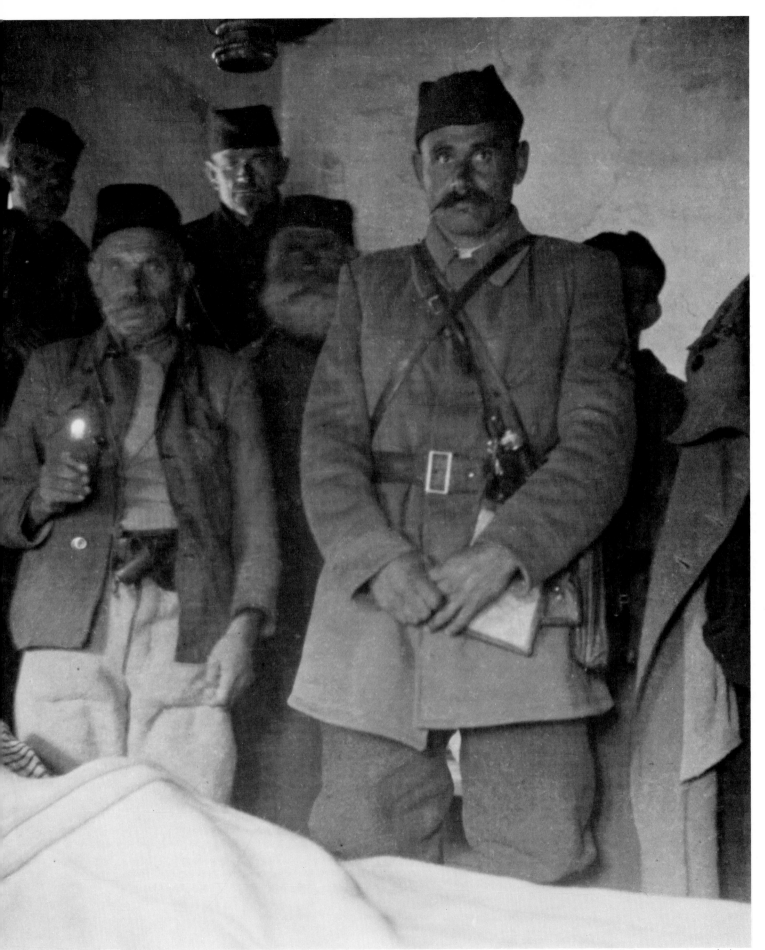

commander comports himself stoically during a funeral service for his son. The mustachioed brigade commander on his left was killed in action six weeks later.

Using a 50mm armor-piercing gun captured from the Germans, Partisan artillerymen fire on advancing tanks in Bosnia in December of 1943. Within a month they began receiving large shipments of Allied armaments. Before 1944 ended they had been sent 100,000 rifles, 50,000 light machine guns and 97.5 million rounds of small-arms ammunition from the West.

Breaking out of an enemy encirclement that threatened them with annihilation, Partisans scramble on all fours across the wrecked Jablanica bridge spanning the Neretva River in March of 1943. The crossing, which was made under air and artillery attack, involved 25,000 Partisans, including more than 4,000 wounded, and took longer than a week.

FOILING SEVEN AXIS OFFENSIVES

The Partisans were more than a thorn in the side of Yugoslavia's occupiers: they were a menace. In an effort to wipe them out, the Germans mounted seven major offensives against them—and failed. Using armor, artillery and aircraft, they inflicted heavy casualties, but each time the Partisans managed to get away. "By concentrating our efforts against one point," Tito explained, "we could always break out of any encirclement."

After the Partisans escaped enemy encirclement at the Neretva River in early 1943 (right), Hitler was determined to an-

nihilate them once and for all. For Operation *Schwarz*, as the fifth German offensive was called, the 1st Mountain Division was pulled back from the Eastern Front and a fresh division sent from Germany. By late May of 1943, an overwhelming force of 12 German and Italian divisions had trapped four Partisan divisions in several narrow river valleys and in the mountains. The German commander gave orders that "no man capable of bearing arms must leave the circle alive."

As the ring tightened, German bombers flew 100 sorties a day, and mountain troops captured the surrounding heights. Sensing his desperate situation, Tito had the Partisan archives buried and all heavy weapons destroyed or concealed. Then he

ordered two divisions into an all-out attack, which involved moving them down a 3,000-foot canyon wall and up the other side. Finally, after a month of continuous and bitter fighting, the Partisans opened a small breach with a suicidal attack on exhausted German troops. The surviving Partisan units broke through and escaped to mountains to the north.

The breakout cost the Partisans heavily; their 3rd and 7th divisions were decimated and many of their critically wounded were killed by the enemy. But the operation was a bigger failure for the Germans. They had hoped to free divisions for the battle on the Russian front. Instead, they were forced to commit even more troops to the fight in Yugoslavia.

THE BRUTAL OCCUPATION

Intended as a grim warning to anyone daring to resist the Germans, four Yugoslavs dangle from a gallows in Serbia in 1942 while occupying troops look on.

A VICIOUS CIRCLE OF VENGEFUL MASSACRES

After being tortured by the Germans in August 1942, a Partisan is forced to carry a placard reading, "I am a murderer, the bandit leader J. Latko."

The fighting in Yugoslavia triggered an orgy of violence that ranks among the War's most grisly. Hitler was determined to crush Yugoslavia with "unmerciful harshness." He demanded that his troops slaughter 100 Yugoslavs in reprisal for every dead German—and orders were issued requiring that the executions be carried out with "frightening effect." Villages were burned, and people were dragged from their houses, shops and cars, and publicly hanged or shot by firing squads.

The brutality took on added ferocity as ethnic and religious groups turned against one another, and even the Germans professed to be shocked by the atrocities Yugoslavs inflicted on Yugoslavs. The Ustashi—an organization of Croatian Catholics who sided with Hitler—massacred 60,000 Jews, 26,000 Gypsies and 750,000 Orthodox Serbs. They chopped off victims' noses, ears, breasts and limbs, poured salt into their wounds, gouged out eyes, and buried or burned people alive. "We Ustashi are more practical than you Germans," said one of the collaborators. "You shoot, but we use hammers, clubs, rope, fire and quicklime. It's less expensive."

In one incident an Orthodox priest was half buried and Ustashi danced around him, taking turns slicing off pieces of his flesh with their swords. In another incident a woman was forced to hold a basin and catch the blood of her four sons while they were slaughtered.

The Chetniks, Serbian irregulars who fought Germans and Partisans with equal ferocity, went on a rampage, annihilating 9,200 Moslems in the Sandjak region bordering Bosnia and Serbia, raping young girls and, in a frenzy of sadism, roasting their victims to death over fires.

The photographic record that survived was sifted and censored by the people who won the war, of course, and it shows what they wanted it to show. But this much is known for sure: the Partisans themselves capped the four-year bloodbath by killing 20,000 of their own countrymen—Chetniks, Ustashi and other Yugoslavs who had collaborated with the Germans.

German soldiers watch the village of Radovna go up in flames after they set it afire and killed 20 women and children in reprisal for guerrilla activity.

An impatient Italian officer viciously jabs one of his prisoners with his knee while leading a group of captured Partisans to their death by firing squad.

The corpses of an entire family lie in a house in Croatia, after Ustashi terrorists—in search of Jews, Gypsies and Serbs—raided it in 1941.

A German firing squad stands ready while soldiers position female hostages for execution. The five women were among 100 Yugoslavs shot in relays in the village of Celje in 1942.

Yugoslavs in business suits who were picked up indiscriminately off the street hang from trees in the village of Panchevo in 1941. They were killed after the Germans began their policy of retaliation for attacks on German soldiers, announced in the notice pinned to a tree (inset).

Grinning Ustashi storm troopers show off a severed head in Bosnia in 1942.

Chetniks murder a Partisan with a dagger and sword in Serbia in 1942.

Standing before the bodies of executed comrades, Partisans await their death by firing squad. The signs identify them by name and brand them as "bandits."

Until early 1943, Partisans and Chetniks fought the Axis— and each other—in relative isolation. Though their exploits inspired the Allies and irritated the enemy, they counted for little in the grand strategy of the struggle being waged around the globe. Now, however, the attention of the great powers began to focus more and more on the embattled mountains of Yugoslavia, and a war that had been shrouded in obscurity and confusion began to loom larger in the thinking of Allied strategists.

Yugoslavia's new importance stemmed from the turn taken by the Allied campaign in North Africa. The Americans had landed there in November 1942 and pushed eastward to Tunisia. The British, after a year and a half of retreat, were now advancing westward in pursuit of General Erwin Rommel's Afrika Korps. The final showdown in Africa was fast approaching. Already Allied strategists were looking north, to the Mediterranean—and an invasion of Sicily. If the Yugoslav guerrillas could be strengthened, they might play a useful role in the Allies' success by diverting Axis divisions that otherwise might be used in Sicily.

British policy now underwent reassessment. Throughout most of the war, the British had given moral support to Drazha Mihailovich's Chetniks and ignored Tito's Partisans. The reason was political: Mihailovich represented the Yugoslav royal government-in-exile, which enjoyed Britain's formal recognition and was ensconced in London. In supporting Mihailovich the British had gone along with his strategy of waiting for an Allied invasion before ordering full-scale guerrilla warfare against the occupation. But they were beginning to have serious doubts about Mihailovich and the Chetniks. They knew from their liaison officer on the spot, Captain Hudson, that Chetnik claims of their effectiveness against the Germans were exaggerated. The British had also begun to wonder whether they might be backing the wrong horse, and were determined, as Churchill later put it, to find out "who was killing the most Germans and suggest means by which we could help them to kill more."

The Germans also had cause to review their policies in Yugoslavia. They were convinced that the next Allied strike would occur not in Italy but in Greece or along Yugoslavia's Adriatic coast, in Dalmatia. Determined to destroy both the Partisan and the Chetnik guerrilla movements and thus

4

A Partisan dash to evade an encircling enemy
Hairbreadth escape across a downed bridge
Hunting the Chetniks
British backing for both horses
Allied supplies from the "Splinter Fleet"
The Prime Minister's son and a daring Scot
Last chance for Mihailovich
A surprise airborne kidnap attempt
Tito takes refuge under British guns

HELP FROM THE ALLIES

prevent a linkup with the Allies, they launched their largest offensive to date on January 20. This effort—known as Operation *Weiss* (White)—involved five German divisions, three Italian divisions, assorted Croatian puppet units and, for the first time, substantial close air support. *Weiss* was aimed initially at encircling the large, liberated area the Partisans had carved out around Bihach in western Bosnia. For this phase of the operation, Axis troops were to have the help of some 12,000 Chetniks who were now collaborating with the Italians. According to the plan the Italians would turn against their Chetnik collaborators and disarm them once the Partisans were defeated.

Even before he knew about *Weiss,* Tito had decided to march a greatly outnumbered Partisan force of 20,000 guerrillas into Herzegovina and Montenegro to the southeast, returning to the area they had abandoned eight months earlier. He wanted to get closer to Serbia, which was not only the great Chetnik stronghold but, by virtue of its size and population, the key to postwar control of Yugoslavia. Now, with *Weiss* under way, this move seemed doubly attractive to him, for he had learned that the southeast sector of the enemy line was manned by Italians and Chetniks, making it the weakest point in the trap the Germans were laying for him. Leaving behind one division to hold off a German sweep from the north, Tito sent the bulk of his army marching toward the Neretva River, some 100 miles to the southeast.

This maneuver was complicated by the presence of the 3,500 sick and wounded who accompanied the march. They were transported about half the way to the Neretva on a train the Partisans had assembled by cannibalizing half a dozen damaged locomotives. At the end of the line they were divided into three groups—those who were able to walk, those who were able to sit on a horse and those who had to be carried on stretchers—and each of them was given a weapon.

The march was further slowed by some 40,000 civilian refugees, mostly women and children, who insisted on staying with the Partisans most of the way to the Neretva. The refugees had little food, and many were suffering from typhus. They struck the diarist Vladimir Dedijer as "one of the most terrible sights of this war, as they struggled along in the freezing cold, barefoot, hungry, and ill-clad." Dedijer

saw one mother actually try to strangle her child and another give her child away.

Painfully, the column inched toward the Neretva. At the end of February the Partisans at last reached the river's bank. Though they had eluded the enemy in the northwest, they were still not out of danger. The Germans and Croatians were closing in from north, east and west, the Italians from east and west. And across the Neretva, massing on the slopes of the 6,000-foot Mount Prenj, were 12,000 Chetniks eager to deal the Partisans a deathblow. A written order from Mihailovich to his men proclaimed: "Now is the time to beat the Communists to their knees, if we act wisely."

The Partisans' position seemed hopeless. Tito's pleadings for help from Moscow brought only "profound fraternal sympathy." Tito asked his Soviet ally: "Is it really impossible, after 20 months of heroic, almost superhuman fighting, to find some way of helping us?" It was perhaps the most tense period of the war for Tito. He was irritable and uncharacteristically indecisive. Even his usually immaculate personal appearance reflected the strain. For the first time, a comrade noted, he did not shave punctually every morning.

Tito knew there was only one way out—across the Neretva and through the Chetniks. The manner he chose for getting across the turbulent, 70-yard-wide river would later be celebrated by Partisan historians as a brilliant stroke of tactics. In truth, it was forced upon Tito by circumstance and miscalculation. Thinking he could cross the bridge to the town of Konjic, where a Partisan unit had secured a temporary bridgehead, he had ordered the demolition of the other bridges over the Neretva. But a German unit rushing westward from Sarajevo seized Konjic, and the Partisans were forced to attempt the crossing on the twisted wreckage of the Jablanica bridge, 15 miles to the west. "Well," Tito told his staff as his troops approached the badly battered bridge, "maybe we can turn that demolition into a strategem of war."

Tito ordered a counterattack against German columns advancing from the west. His purpose was to give the Partisans time to assemble their wounded at Jablanica and to fool the Germans into thinking that he might try to break out to the west instead of crossing the river.

The counterattack succeeded in pushing the Germans

back 15 miles. The crossing began on the night of March 6, when a small group of Partisans crept over the girders of the wrecked railroad bridge and stormed the Chetnik blockhouse on the far shore. Six Partisan battalions followed and set up a bridgehead on the slopes of Mount Prenj. The next day wooden planks were placed on the girders to create a narrow walkway a few feet above the raging water.

On the night of March 7 the wounded—now more than 4,000—inched out onto the slippery planks. Many crawled. Others were carried by Italian prisoners. At first the disabled Partisans hid in a tunnel by day and crossed only by night to avoid air attacks. But as the German infantry pressed down on Jablanica, the wounded streamed across the river around the clock; once they were over, the able-bodied followed. By March 15 the crossing was completed: nearly 25,000 Partisans had made it to the opposite bank.

The Chetnik commanders had greatly underestimated the Partisans' strength; some had been so overconfident, in fact, that they had fallen to squabbling over who would claim credit for the expected victory.

As the surprised Chetniks scattered, the Partisans pursued them south into Montenegro. Tito's troops were now doing the job that the Germans had entrusted to the Italians for the final phase of Operation *Weiss*—disarming and annihilating the Chetniks. As the Partisans closed in, the bearded Chetniks frantically begged villagers for water and razors so that they could shave off their beards and elude detection by their pursuers.

The Partisans had paid a heavy price for the success of their escape over the Neretva. According to the German estimate, some 16,000 troops and accompanying civilians had been killed, wounded or captured.

Unbeknown to Tito in his hour of need, help was in the making—not in Moscow but in London. The Partisans certainly did not look there for help; the British were supporting the hated Chetnik enemy. "Remember," one of the Partisan leaders, Milovan Djilas, had cautioned, "the sun will not rise in the West."

Over the past several months, however, the British had formed a clearer picture of the resistance in Yugoslavia. Their emissary to Mihailovich, Captain Hudson, who had been rejected by the Chetniks after British aid failed to materialize, found himself accepted again by Mihailovich after a trickle of supplies began to flow. Alarmed by what he discovered, Hudson radioed London of Chetnik inactivity and of collaboration between Mihailovich's commanders and the Italians. His reports were subsequently confirmed when a high-level mission headed by Colonel S. W. Bailey was parachuted to Mihailovich's headquarters close to the Montenegrin border on Christmas Day, 1942.

The British were willing to wink at collaboration with the Italians—the Chetniks' avowed purpose was to obtain arms and ammunition—but they were growing impatient for action against the enemy. Mihailovich, in turn, was growing disenchanted with the British; they were always calling for action but they failed to deliver enough arms for him to carry it out. Over more than a year they had supplied only a few tons by air and submarine, and during the 10 weeks following Colonel Bailey's arrival they made just two airdrops. Adding insult to injury, the shipments included several hundred boxes of tropical antisnakebite serum and 30 million worthless lire that the Italians had specially printed for their occupation of Ethiopia. Bailey wrote later: "Mihailovich's rage was matched only by my own when I got instructions from Cairo to the effect that I was to count the lire myself, then have them checked independently by Hudson and the other officer on the mission, before formally acknowledging receipt."

Mihailovich gave vent to his anger at a small village near his headquarters on February 28. The occasion was the christening of the mayor's youngest child, and Mihailovich had drunk quite a lot of plum brandy. According to Bailey, the Chetnik leader charged "that the British were trying to purchase Serb blood at the cost of a trivial supply of munitions." He termed the Italians his "only adequate source of help" and vowed he would fight the Germans and Italians only after he had dealt with his internal enemies.

Less than a month later the British decided to send a military mission to the Partisans. Their intention was not to abandon the Chetniks but simply to back both groups. To the British, Tito still was something of a mystery; they did not even know his real name.

One of the two captains in the mission was Frederick William Deakin, 31, a personal friend of Churchill. Deakin bailed out over the slopes of Mount Durmitor, the same

SUPPLYING THE PARTISANS BY RAGTAG FLEET

The fast schooner Marija (right) docks in Bari, Italy, beside the steamer Morava, a slow vessel that needed luck to avoid German patrol ships.

In October 1943, Partisan representatives Sergije Makiedo and Joze Poduje left Yugoslavia to seek Allied help in setting up a seaborne delivery service to help supply their guerrillas. Their proposal was enthusiastically received by intelligence officers of the American Organization of Strategic Services. In fact, two OSS men, Robert Thompson and Hans Tofte, had already formed a plan for just such a supply line.

With Allied approval, operations speedily began. To beef up the Partisans' hodgepodge fleet of fishing boats and old steamers, the OSS contributed sleek schooners and ketches. The vessels sailed from southern Italy to the Partisan island base of Vis. Returning ships brought out wounded Partisans for treatment in Allied hospitals.

The cooperative venture paid off handsomely for the Yugoslavs: in a four-month period, the ships delivered 50 times more supplies than British airdrops.

Sergije Makiedo (far left) and other Partisans chat with OSS officer Thompson (left).

place where, during the previous year, the Partisans had awaited the Soviet supply planes that never came. As he floated down he could see flashes of gunfire. Deakin had arrived at precisely the right time and the right place to appreciate the predicament of the Partisans.

They were in the midst of another ordeal, their worst of the war. Operation *Schwarz* (Black), the successor to *Weiss*, was under way. The Germans had mustered 119,000 troops for an offensive aimed at destroying both the Partisans and the Chetniks, and they had clamped an iron ring around the Partisans' main force of 19,000.

Immediately following the arrival of Deakin, the Partisans were forced to withdraw into Bosnia. Though they succeeded in breaking through the enemy trap, they lost 6,500 troops, including half of their sick and wounded. During this action a German bombing attack killed the British mission's intelligence officer, Captain W. F. Stuart, and almost got Tito and Deakin. Tito flung himself to the ground and might have been struck by a bomb fragment but for his dog Lux. The shrapnel struck Lux instead, killing him. Tito caught a splinter in the left arm, and fragments from the same bomb wounded Deakin in the foot.

The brush with death helped cement the personal relationship between the British officer and the Partisan leader. Deakin was now close to Tito and could report from personal observation that the Partisans were tying down large numbers of Germans who might otherwise be dispatched to fight the Allies. On the strength of Deakin's recommendation, the British began sending arms, medical supplies and food to the Partisans.

Inspired by his young friend's favorable reports, Churchill took an increasing interest in the Partisans during the summer of 1943. But the Prime Minister was still backing both horses. He directed that aid to both the Partisans and the Chetniks be stepped up to 500 tons every month. Since only four British Liberators were available for supplying the guerrillas in Yugoslavia, as well as those in Greece, he issued orders that additional aircraft be made available—"if necessary, at the expense of the bombing of Germany and of the U-boat war."

In late July Churchill appointed another young friend of his, Brigadier Fitzroy Maclean, a 32-year-old Conservative member of Parliament and former diplomat, to head a new, higher-level mission to Tito. "What we want," Churchill said, "is a daring ambassador-leader to these hardy and hunted guerrillas."

Events in Italy, however, quickly outpaced the British moves. On September 8—before Maclean reached Tito and before aid to the Partisans and Chetniks could be stepped up substantially—the Italian government surrendered. The surrender took Tito and Mihailovich by surprise, and both were furious because the British, who had been engaged in negotiations with the Italians for weeks, had not given them advance word of the outcome.

The Italian capitulation set off a frantic three-way race among the Partisans, Chetniks and Germans to disarm the 14 Italian divisions in Yugoslavia and take over their occupation zones in Montenegro, Slovenia and especially along the Dalmatian coast, where the Germans and the Yugoslavs believed the Allies might still land.

The Partisans reached Dalmatia first, seizing the port of Split and most of the offshore islands. Racing to Split from

Prime Minister Winston Churchill's son Randolph (left) meets with Vlada Cetkovich (far right), commander of the Partisan VIII Corps, and his staff in Jadovnik, Yugoslavia. Churchill was chosen for assignment to Tito's forces by Brigadier Fitzroy Maclean, head of the British mission to the Partisans. Maclean, who had served with Churchill in North Africa, selected him in the belief that he "would get on well with the Yugoslavs, for his enthusiastic and at times explosive approach to life was not unlike their own."

western Bosnia, one Partisan unit covered the first 45 miles on foot in less than 24 hours. Deakin, who accompanied the unit, marveled at the swiftness and organization of the march—"in ordered columns, day and night, pausing only at intervals for a few minutes' rest."

The reoccupation of Split was short-lived. In the wake of the Italian surrender, the Germans had also rushed troops into Montenegro, Slovenia and Dalmatia to take areas formerly occupied by the Italians. In a series of swift attacks, they drove the Partisans out of Split and all of Dalmatia, and into Bosnia. But before they departed, Tito's forces gained some valuable booty. They captured enough arms from half a dozen Italian divisions to equip some 80,000 new recruits—among them several thousand Italian soldiers who joined the new Partisan-created Garibaldi Division. Partisan units were now able to move effectively against Chetniks who had established themselves in Montenegro during the summer. More important from the Allied standpoint, the Italian surrender and Partisan aggressiveness forced Germany to increase its occupation army in Yugoslavia to 14 divisions—a total of 140,000 men by the end of 1943.

The aggressiveness of the Partisans had another crucial effect: it prompted a drastic change in U.S. policy. Until now the American attitude had been characterized by President Roosevelt's cynically pragmatic remark about Mihailovich and Tito: "We should build a wall around those two fellows and let them fight it out. Then we could do business with the winner."

The United States had been content to follow Churchill's lead in Yugoslavia, though it tended to be suspicious of his political motives there. It had given Mihailovich's Chetniks propaganda support, but little else. An American shipment of 400 tons of concentrated food earmarked for the Chetniks had been sent to Egypt in 1942 for distribution in Yugoslavia. The food was wrapped in the Yugoslav tricolor and bore greetings in Serbo-Croatian to the Chetniks from President Roosevelt, but most of it was misrouted and ended up in the hands of the civilian population on Malta.

The capitulation of Italy raised the possibility that the Partisans could be supplied in volume from Italy's east coast, and a group of American officers in the Office of Strategic Services in the Middle East came up with a daring plan for a seaborne operation from Italy. The senior OSS officer was Major Louis Huot, a former newspaper reporter with a passion for liberal causes. In early October Huot flew to Algiers where he secured the personal approval of General Dwight D. Eisenhower, the Allied Commander in Chief in the Mediterranean. While in Algiers, Huot came across two Partisans who had sailed a small vessel from Yugoslavia to Bari, Italy. They were just what he was looking for.

Returning to Italy together, Huot and the Partisans put together a makeshift fleet of old fishing vessels, and in a few days they ferried 400 tons of supplies to Vis, the outermost of the Yugoslav islands. Huot was on one of the ships; though his orders did not authorize him to enter Yugoslavia, which fell under British military jurisdiction, he was determined to meet Tito. He made his way to the Yugoslav mainland and Tito's headquarters in the town of Jajce in the western part of Bosnia. "One day, a rather strange man appeared on Partisan territory," wrote Dedijer. "He asked

Brigadier Fitzroy Maclean, chief of Great Britain's military mission to the Partisans in Yugoslavia, was parachuted into Yugoslavia in September of 1943. In December he was ordered to Cairo, where he met with Prime Minister Winston Churchill. "He asked me whether I wore a kilt when I was dropped out of an aeroplane," Maclean later reported, "and from this promising point of departure, we slid into a general discussion of the situation in Yugoslavia." Largely on the strength of Maclean's recommendation, Churchill decided to give all-out aid to Tito.

A sheepskin coat and hat protect a Cossack against the Yugoslav winter.

A commander wears traditional fur cap and coat with cartridge holders.

A GALLERY OF STYLISH WARRIORS

The most colorful army unit in Yugoslavia during the War was the XV Cossack Cavalry Corps—21,000 Russians who fought for the Germans. During the Russian Revolution, Cossacks had ridden against Communists, and when the Communists won, thousands fled to the West. With the German invasion of the U.S.S.R., many Cossacks cast their lot with the Germans in the hope of overthrowing their old enemies.

Although most of the Cossacks' time was spent fighting Yugoslav Partisans—it was while they were thus engaged that German combat artist Olaf Jordan made the painting shown here—they also fought against the Russians near the Yugoslav-Hungarian border. There, on Christmas Day in 1944, they scored their greatest victory, trapping a Red Army division twice their size. But in May 1945, with Germany's defeat, they surrendered to the British who—responding to Russian wishes—handed them over to the Red Army. Most were executed or sent to Siberian camps.

A rifleman with a German shirt carries a German-supplied carbine.

The picture of aristocratic hauteur with his cape draped over one shoulder, a Cossack colonel clutches his saber while displaying a German Iron Cross.

to see Tito, but inquired all the time whether there were any British officers in the vicinity. At that very moment a British officer came along. The American immediately asked the town major to hide him in another room so that the Englishman should not see him."

Huot met with Tito and engaged in a long conversation that convinced him that "here was a force to reckon with, a leader men would follow through the very gates of Hell." He even concluded that Tito "was planning no Communist revolution." The British learned of the meeting, and when they protested Huot's unauthorized presence in Yugoslavia, the OSS quickly transferred him to a desk job in London.

Even after Huot's transfer, the "Splinter Fleet"—as the fishing vessels he had assembled came to be known—continued to ply the Adriatic under American auspices until the end of 1943. Its ships made more than 70 crossings and ferried more than 6,000 tons of food, weapons and medical supplies to the Partisans. During the same period, British aircraft managed to drop only 125 tons of supplies to Tito's army, despite Churchill's ambitious goal of 500 tons each month. The Splinter Fleet also evacuated thousands of sick and wounded Partisans for treatment in Italy. And on one voyage it transported to Vis an American newsman, Associated Press correspondent Daniel De Luce, whose stories on the Partisans helped stir enthusiasm for Tito's cause in the United States.

The Yugoslavs found another supporter in Brigadier Maclean, Churchill's friend who had parachuted in a week after the Italian surrender. Maclean had served as a diplomat in Moscow during the 1930s, and at Tito's headquarters he recognized "the familiar Communist jargon on everyone's lips, the same old Party slogans scrawled on every wall and red star, hammer and sickle on the cap badges." Nonetheless, he hit it off well with Tito and his top commanders. They were impressed by his bravery under fire, by the colorful kilt he wore on ceremonial occasions and, not least, by his intimacy with Churchill. Maclean, in turn, was impressed by Tito. He found that Tito, in spite of his Communist training, showed an "unexpected independence of mind." The Partisan leader, wrote Maclean, had "experienced the satisfaction of building up from nothing his own powerful military and political organization, of which he

himself was the absolute master." Even more important, Maclean was convinced that whether Britain supported Tito or not, Tito was going to win in Yugoslavia.

Tito's army of 150,000 men, which outnumbered the rival Chetniks by probably 2 to 1, had attained such size that it no longer needed to be concentrated as a single main force, vulnerable to German encirclement. Its 26 divisions were now dispersed as self-contained units all over Yugoslavia, except for the remaining Chetnik stronghold, Serbia.

In October Maclean backed up his favorable written reports on Tito by returning to British headquarters in Cairo to brief his superiors personally. He was the first British liaison officer to come out of Yugoslavia, and he made his way from Jajce to the Dalmatian coast by an extraordinary variety of conveyances—railroad, car, horse, truck, pole raft and a bus driven by a captured Italian pilot who insisted on singing arias from Italian operas and "maneuvering his clumsy vehicle as if it had been a dive-bomber."

In Cairo Maclean had the good luck to have an audience with Prime Minister Churchill, who was on his way home from the Big Three Conference with Roosevelt and Stalin at Teheran. On the basis of Maclean's previous written reports to the Prime Minister, the Big Three had decided to give all-out support to the Partisans—without even mentioning Mihailovich's Chetniks.

Churchill was "installed in a villa out by the Pyramids," Maclean recalled. "He was in bed when we arrived, smoking a cigar and wearing an embroidered dressing-gown." The two men discussed the political and military situation in Yugoslavia, and Maclean—in spite of his favorable view of Tito the man—expressed his concern about the long-term political consequences of aid to Tito's Communists. "The Partisans, whether we helped them or not, would be the decisive political factor in Yugoslavia after the war," he said. "The system which they would establish would inevitably be on Soviet lines."

But Churchill was more concerned with the military than with the political consequences of the war in Yugoslavia.

"Do you intend to make Yugoslavia your home after the war?" he asked Maclean.

"No, sir," replied Maclean.

"Neither do I," said Churchill. "And, that being so, the less you and I worry about the form of government they set up, the better. That is for them to decide. What interests us is, which of them is doing most harm to the Germans?"

Soon thereafter Churchill began a personal correspondence with Tito, enclosing an autographed picture of himself in one of his letters. He even assigned his son, Randolph, to the British mission at Partisan headquarters. "I wish I could come myself," Churchill wrote Tito, "but I am too old and heavy to jump out on a parachute." The symbolic significance of the Prime Minister sending his only son was not lost on the Partisans. Young Randolph "soon enchanted our commanders and commissars with his wit and unconventional manner," observed Milovan Djilas, "but he revealed through his drinking and lack of interest that he had inherited neither political imagination nor dynamism with his surname."

The British now agreed to receive a Partisan mission in Cairo to discuss military needs. This act, in effect, gave formal recognition to the Partisan army, though it led indirectly to the loss of one of Tito's youngest and most promising associates, Ivo-Lola Ribar, who had been a highly successful organizer of young people, the Partisans' primary source of both soldiers and political workers. On November 27 the mission headed by Ribar was about to take off from an improvised airfield in a captured German bomber. A German reconnaissance plane spotted the craft and attacked with bombs and machine guns, killing Ribar. For Ribar's father, who was president of the Partisan Anti-Fascist Council, AVNOJ, the death was a double tragedy. Only one month before, Ivan Ribar had lost his other son in the civil war with the Chetniks.

Nonetheless, two days after Ivo-Lola's death, Ribar presided over the second nationwide session of AVNOJ—a meeting in Jajce that brought further recognition to Tito and an audacious declaration of political independence by the Partisans. Tito was named to the newly created military rank of marshal of Yugoslavia—an honor for which he had designed his own insignia, a heavily embroidered wreath of oak leaves. The Partisan leader was also elected Premier of the new provisional government, which, with the Chetniks on the run, was now proclaimed the only legal government of Yugoslavia. The country's sovereign-in-exile, young King Peter, was forbidden to return home unless formally invited "by the will of the people."

These were sweeping decisions, and Tito had not bothered to clear them beforehand with Moscow. Stalin was so angry at Tito's defiance that he sent a message to Tito labeling the conference "a stab in the back." He feared that the emergence of a Communist government in Yugoslavia would lead Britain and the U.S. to recast their thinking about the Balkans—perhaps even intervene there. If they

A group of young Partisans leaves Drvana after the Second Anti-Fascist Youth Congress held on the night of May 22, 1944, which was highlighted by an appearance by Marshal Tito. Of the original 103 in this delegation that set out from Montenegro, Sandjak and Herzegovina, only 54 made it; the others succumbed to exhaustion from the 36-day journey and the depredations of Italians and the Ustashi, troops of the puppet Croatian state. Among the 54 who reached Drvana was Stana Tomashevich (center), the young woman who was elected to chair the congress.

HOMELESS WANDERERS IN A LAND OF WAR

Homeless children take shelter from the elements in a cliffside cave in Montenegro. Caves also protected refugees from strafing by German planes.

A lucky young refugee savors a few morsels of scarce food.

Hundreds of thousands of helpless Yugoslavs—women and children and old people—were uprooted and whipsawed in the never-ending warfare between the guerrillas and the occupation forces. Burned out of their homes and villages by marauding troops, the civilians flooded the countryside, blindly fleeing their oppressors. Many who failed to escape were sent off to concentration camps or shot. A Partisan army unit from Dalmatia found the bodies of 50 women and children in a cave.

The refugees' goal, which shifted constantly with the tide of battle, was some remote region that reportedly had been liberated by the guerrillas. Along the way, thousands died of starvation, exhaustion or disease. Inured to pain and hardship, the ragged legions marched silently on and on. Wrote one refugee, "It was only the children who showed their suffering: they did not moan, they did not cry, but they simply squeaked sadly like little puppies who had lost their mothers."

Carrying a baby, a mother from Knezpolje leads her daughter across a field in January 1944. The bag on her back contains a quilt and several pots.

were to intervene, they might revoke their promise to open a second front in Western Europe in 1944, something Stalin had been pressing them to do for two years.

When the U.S. and Britain showed no signs of alarm, Stalin relented. The Soviets then publicly praised Tito's decisions and announced they would finally send a military mission to the Partisans. This, of course, was the supreme moment of recognition for Tito, though the irony of the situation was not lost on him. While the British and Americans had been sending him arms, the Russians had provided only advice and moral support from a propaganda station called Radio Free Yugoslavia, located in the Soviet Union.

There was irony, too, in Stalin's choice of the chief of the Soviet mission that arrived at Tito's headquarters in late February, 1944. In contrast to the high personal connections of Fitzroy Maclean and Randolph Churchill, the Soviet emissary, Lieut. General N. V. Korneyev, was a former Army group chief of staff whom Stalin held in low regard. "The man is not stupid," Stalin said, "but he is a drunkard, an incurable drunkard." Korneyev had been wounded at Stalingrad and had a limp. The Soviet mission, therefore, refused to parachute in and had to be transported to Yugoslavia in ski-equipped gliders borrowed from the British.

The Partisans greeted their long-awaited comrades joyfully, but their enthusiasm was not reciprocated. Korneyev told Maclean he would have preferred an assignment in Washington. He also complained about the lack of lavatory facilities in the quarters assigned to him, an omission Partisan plumbers immediately set about correcting by building some to Soviet specifications. And although Soviet supply planes based in Italy brought the Russians copious quantities of vodka and caviar, they managed very little in the way of arms for the Partisans—a fact that Tito noted dryly at his formal weekly meetings with the Allied mission chiefs.

As Tito's star rose, Mihailovich's plummeted. An indicator of the Chetnik leader's eclipse was the bizarre history of a movie about the Yugoslav resistance filmed in a British studio. When the film was begun early in 1942, Mihailovich's image outside his country was at its zenith, and the film had the working title *Chetniks*. But when the film was shown at theaters in London in 1943, Mihailovich was no longer in the picture. The title of the movie had been changed to *Undercover*, and the *London Daily Worker* praised it for its portrayal of Partisan heroism.

Everything seemed to go wrong for Mihailovich. The surrender of the Italian divisions in Yugoslavia had deprived him of his principal source of supplies. During the previous summer the British had promised equal aid to the Partisans and the Chetniks, but deliveries did not work out that way at all. A British liaison officer with Chetnik units in eastern Serbia reported that not a single parachute drop was received in his area after October 1943, a period when the Partisans benefited from as many as 60 sorties on one night.

The paucity of British aid had political as well as military consequences for Mihailovich. In Yugoslavia each parachute drop was an occasion for celebration for everyone in the area, guerrilla and civilian alike. It brought not only arms but also parachute silk that the women sewed into dresses and metal supply canisters that the men fashioned into stoves. The delivery was a symbol of contact with the outside world, a sign of hope that the Allies would soon arrive. The drop-off in British aid demoralized the Chetnik fighters and sent the noncombatants flocking to the Partisans, whom the British now obviously favored. Only in their native Serbia did the Chetniks still enjoy widespread support from the population. And even there several of their regional commanders had concluded local nonaggression pacts with the Germans.

The disenchantment of Mihailovich with the British was matched by their growing impatience with his inactivity. The British had so inflated his image early in the war that inevitably they were disappointed by the Chetniks' performance in the field. Colonel Bailey, the chief British liaison officer with the Chetniks, was struck by Mihailovich's obsession with petty military administration. Even when Mihailovich bestirred himself on rare occasions to fight the Germans, his rivals got the credit in the outside world—just as the Chetniks earlier had been erroneously honored for the exploits of the Partisans. In October 1943 the Chetniks destroyed an important railroad bridge over the Drina River in eastern Bosnia. A week later they heard the BBC credit the attack to the Partisans. And they had other proof of the outside world's lack of interest in them: when the Germans announced a reward of 100,000 gold marks for the capture of Tito or of Mihailovich, only the price on Tito's head was reported by the press in Britain and in the United States.

Mihailovich fell to quarreling with the British mission at his headquarters. Bailey, the mission chief, was superseded in September 1943 by a rather stiff brigadier named C. D. Armstrong. It was hoped that a man of higher rank would carry more weight with Mihailovich and perhaps even manage to persuade him to cooperate with Tito. But the Chetnik leader was contemptuous of Armstrong and referred to him as "a common sergeant." Feelings reached the point where he would only communicate with Armstrong by letter. He lavished attention on the more sympathetic U.S. liaison officers, even honoring them on Thanksgiving Day in 1943 by lighting 11 huge bonfires in the shape of the letter A, for America, on the mountains around his camp.

In December 1943 the British government decided to give Mihailovich his last chance to demonstrate his value to the Allied cause. The Chetniks were asked to blow up two bridges, which would paralyze all north-south rail traffic. Mihailovich agreed to the request, moved Chetnik units into place and then, inexplicably, never gave the order to attack. In February the British halted their on-again-off-again supplies to the Chetniks and ordered the 30 liaison officers with them to leave the country. Churchill later explained to Parliament his rationale for abandoning Mihailovich: "He has not been fighting the enemy and, moreover, some of his subordinates have made accommodations with the enemy."

Churchill was not aware that Tito—whom he lauded as "glorious in the fight for freedom"—also had attempted to make an accommodation with the enemy on at least one occasion. The details of that remarkable episode remained shrouded in official Yugoslav silence for more than 30 years until Milovan Djilas' memoirs *Wartime* were finally published in the West.

Djilas told how the Partisans attempted to gain a truce in their fight against the Germans. The occasion was a series of negotiations conducted during March 1943 at the height of Operation *Weiss*. Ostensibly, the talks were aimed at an exchange of prisoners, including a Slovenian Communist woman named Herta Has, who had lived with Tito as his common-law wife immediately preceding the War and by whom she had had a child. Djilas—using a pseudonym to hide his identity—and two other top-level representatives were trying to get the Germans to accord the Partisans formal status as a belligerent, which would mean that prisoners, and particularly the wounded, would be treated in keeping with international conventions. More significantly, the three men had been entrusted by Tito to explore the possibilities of a temporary truce that would relieve German pressure near the Neretva River and enable the Partisans to pursue their civil war against the Chetniks.

Before the talks, Tito had radioed Moscow that he was negotiating with the Germans for an exchange of prisoners. This news—with no mention of his further aims—precipitated a rebuke from the Soviets. In turn, the rebuke drew a sharp response from Tito: "If you cannot understand what a hard time we are having and if you cannot help us, at least do not hinder us."

After preliminary meetings with a German division commander, Djilas and his delegation were taken by car and by train to Zagreb, the Croatian capital, for further talks. The Partisan delegates committed to writing their conviction that the Chetniks were their "main enemy" and announced their intention to "take up combat against the English" if British forces landed in Yugoslavia. The negotiations came

At a special school on the island of Vis, British Major Geoffrey Kup instructs Partisans in artillery techniques. Partisans were trained in the use of 75mm howitzers; the chief of the British mission to the Partisans, Brigadier Fitzroy Maclean, observed that raw recruits learned to handle the artillery pieces "as if they had done nothing else all their lives."

THE PRISONER WHO SAVED HIS CAPTOR'S LIFE

When Lieut. Colonel Jack Churchill, commander of the British Number Two Commando unit, was captured by the Germans in June 1944 on the Yugoslavian island of Brac, he could not have guessed that he would later play a crucial role in the life of his captor.

The man who took Churchill into custody was Captain Hans Thorner of the 118th Division. Thorner disregarded a standing order that all Commandos were to be executed and saw to it that his prisoner was treated correctly. Before leaving Thorner's care, Churchill wrote a letter to the German officer thanking him.

From Yugoslavia, Churchill was shunted to various prison camps in Germany, including Dachau, but escaped near the end of the war. Thorner was subsequently captured by the Americans near Vienna, and the Partisans demanded that he be turned over to them to be tried for war crimes.

To convince the Americans of his good character, Thorner showed them the letter from Churchill. Back home in Great Britain, Churchill guessed that Thorner had probably been taken prisoner, and went to Allied authorities in London and offered to appear in Thorner's defense if the German was court-martialed. As a result of Churchill's timely intervention, Thorner was not delivered over to the Yugoslavians—who angrily denounced Churchill as a "swine" for his interference—and was sent back to Germany instead.

Lieut. Colonel Jack Churchill was the prisoner of the man below for three days.

No PI 633 Neresche
Brac
6 - VI - 44

Dear Captain,
        Just a short note to thank you & your men, down here, for our correct treatment during our stay with you.
    The food was rather short, & less than we are used to, but that could not be helped under the circumstances.
    I hope that, after the war we shall meet again, & in any case should you at any time find yourself in England do ring up HELENSBURGH 222 or GERRARDS CROSS 2120, where you will find me & I hope will dine with my wife & I.
        Farewell.
                    Jack Churchill.

Churchill's note thanks his captor.

Captain Thorner was an honored German officer.

to a standstill, however, when Hitler got wind of them. "One does not negotiate with rebels," he declared. "Rebels must be shot."

Even so, the prisoner exchange was completed (the Germans had no idea they were releasing the mother of Tito's two-year-old son), and the Partisans fulfilled a pledge they had made to stop all sabotage against the Zagreb-Belgrade rail line. In his account of the negotiations, Djilas recalled that the truce attempt brought "no pangs of conscience." Ironically, the rationale advanced by Djilas—"military necessity compelled us"—echoed that of Chetnik commanders whose local truces with the Germans made them traitors in the eyes of the Partisans.

By the spring of 1944 the Partisan position had greatly improved. The Chetnik threat had been confined to Serbia, and though the Germans, together with their Bulgarian and local allies, still controlled more than half of Yugoslavia, Tito's army had grown by another 150,000; it now numbered an estimated 300,000 men and women. The Partisans were approaching parity with the Axis occupation armies in manpower, if not in firepower.

American and British aid now poured in at the rate of nearly 3,000 tons per month. The fact that only a minuscule quantity came from the Soviet Union—which Tito had praised as "our greatest protector"—proved embarrassing to many Partisan commanders. One political commissar explained to his unit that the initials U.S. on the planes that flew in from Italy to make the parachute drops obviously stood for "Unione Sovetica."

The British helped the Partisans in still another important way. They set up military missions with Tito's units throughout most of Yugoslavia to provide direct assistance. These missions consisted largely of specialists—artillery instructors, demolition experts and doctors, who were called upon to endure with the Partisans privations and hardships such as many of them had never known.

As the Partisans grew stronger and more confident, the normally cautious Tito let down his guard. One morning in May 1943 a German reconnaissance plane flew over Partisan headquarters at Drvar and lingered so long that its picture-taking purpose was clear. But no special precautions were taken, and a few days later—just as the Partisans were preparing to celebrate Tito's 52nd birthday—the Germans struck. Some 600 SS paratroopers, each armed with a picture of Tito, descended on Drvar by glider and parachute, battled it out with the Partisans, massacred the civilian population and began looking for the Partisan leader.

Tito's headquarters was in a cave outside town. At one point, German rifle fire crackled so close to the mouth of the cave that Tito's secretary Zdenka cried, "They'll kill us! They'll kill us!" But Tito was reluctant to leave his shelter. His associates urged him to leave—to remain in hiding in the cave, they said, was not only dangerous but could also be embarrassing.

With German reinforcements converging on Drvar, Tito, his high command and his new dog Tiger fled into the woods. "There, on a siding in the woods was drawn up the Partisan Express," wrote Fitzroy Maclean, "with steam up and smoke and sparks belching from the funnel. Solemnly, Tito, his entourage and his dog entrained; the whistle blew; and, with much puffing and creaking, they started off down the five miles of track through the woods, with the enemy's bullets whining through the trees all round them."

At the end of the short run the Partisans got off and proceeded on foot. British bombers and fighters flew more than a thousand sorties in support of their retreat, and after a week of dodging the Germans, Tito finally agreed to a Soviet suggestion that he needed a safer base of operations. The rescue effort that followed was perhaps the ultimate example of Allied cooperation. Tito was transported from Bosnia to Italy in an American-built DC-3 under the operational control of the British; the plane was manned by a Soviet crew who had wangled the mission so the Communists could claim credit for saving their Yugoslav disciple.

From Italy Tito was taken by a British destroyer to Vis, an island in Partisan territory that was heavily fortified and defended by British artillery and Commando forces. On board the ship Tito's hosts plied him with hospitality, including rounds of gin, wine, liqueurs, champagne and brandy. The marshal of Yugoslavia, in rare good humor, entertained his hosts by reciting for them, in English, an old nursery rhyme, "The Owl and the Pussycat." Less than half an hour later, Tito arrived at Vis. He would remain there for three months, consolidating his position, before returning to the mainland.

HEROES AND ENTERTAINERS

Dressed in Partisan uniforms, members of the Theater of National Liberation—formed in 1942 by seven Zagreb entertainers—assemble for a portrait in 1944.

A TOUGH TROUPE OF DEDICATED PERFORMERS

"How long are we to walk?" asked the actor. "I've come to do acting, not walking." But walking was one of the chief activities he and the other members of the Partisans' Theater of National Liberation engaged in during the War as they traveled from camp to camp and village to village to put on their morale-boosting shows.

The troupe shared with the Partisans almost every hardship and danger short of actual combat. They endured attacks by German and Chetnik forces and heavy poundings from the air. They went on marches that lasted up to 37 hours and took the troupe through waist-deep snow, across terrain exposed to enemy fire and over passes more than 3,000 feet high. Escaping from the Germans, they made the perilous crossing of the Neretva River with the Partisans. They crossed by night, on the planks of the makeshift, rickety bridge built over the raging water, and when they confronted the looming mountain on the other side, one of them commented dryly, "There you are, Comrades. We have entered history, but who will get us out of it?"

Yet even after a half day's hike on the most rugged paths the actors would go on with their shows. For their peasant audiences, they provided some of the few bright spots in the War. So popular were they that on one occasion when they arrived late for a performance, the village school was packed with people who had been patiently waiting for them—many standing—for 10 hours.

On their long marches food was scarce, and the actors ate what they could find. Occasionally they dined on nettles and dry pear peelings, which the peasants normally fed to poultry. When there was no food at all, they gulped water to subdue their hunger pangs and tried to conserve their strength.

One of the actresses carried a baby girl with her (left) and grew so weary that her milk ran out before the infant was three months old. Keeping the child alive became a concern of the entire troupe; all they were able to give the baby at one point was a little watered cow's milk and some sugar. Amazingly, the child survived.

As Partisans march through Yugoslavia, actress Ivka Rutich walks beside them carrying the baby girl she gave birth to after joining the troupe.

All seasoned travelers, the performers linger by the Partisan train that transported them to villages along a 19-mile-long track in west-central Yugoslavia.

Dressed as peasants, George Skrigin and Mira Sanjina perform a folk dance in Jajce, a Bosnian town.

In Jajce, the actors present Gogol's The Inspector General, a satire about pre-Communist Russia.

PUTTING ON SHOWS WITH MAKESHIFT PROPS

The Theater of National Liberation was, understandably, operated on a shoestring. Equipment was almost always primitive: wooden planks were used for a stage, two sheets for a curtain, and carbide or gas lamps for the spotlights. Party officials furnished the performers with fabric for their costumes. It was of such cheap quality that during one downpour the sizing washed out of the velvet, and it took the artists two days of sand-and-soap scrubbing to get the sticky residue off their bodies.

Like everything else, ballet shoes were scarce, but dancer George Skrigin was so insistent on being properly dressed for his performances that to go on without the right shoes was unthinkable: he drew a pair with India ink on his woolen socks.

Under a banner reading "Long Live the People's Liberation Struggle," Vjeko Africh recites a poem about a Croatian who led a 1573 revolt against landholders.

In a cave, refugees find protection while Ivan Goran Kovacich (far right) finishes writing a poem.

In a secluded glen, actor Vjeko Africh chats with two Partisan women who are cooking the day's lunch.

A German scout plane, armed with machine guns, zooms above the troupe. Because of its small size, Partisans called this kind of aircraft a "cigarette butt."

UNDER ATTACK BY AXIS PLANES

The performers, and the Partisans and refugees they traveled with were constantly harassed by enemy planes. To reduce the risk, they often moved at night and sheltered in caves or forests during the day.

On one occasion, three male performers taking a bath in a brook were spotted by a German reconnaissance plane. The men ran naked into the woods and hid behind trees. The pilot, who seemed to be enjoying himself immensely, fired his machine gun at them till he ran out of ammunition, then flashed a Nazi salute and flew away.

As the actors came out of the forest "like three soaked and downcast pigeons" to pick up their clothes, they were greeted by the laughter of female Partisans who had been hiding close by. The women, said one of the men, found this "the biggest show their actors had ever given them."

137

At Tito's headquarters Partisan officials listen to a Communist broadcast.

The troupe clusters around Tito and his dog Lux in the summer of 1942. They

met Tito several times during the War; one such session occurred amid a nine-hour bombing—one of the Partisan leader's many close calls (following pages).

YUGOSLAVIA'S MARSHAL TITO

In his cave headquarters on the island of Vis, Marshal Tito works at a desk covered with a U.S. Army blanket. A map of Yugoslavia hangs on the sandbag wall.

A MAN OF MANY FACES

In 1941, when Hitler's forces knifed through the Balkans, the head of the outlawed Communist Party of Yugoslavia was a shadowy figure named Josip Broz. His comrades-in-arms knew him as Tito. In the outside world there was so much confusion about his identity that some people thought the name Tito stood for a terrorist organization, and others believed the guerrilla leader was a young woman, a Ukrainian Jew, a Russian general, even an American citizen who had once been an organizer in the U.S. Communist Party. He had traveled under at least two dozen aliases, and his Soviet patron Josef Stalin still referred to him by the last name Walter.

But in Yugoslavia there was soon no question of his identity. He was the iron-willed head of the Partisan army, an old-line Communist driven by fierce nationalism. He fought alongside his Partisan followers and was wounded with them. On the march he covered long distances with such speed that one member of his entourage remarked that someone ought to give Tito a horse so the pace could be slowed. Tito established his headquarters in the most secluded places—a hut, a cave, a castle or a shelter made of branches in the forest—and shared the privations of guerrilla fighting with his men.

His career was marked by narrow escapes, and in these he was aided by his uncanny ability to remain cool in the most dangerous situations. On one occasion before the War, Yugoslav police burst into the Metalworker's Union headquarters in Zagreb looking for Tito, who happened to be there at the time. "Is Josip Broz here?" they demanded. Tito spread his arms in surprise and replied, "Don't you see that he isn't here?" The police studied the faces of those present, turned toward Tito, saluted, thanked him and then walked away.

Tito's knack for being able to wriggle out of tight situations saved him and his followers many times during the war. "He was always encircled," remarked the exasperated German SS chief, Heinrich Himmler, "and the man found a way out every time."

The Communist Central Committee was headquartered in the Hotel Palace in Uzice until the Germans forced Tito out of town in November 1941.

Passport photographs show four of the guises Tito employed to elude the police in the years immediately before the War. The wily Communist sometimes donned spectacles, dyed his hair red and grew a moustache to conceal his identity. Clockwise from top left are photos used with aliases Friedrich Walter, Ivan Kostanjsek, Spiridon Mekas and Slavko Babich.

At a camp in Bosnia, Tito dictates a military order to his secretary Zdenka.

Tito (front row, center) meets Partisan leaders at Bihach, December 1942.

As commander in chief of the Partisan army, Tito reviews the elite First

144

Proletarian Brigade, mustered in a field near the town of Bosanski Petrovac in November 1942. At the time, Tito's army claimed a strength of 150,000 men.

FROM HARRIED FUGITIVE TO VICTORIOUS LEADER

The year 1943 brought Tito from the brink of annihilation to the pinnacle of power. He spent the first six months of the year in the forests of Yugoslavia, trying to stave off two German offensives that threatened the Partisans with extinction. To defend himself he carried a pistol and hand grenades.

In June he narrowly escaped death at Sutjeska when a bomb landed a few feet away from him, killing several of his party and blowing him into the air. His life was spared only because, at the last second, his dog Lux had crouched at his head and absorbed the full force of the blast.

Even when the Partisans' lot was bleak, Tito's determination never faltered. "Our units are on the march day and night, without sleep or food," he wrote. "Our position is hard, but we shall get out of it. The enemy is making an extreme effort to annihilate us, but he will not succeed."

Tito held his group together by addressing his soldiers' problems in a patient, undogmatic manner. "When you put a question to him," said Edvard Kardelj, one of Tito's closest confidants, "he did not always answer with a quotation from Marx, or Engels or Lenin—he spoke in practical, common-sense terms." Although he ruled the Partisans firmly, he was receptive to their suggestions. "If none of us had any conflicting opinions to put forward," said Kardelj, "he would urge us to think again."

Tito's down-to-earth demeanor and his fearless leadership attracted thousands of new conscripts to his army and won him worldwide fame. In November, at the second session of the Anti-Fascist Council of National Liberation in Jajce. his country was declared an independent, sovereign nation, and he was named President, as well as marshal, of Yugoslavia.

His wounded arm in a sling, a weary Tito rests with compatriot Ivan Ribar during a rugged march in 1943.

On the way to the Anti-Fascist Council meeting in Jajce, Partisans use a rope to pull a boatload of fellow delegates across the Sana River in November 1943.

Standing in front of a bust of himself, Tito delivers a political report to the second session of the Partisan Anti-Fascist Council, held on November 29, 1943.

Partisan sentries guard Tito's concealed headquarters outside Drvar. The camouflaged house at the mouth of a cave was Tito's capitol for three months in 1944

DESPERATE ESCAPE FROM A HILLSIDE REDOUBT

Although his Partisans had pushed the Germans back on virtually every front by 1944, Tito himself was not out of danger. His rise to prominence had made him a more inviting target; on May 25—his 52nd birthday —enemy forces launched a daring paratroop raid on his headquarters at Drvar.

Tito had established his command post in a camouflaged wooden house at the mouth of a cave halfway up a steep hill above the village. As crack German paratroopers poured a withering fire on his hillside hideout, the Partisan leader made his break. Using a rope, Tito and several others, including his newly acquired dog Tiger, scrambled through a narrow tunnel, which had been carved in the cave's roof by a stream, and escaped.

The Germans had some small consolation for their effort: they seized a pair of Tito's boots and a uniform, which was at a tailor's shop in Drvar. The trophies were rushed to Vienna for public display.

Hunting for Tito, German soldiers interrogate a captured Partisan girl during their raid on Drvar.

Amused by their find, German troops display Tito's uniform, which they seized after the attack.

149

Puffing a cigarette, Tito strolls with Churchill at Naples in August 1944.

THE FINAL SUCCESS: WORLD RECOGNITION

After his close call at Drvar, Marshal Tito was forced to flee the mainland of Yugoslavia and set up his headquarters in a tightly guarded cave on the Adriatic Island of Vis, 33 miles offshore. From there he directed military operations in Yugoslavia.

Tito's international prestige had never been higher. In August 1944 he traveled to Italy to confer with the Allied High Command and was met at Naples by Prime Minister Churchill. It was Tito's first official public appearance outside Yugoslavia.

Churchill was so impressed by Tito that he said of the Partisan leader, "Marshal Tito has shown himself to be not only a great soldier but also a remarkable statesman." For his part, Tito was pleased with the two days of "very frank" talks with Churchill covering everything from military aid to the Partisans to Tito's Communist vision of postwar Yugoslavia.

After his conference with Churchill, Tito flew back to Vis. In the remaining nine months of the war, he waged his battles so skillfully that he gained another tribute from an unlikely source. Said Germany's SS chief Heinrich Himmler: "I wish we had a dozen Titos in Germany. . . . He is an uncompromising and steadfast soldier, a steadfast commander."

After returning from Italy to Vis, Tito splashes in the Adriatic with his dog Tiger.

Tiger was captured from a German colonel in 1943, became Tito's constant companion and soon learned to obey his master's commands in Serbo-Croatian.

151

5

After the Germans occupied Greece in April 1941, the parlors of Athens were abuzz with talk about organizing armed resistance. Bearing testimony to the old joke that the number of political parties in Greece is roughly equal to the number of inhabitants, politicians and former Army officers founded dozens of clandestine committees. These groups, known by their initials in Greek, formed an alphabet soup of political factions—AAA, EKKA, and eventually even one known simply as X.

At first the underground committees were too busy getting organized—all political activity had been curtailed during the previous four and a half years of Premier Metaxas' dictatorial regime—to put guerrillas in the field. But as the months passed, the Greeks were galvanized to action by the hardships of the occupation. Though Axis tyranny was less severe than in Yugoslavia, which Hitler deliberately set out to destroy, Greece suffered grievously at the hands of the conquerors. The Germans, anxious to minimize the costs of occupation, maintained control over only a few key areas, including the ports of Salonika in the north and Piraeus near Athens, and part of Crete, which was important as a supply base for Rommel in North Africa. The Bulgarians took over most of Macedonia and Thrace. The Italians got the rest.

The administration of Greece was left largely to a puppet government, which initially was under Italian direction. But the government was so ineffectual that Greece was almost immediately plunged into economic chaos. Inflation soared and citizens of Athens had to carry packages of bank notes just to pay streetcar fares. Even worse was the food shortage. With the Germans using the country's only north-south railway to supply their forces in Crete and Africa, food shipments to the large cities practically ceased. In order to survive, young men of Athens foraged in the countryside. In Athens during the first winter of occupation, tens of thousands of citizens died from starvation and cold and from related diseases.

All the while, talk of organized resistance continued. But it took until the end of September of 1941 for something to finally happen.

Not surprisingly, the first political faction to act was the small but vigorous Greek Communist Party. The Communists had thrived on adversity; banned by Metaxas, they had maintained their organization and gained valuable experi-

GREECE'S MOUNTAIN WARRIORS

ence in clandestine operations. Realizing that the Moscow party line had little appeal to the Greeks, with their strong allegiances to family, church, democratic process and national independence, the Communists set up a series of front organizations that preached resistance to the occupation and free elections after the War. These were goals shared by the great majority of Greeks.

The most important Communist front was a coalition of six purportedly independent parties, which was known as EAM. Through the winter of 1941-1942, efficient propagandists for EAM spread those initials everywhere—printed them on leaflets, painted them on walls and even burned them into the underbrush on the side of Mount Hymettus near Athens. Thousands of hopeful Greeks joined EAM (usually in total ignorance of the fact that Communists dominated it). The recruitment drive was so successful that in April of 1942, EAM spun off a military organization, ELAS, and urged citizens to join it and take up arms against the occupation forces.

The guerrilla nucleus of ELAS was put together in the mountainous Roumeli region of central Greece by a muscular young Communist named Athanasios Klaras, who had taken the *nom de guerre* Aris Velouchiotis (this was common practice among guerrillas to prevent Axis reprisals against their families). Aris was a former schoolteacher and professional revolutionary who had been trained in Moscow and seasoned in Greek jails where he was confined for illegal Communist activities. A charismatic leader with a strong streak of cruelty, he had a knack for communicating with peasants in the simple but subtle language of the mountains and possessed a flair for the dramatic. He draped his short, powerful figure with bandoliers, wore a black Cossack-style hat flamboyantly and was surrounded by a personal bodyguard of a score or more men, who adopted his headgear and hence were known as "black bonnets." Even his pseudonym was chosen for effect: the last name for his birthplace near the mountain Velouchi and the first after Ares, the Greek god of war.

Shortly after the Communists launched ELAS, a second major guerrilla band took shape in the mountains of Epirus along the Albanian border. This group, known as EDES, represented an Athens-based faction whose political color-ation was unmistakably republican. The military-leader of EDES was Napoleon Zervas, a plump, jovial former colonel in the Greek Army, who carried a jeweled dagger at his ample waistline and had made his living as a professional gambler in Athens. His participation in a coup d'état against the monarchy had resulted in his dismissal from the Army 16 years before.

Zervas had proved himself to be a capable officer during the First World War but had been reluctant to take the field in World War II. The British, who were impressed by Zervas' military and political background and who maintained contact with Athens through a secret radio system, first attempted to bribe him into action by smuggling in 24,000 gold sovereigns—then worth nearly $200,000 (and far more than that in inflation-ravaged Greece). Then, while he vacillated, they resorted to the ugly expedient of threatening to expose him to the Germans for plotting against the occupation—an activity that so far had been confined mostly to talk. Acceding to the pressure, Zervas took to the mountains in his native Epirus, promoted himself to general and proceeded to attract experienced officers from the prewar Army and to enlist the help of the local peasants.

In the summer of 1942, Zervas led his band—then about 100 strong—in the first noteworthy guerrilla operation in Axis-occupied Greece. Italian supply columns, leaving the town of Ioannina every noon for their base at Arta, had to pass through the long, narrow, cliff-sided defiles of the Louros River valley. Zervas chose to attack there, using a classic guerrilla tactic. First he ordered his men to block the road with mines. Then he deployed the men along the cliffs above the road. Late in the afternoon the daily convoy—20 trucks bearing guns and ammunition and guarded by two tanks—advanced into Zervas' trap.

When the lead tank was crippled by a mine, guerrillas at the rear of the column blew up a bridge over the river, blocking the convoy's retreat. The Italians' response was later reported condescendingly by German General Hubert Lanz, whose XXII Mountain Corps eventually took over control of the area. The Italians at the head of the column, Lanz wrote, "were demoralized. Nobody attempted to offer resistance. All were possessed of but one thought: every man for himself!"

The Italians in the rear-guard tank were among the few

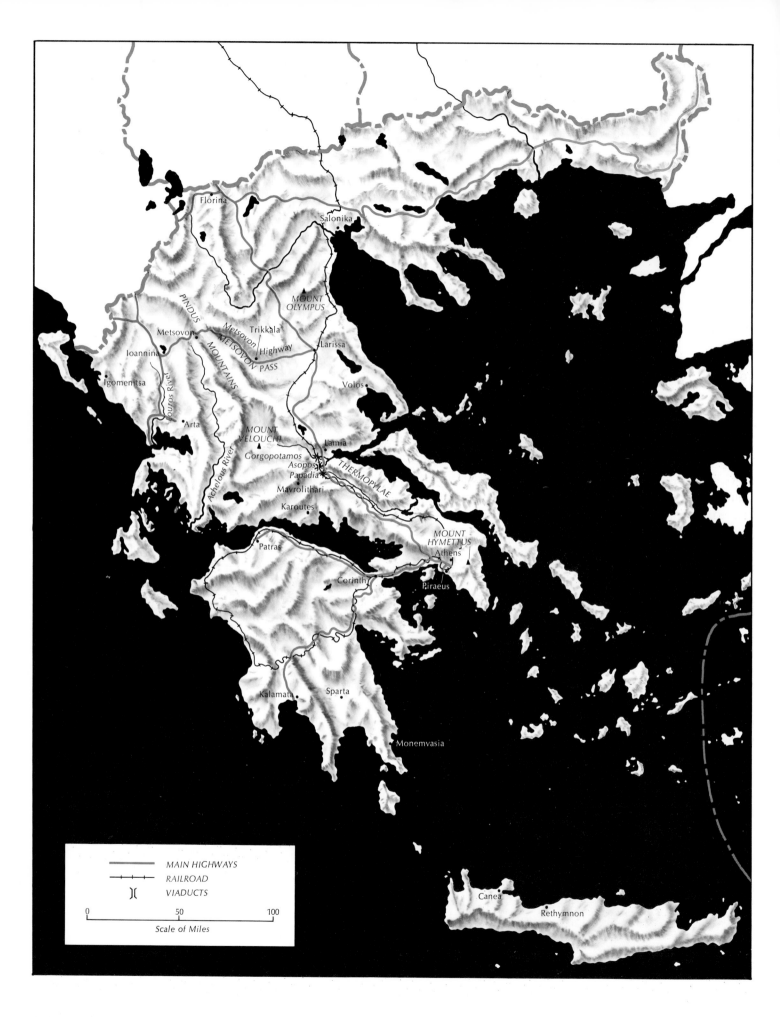

Florina

Salonika

MOUNT
OLYMPUS

PINDUS

Metsovon
Trikkala

Metsovon
Highway

METSOVON

Larissa

Ioannina

PASS

MOUNTAINS

Igomenitsa

Volos

Arta

MOUNT
VELOUCHI

Gorgopotamos
Asopos
Papadia

Lamia

THERMOPYLAE

Mavrolithari

Karoutes

Patras

MOUNT
HYMETTUS

Athens

Corinth

Piraeus

Kalamata

Sparta

Monemvasia

MAIN HIGHWAYS
RAILROAD
)(VIADUCTS

0   50   100

Scale of Miles

Canea

Rethymnon

who did put up a fight. "From behind steel-shielded ports, machine gun bursts cut into the nests of the guerrillas on the escarpments," continued Lanz. "They were scoring effective hits when fate overtook them too. The daring bandits had exploded a concentrated charge under the chassis. Its body suddenly split open and the heavy tank tipped over, burying its brave crew in fire and smoke. The last pocket of resistance had been broken."

At this juncture Zervas' men swarmed down on the column. They killed the survivors and stripped the 60-odd victims of valuables. Then they brought up their pack mules and loaded them with wounded guerrillas and all the armaments they could salvage. Finally they set fire to the trucks and tanks and disappeared into their mountain fastness.

There was no immediate follow-up to this promising success. By the end of the summer of 1942, Zervas' EDES and Aris' ELAS had grown only modestly; each numbered no more than several hundred men. These units operated in adjacent regions, tacitly respecting the Achelous River in northwestern Greece as the boundary between them. Both outfits were ill equipped, inexperienced and incapable at this point of conducting anything more than minor and sporadic forays against the enemy.

Then, on September 30, the whole course of the resistance movement was suddenly transformed by an airborne drop from Cairo. That night a team of eight British soldiers, headed by Colonel Eddie Myers of the Royal Engineers, parachuted into the seldom-patrolled mountains of central Greece, somewhere near the village of Karoutes. Several men in the group were demolition experts, and their mission was to blow up one of three viaducts bridging the ravines of Gorgopotamos, a 10-mile stretch of rugged terrain south of the town of Lamia. Greece's north-south railroad ran over those viaducts, and by destroying any one of them the British would put the railroad out of commission for at least six weeks, stopping German supplies bound for Piraeus and thence by ship to Rommel's Afrika Korps.

In the days after the British landed, reports of their arrival were passed from village to village throughout the surrounding countryside. One villager who helped spread the word was "Uncle Niko" Beis, a mountain shepherd who had lived in America for several years and could speak English.

On learning that parachutists had landed, Uncle Niko said to himself, "God has sent us Englishmen from heaven; it is my duty to help them."

When the friendly shepherd found the British in the wilderness, they were badly in need of his help. Their radios were defective, and they could not establish contact with Cairo. Moreover, Colonel Myers had planned on enlisting Zervas' band to aid his mission, and the team had landed fully a hundred miles to the east of the EDES camp. The British were closer to Aris' band, but they were not even aware of its existence.

Uncle Niko led the British to a large cave and, with help from other villlagers, supplied them with food, cooking equipment and mules for transporting their bulky gear. Meanwhile, the British reconnoitered the Gorgopotamos area and chose for their target the northernmost of its three viaducts. Back at the cave, they built a wooden model of the steel girders that supported the viaduct and molded their plastic explosives to fit the stanchions. Practicing long hours with the model, they learned to attach their charges and prepare the fuses blindfolded.

Meanwhile, cooperative Greeks had arranged for Zervas and Aris to meet separately with the British. On November 19, Zervas arrived at the cave with his bodyguard and made an immediate hit with Myers. "He kissed me warmly on both my now bearded cheeks," Myers later wrote. "Undaunted, I kissed him back."

Next afternoon, after plodding for hours through a heavy snowfall, Myers reached the village of Mavrolithari and rendezvoused with Aris, who "gave me the impression of being on guard against someone or something." While Zervas had shown himself eager to cooperate in the raid on the viaduct, Aris hung back, stating that he had orders from his superiors in Athens to avoid enemy forces of the size of the 80-man Italian detachment guarding the target. But Aris did not want Zervas to get all of the credit if the raid was successful, and he grudgingly agreed to commit 100 men. It was decided that all three of the leaders would share the command.

The guerrillas launched the attack on the viaduct just after 11 p.m. on November 25. One group assaulted the southern end of the 200-yard bridge and after a stiff skirmish managed to secure it. But a second group of 30 inexperienced

Guerrilla warfare harassed the Axis forces from Thrace in the northeast to the island of Crete about 400 miles to the south. Most of the guerrillas' sabotage missions, including the destruction of the Gorgopotamos viaduct, were staged in barren mountainous areas, which constitute about 75 per cent of the country's surface. This rugged terrain—cut with deep gorges and rising to peaks more than one mile high—abounded in hiding places for the guerrillas and enabled them to make hit-and-run attacks that helped to offset the superior firepower of the Axis occupation troops.

men bogged down under heavy fire from Italians at the northern end. After 20 tense minutes, Zervas was on the verge of aborting the operation, but he could not locate the signal pistol to fire the appropriate green flare.

While the fighting was under way the British demolition crew descended into the gorge from the southern end of the bridge and reached the base of one of the viaduct's 70-foot-high steel piers. There they discovered to their horror that they had molded their plastic explosives to fit V-shaped girders—and the girders were actually U-shaped. Working hastily under Italian mortar fire, they remolded their plastic charges, a task that took nearly an hour. Through the long wait, a guerrilla detachment guarding the northern approaches to the bridge engaged in a sharp battle to hold back a patrol train carrying enemy reinforcements.

Finally, a shrill whistle was sounded by the demolition crew—the signal that the fuses were about to be lighted. "Two minutes later," Colonel Myers wrote, "there was a tremendous explosion, and I saw one of the seventy-foot steel spans lift into the air and—oh, what joy!—drop into the gorge below, in a rending crash of breaking and bending steel-work." The explosion—plus a second one that the engineers quickly wired and set off for good measure—tore a huge gap in the viaduct. Then the British and the guerrillas beat a jubilant retreat.

The Gorgopotamos mission had taken so long to mount that its basic purpose—to impede the movement of German supplies through Greece to North Africa—had meanwhile been accomplished by other means; in October the British had broken out of El Alamein and were driving Rommel's Afrika Korps so far to the west that German reinforcements and matériel were sent by the shorter route through Italy. But the sabotage did disrupt the Axis supply pattern inside Greece, and it also gave the hard-pressed Greeks a much-needed boost in morale. Colonel Myers was so delighted with the results that he informed Zervas, Aris, Uncle Niko and a number of other helpful Greeks that he was recommending them for British decorations. Aris replied dourly, "I would much sooner have boots for my guerrillas." From a fund of gold coins, Myers gave Aris 250 sovereigns to purchase necessities and promised him an airdrop of boots and other supplies.

Myers' superiors in Cairo were encouraged by the success at Gorgopotamos. It indicated that Greek guerrillas—even the uncooperative ELAS band—could be coordinated by British officers and involved in major tactical operations that dovetailed with Allied strategic plans. Myers was ordered to remain in Greece to encourage the build-up of guerrilla forces and coordinate their operations.

The assignment came as a shock to Myers. His original orders had called for him and most of his demolition team to be evacuated from Greece by submarine, while a small cadre stayed behind to maintain liaison with Zervas. Instead, he now found himself thrust into a role for which he felt ill equipped. He was a four-square field soldier with no knowledge of Greece, its people or language—and no taste for intrigue. Nevertheless, Myers went to work with soldierly diligence and growing enthusiasm.

In the weeks that followed Gorgopotamos, things began to pick up. The joint British-guerrilla mission inspired thousands of patriotic Greeks to turn guerrilla. They formed new bands and joined EDES and ELAS in droves. It soon became clear that ELAS was rapidly outgrowing EDES, with Aris

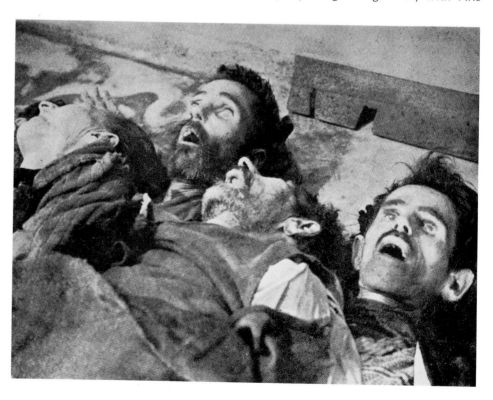

Emaciated victims of famine lie in a morgue in Athens. More than 30,000 Athenians starved to death in the last months of occupation. The urban hunger was caused primarily by the Axis' preemption of Greek transportation facilities to ship military supplies instead of normal food consignments. But even the peasants in the countryside had a hard struggle to survive, as their crops and farm animals were frequently confiscated by the Germans.

gaining about five new recruits to every man who joined Zervas. And that was worrisome, for Aris' unpredictability and intransigence grew apace with the size of his band. Though the British did not yet know that ELAS was controlled by Communists, their suspicions were rising steadily.

Both Aris' ELAS and its controlling body in Athens, EAM, used Communist-like tactics to recruit more guerrillas. In the cities, where EAM's efforts were concentrated, its recruiters had no compunctions about forcing men to enlist in ELAS. In the field, where Aris himself got most of his recruits, ELAS expanded by absorbing the many small, independent guerrilla bands that were forming up. Aris took them over by persuasion, by intimidation (e.g., threatening to denounce the members as collaborators) and, if everything else failed, by force. ELAS guerrillas even invaded the territory of the big EDES band, and a clash was avoided only by Zervas' discreet retreat.

Politics apart, the British continued to prefer Zervas to Aris. Zervas cheerfully followed Myers' orders, and at British request he even sent a conciliatory message to the exiled Greek monarch whom he had plotted to overthrow. ("For that," Major Christopher Woodhouse, Myers' deputy, observed dryly, "there are two names: one is unscrupulous opportunism; the other is unquestioning loyalty.")

Aris, on the other hand, was both uncooperative and unreliable; he also had a fanatical, even barbaric, streak. He was quoted as saying he would rather execute 10 innocent men than let one guilty one go free—and, indeed, he had presided over many executions and seemed to relish them. A British liaison officer, Captain Denys Hamson, wrote of him: "I suppose he was the most ruthless man I have ever met, the most cold-blooded, the cruelest. . . . I had no doubt that after one of our all-day drinking sessions in the most friendly atmosphere, he would have literally flayed me alive if it had suited his purpose."

Yet the British had no choice but to court Aris. His resistance movement had grown from a handful of men to an army of several thousand that now vied with the Axis for control of most of Greece, including areas in which lay most of the prime targets that Colonel Myers had earmarked for sabotage. The British needed not only Aris' manpower in their operations but also his permission to work in his territory. Meanwhile, Zervas' EDES band—which had grown less rapidly in the interim—was confined chiefly to a smaller, less important area of northwestern Greece.

Early in 1943, Myers' deputy, Major Woodhouse, uncovered evidence that ELAS was run by Communists. Unlike Myers, Woodhouse had the background to pick up that kind of information. He spoke fluent Greek, was well versed in the country's labyrinthine politics and had already spent nearly a year on intelligence missions behind enemy lines in Crete. He was only 25 and something of a prodigy—a year later he would become the youngest colonel in the British Army. A strapping six-footer, Woodhouse was so fit that he often wore out the wiry guerrilla guides assigned to escort him around the Greek mountains.

In January, six weeks after Gorgopotamos, Woodhouse walked more than a hundred miles to enemy-occupied Athens to talk with various resistance committees. His most important meeting was with five representatives of EAM. While he was there, Woodhouse heard one of the EAM leaders let slip a remark—"We have all been outlaws for years"—that could only mean that they were Communists. Woodhouse subsequently established that at least two of the EAM leaders, George Siantos and Andreas Tsimas, were top members of the Greek Communist Party. And if further evidence was needed, the EAM leaders supplied it when, on learning that the Germans had heard of Woodhouse's presence in Athens, they helped him escape to the mountains with a deftness that bespoke the Communists' long experience in underground operations. They even dyed his red hair black so that he would not stand out quite so prominently among the short, dark Greeks. In sum, Woodhouse's Athens visit "removed all doubt," he later wrote, "that EAM was effectively dominated by Communists."

As far as could be discerned, however, the EAM leaders seemed to be independent of Soviet domination. The Greek Communist Party included a considerable number of nationalists, and it apparently had no direct contact with the Russians. Nor were the Greek comrades following the Moscow party line as it was enunciated secondhand by Tito's Partisans during joint strategy meetings in this period; the Communists shrugged off Yugoslav advice as stubbornly as they resisted British efforts to control them.

But the fact that they were Communists influenced British

policy much more sharply than did the fact that Tito's Partisans were Communists too. The British had little to lose in Yugoslavia but were heavily committed in Greece by capital investments and they needed Greece in order to protect the Suez Canal—the lifeline of the British Empire. Judging by the pattern of Communist take-overs elsewhere, EAM and ELAS would—sooner or later—grab for national power and attempt to communize Greece, and the British did not have any desire to help them at the expense of their postwar interests there. Following Woodhouse's discovery, Churchill and the British Foreign Office were reluctant to aid the ELAS guerrillas in any way.

Yet of necessity the British continued working with ELAS. Eddie Myers regularly informed Cairo of his need for ELAS' support, and SOE (Special Operations Executive), the OSS-like intelligence agency in charge of British relations with the resistance movements in Europe and elsewhere, authorized Myers to deal with ELAS as circumstances and his best judgment dictated. Myers also acted with the approval and cooperation of the Allied Middle East Command, under General Jumbo Wilson.

In February 1943, Myers tried again to coordinate all the guerrilla bands. He discussed the subject with Zervas and Colonel Stephanos Saraphis, the leader of a small republican band. Saraphis, like Zervas a once-promising career officer who had been cashiered for an unsuccessful coup against the monarchy, suggested that all the independent non-Communist guerrilla forces form a united nonpolitical front, to be known as the National Bands. Then they would have the strength in numbers to invite ELAS to join and, perhaps, to make Aris cooperate and curb his vicious practice of attacking other guerrillas. Myers liked the idea and, after receiving approval by radio from SOE, Cairo, started months of work to put the plan into effect.

Myers' concern over Aris' excesses was shared by the Communist bureaucrats who decided ELAS policy in Athens. They disliked entrusting any one man with full field authority, and besides, they sorely needed a dedicated professional officer to train the new recruits who were swelling ELAS' ranks. Though Aris was considered by some to be the fighting genius of ELAS, the Communist politicos decided to look for someone to replace him as military leader.

The Communists' search bore strange fruit in March 1943. A group of ELAS men captured the little republican band of Colonel Saraphis, who was working with Myers for a National Bands agreement. The Communist leaders thought enough of his military experience to offer him Aris' post. Saraphis emphatically turned them down.

But the Communists would not take no for an answer. Working unsubtly to change Saraphis' mind, they charged him with collaboration and paraded him in chains through mountain villages where peasants greeted him with shouts of "Traitor!" According to Saraphis' account, during his five weeks of captivity he came to realize that ELAS was his nation's best hope for effective resistance against the Axis. He might well have been sincere, for other republicans had reached the same conclusion and were now joining EAM and ELAS knowing full well they were Communistic but hoping to moderate their left-wing policies. Saraphis made a Balkan about-face, joined ELAS and was given Aris' post as military leader.

Thereupon, the ELAS high command became a triumvirate, with Aris in charge of recruitment and public relations. The third boss was EAM Central Committee representative Andreas Tsimas, a sort of political commissar whom Woodhouse described as "a man in equal measure intelligent, flexible and reliable. He was the only leading Greek Communist with whom it was an intellectual pleasure to argue." All three had to agree before the band could undertake any operation. It was a cumbersome arrangement at best, and it

Aris Velouchiotis, the fanatic leader of ELAS, cut a savage swath through Greece, attacking rival EDES guerrillas and conducting mass executions of suspected collaborators. His excesses alienated many of his supporters and earned him a reprimand from his Communist superiors. "Even traitors should not be brutalized," the party's secretary general told him. "Our only objective for the moment should be to struggle against the invader."

frustrated the British by obliging them to negotiate endlessly whenever they needed ELAS cooperation.

The Greek resistance came of age in the summer of 1943. ELAS now had as many as 16,000 frontline men, with about the same number of villagers enlisted as part-time reserves. EDES had about 5,000 regulars with an equal number in reserve. To counter increasing guerrilla activity and to defend against a possible Allied invasion, the German occupation forces, which had dwindled steadily in 1941 and most of 1942, were being beefed up again. In June the German General Staff transferred the 1st Mountain Division from embattled Serbia and the 1st Panzer Division from France to support the hard-pressed Italian occupation troops.

In spite of larger and more frequent Axis patrols, and in spite of a spreading network of compact Axis strong points, the guerrillas made sabotage commonplace. They sawed down telephone poles, or climbed them to cut down wire for their own communications systems and then booby-trapped the poles to blow up the Axis telephone repairmen. The Germans quickly learned to use the booby-trap trick against the guerrillas; they embedded explosives in and around poles that the guerrillas were likely to saw down.

Few of Greece's highways were safe for the Axis. Guerrillas strewed the roads with tire-puncturing iron devices and with concrete-covered mines that resembled rocks. They blew up or blocked whole stretches of roadway, and ambushed a number of Axis patrols.

The focal point of guerrilla action was the so-called Met-

Napoleon Zervas, the portly commander of the EDES guerrillas, leads a group of his men through a mountain village in Epirus. Besides fighting the Germans and the rival Communist guerrillas of ELAS, Zervas engaged in a little-known struggle against the Chams—Albanians who lived in his territory and collaborated willingly with the Axis occupation troops. Eventually Zervas defeated the Chams, driving them out of Greece.

sovon Highway, the only major east-west thoroughfare in the north. For Italian troops and convoys, the highway was a long gauntlet, for it ran through the territories of both EDES and ELAS. Guerrillas attacked one stretch so often that it came to be known as "Death Valley."

In late June ELAS agreed to join the British and the non-Communist bands in three weeks of maximum effort, code-named Operation *Animals*. The purpose of *Animals*—a purpose that the British dared not divulge to the guerrillas for fear of a leak—was to deceive the Axis into believing that an invasion of Greece was imminent and thus distract enemy attention from the site of the real invasion: Sicily. To heighten the deception, British intelligence agents planted a grisly piece of counterfeit evidence. Off the Mediterranean coast of Spain, close enough so the tide could carry it ashore for the Spanish to discover and pass on to the Germans, they dumped a corpse dressed in a British officer's uniform and carrying phony documents referring to the coming invasion.

All this evidence convinced the Germans that an Allied army would soon land somewhere in Greece. A staff officer wrote that "the strong concentration of guerrilla bands" on the southwestern coast of Epirus "indicates that it is at this point that the springboard for the support of landing operations must be looked for." The Peloponnesus was also considered a likely invasion site, and in a top-secret message the German Naval War Staff advised that "all measures must therefore be taken to reinforce rapidly the defensive strength of the areas that are specially threatened."

Operation *Animals* was launched on June 21. The guerrillas, hoping that liberation was at hand, struck at Axis supply and communications lines all over the country. In concert with the British liaison officers, who now numbered about 30, they systematically destroyed a 50-mile stretch of highway, severed the north-south railway in no fewer than 16 places, and seized and held an important mountain pass near Mount Olympus for two weeks. So thorough was the job of disruption that German soldiers whom EDES captured in southwestern Epirus said it had taken them 17 days to reach there by road from Athens—some 170 miles away.

Though the guerrillas were disappointed when no Allied liberation army followed Operation *Animals*, their sabotage campaign was a resounding success. It not only pinned down German troops that could have been used to better

A FRIEZE
OF GREEK GUERRILLAS

The Greek guerrillas were a hardy, rugged breed composed largely of farmers, herdsmen and merchants from remote, mountainous regions. There were even Greek Orthodox priests *(bottom, left)* within their ranks. The guerrillas were drawn into the resistance movement by organizers from large towns who told of the horrors of the Axis occupation.

Armed with whatever type of weapons they could find or capture from the enemy—including daggers, old-fashioned rifles and primitive grenades—small groups of guerrillas frequently immobilized substantial enemy forces. On one occasion, a woman from the Peloponnesus named Annetta *(top, center)* singlehandedly captured and disarmed a group of Germans.

The guerrillas lived in small bands in hillside huts and caves and moved their rendezvous areas frequently to avoid detection. They lived off the land and used the terrain to their advantage.

"Each footpath in the mountains, each path in the underbrush is familiar to them," wrote one exasperated German officer. "They are past masters in the art of utilizing the terrain for their own purposes. During the entire period of the occupation hardly a night and, from the summer of 1944, not a single day passed without a surprise attack, a mine explosion or another act of sabotage occurring."

effect in Italy and on the Russian front but it also reinforced the Germans' mistaken belief that Greece was earmarked for invasion. Even after Sicily fell to the Allies, Hitler's High Command continued to build up troop strength and coastal defenses in Greece.

ELAS had contributed heavily to the success of *Animals,* but the organization's behavior was a continuing source of worry and frustration to the British military mission. Even during *Animals,* the Communists had taken time out for an attack on a small independent band, EKKA, and also had assaulted some promonarchy groups in the Peloponnesus. And ELAS' new military leader, Saraphis, had reneged on a promise to help the British blow up the Asopos railroad viaduct, a few miles from the Gorgopotamos bridge. Saraphis' excuse for withdrawing was that the attack would require 1,500 men with artillery support—an explanation that was soon made ludicrous when a British team of six men slipped past the viaduct's German guards and put Asopos out of commission for four months.

By July ELAS' persistent willfulness had convinced Myers that only the long-debated National Bands agreement could insure the Communists' thorough cooperation. The British called for the establishment of a loose confederation of independent guerrilla bands whose operations would be controlled through their liaison officers. Myers redoubled his efforts to get the ELAS leaders to sign the agreement by suggesting the formation of a joint general headquarters; he hoped that genuine authority and a sense of responsibility would improve the behavior of the Communist leaders. Most of the Communists wanted to sign, for they felt the agreement would make ELAS respectable and give them the chance to dominate the resistance movement. But long delays and quibbling ensued.

At last Myers made concessions to get the ELAS leaders' signatures. He agreed that the British would share control of operations with a joint guerrilla headquarters. ELAS was given three of the six seats in the guerrilla headquarters; one seat each went to Zervas' EDES, the socialist EKKA and the British military mission. British gold sweetened the terms. Every month two gold sovereigns—then worth $20 each in Greece because of inflation—would be paid to each band for every guerrilla on its membership rolls. This allowance encouraged flagrant roster padding and the strong-armed recruitment methods of ELAS, and it led many Greeks to sneer at the "Golden Resistance."

Whatever its drawbacks, the National Bands agreement gave all the guerrillas something they valued highly: recognition by Great Britain as a regular military force in the Allied Middle East Command. Having won military recognition, the guerrillas now wanted political recognition from the British and from their own government-in-exile in Cairo. They intended to insist on some sort of guarantee of political freedom in any postwar government. These common goals united them for once in spite of their political differences, and they put their case to Myers.

In this politically supercharged atmosphere, Myers decided to visit Cairo for briefing and instruction by his superiors. To make the trip by air—and also to improve communications with Egypt, as Cairo had suggested—Myers ordered an airfield built on a high plateau in ELAS' territory in central Greece. The guerrilla leaders requested permission to accompany Myers on his trip and to make their own representations to the authorities in Cairo. Myers, realizing how important they considered their case, agreed to let a small delegation come along.

The airfield—the first built by the Allies in occupied Europe—was constructed in little over a month by 700 Greek laborers working two shifts a day under the energetic direction of British Captain Hamson, the liaison officer assigned to ELAS. As the 1,700-yard-long runway took shape, Hamson's workers camouflaged it with pine trees carted in from the surrounding hills and stuck into the ground. The camouflage was so effective that Cairo headquarters, which sent an RAF plane to photograph the nearly completed airstrip, radioed Myers that the field was unusable, and had to be convinced otherwise.

But on the night of August 9, a DC-3 from Cairo landed on the airstrip, homing on oil lamps held by ELAS guerrillas stationed at 150-yard intervals. Myers climbed aboard with the delegation of six guerrilla leaders. Though Myers knew that the guerrillas' visit was vitally important to the political future of Greece, Cairo believed that the meeting would deal primarily with military matters. A diplomatic disaster was in the making.

In Cairo the guerrilla delegates—four from EAM and its

associated organizations, and one each from both EDES and EKKA—sat down to a series of stormy sessions with British officials and pressed a key political point on which all the bands were in full accord. They asked for a pledge from Greece's King George II that he would not return to the country before the people voted for or against the monarchy in a plebiscite. They were confident that such a vote would reject the monarchy.

The Greeks had deep reasons for opposing the monarchy. Many did not like kings in general or this one in particular because he was not a Greek; he belonged to the third generation of a foreign dynasty and still had not adopted Greek ways. Others accused King George of having deserted them—fleeing Greece during the German invasion. But the strongest objection was that seven years earlier the King had authorized Metaxas to dissolve Parliament, suspend personal liberties and impose a virtual dictatorship. The delegates' opposition to the King was further stiffened by his own casual indifference to them. At a lavish British luncheon for the guerrillas, the party ended with a surprise visit by the King; instead of coming dressed for the occasion, he wore shorts and tennis shoes.

The King, who intended to return to Greece before a plebiscite, refused to postpone his plans as the guerrillas demanded. In fact, he refused to give the delegates an answer of any sort for 12 days. In the meantime, his own government-in-exile provoked an internal crisis by endorsing the guerrillas' position. This in turn exposed and brought to a head the long-standing differences among Cairo's British political and military authorities. The Foreign Office, putting postwar political considerations first, supported the royalists' position that any plebiscite should take place only after the King was safety ensconced in Athens. The British Middle East Command and the cloak-and-dagger SOE supported the guerrillas, whose operations were of military import in the War.

Finally, on August 19, the King cabled the British Prime Minister and the American President for advice, and both of them came down squarely on his side. Churchill considered this a "special obligation," he later wrote, because the King had stood on the side of the British against the German invasion of Greece.

Churchill's decision had serious repercussions. The controversial SOE was revamped—one of eight shake-ups it went through in four years. The long-suffering Myers was blamed for the embarrassment that the guerrilla delegates had caused the British. The British Ambassador to the Greek government-in-exile, Reginald Leeper, described Myers as "a very dangerous fool" and insisted that he should not be allowed to return to Greece. Myers was sent to London and his young deputy, Woodhouse, took over the British military mission in Greece—with instructions to keep the guerrillas in their place.

In September the guerrilla delegates left Cairo and returned home, empty-handed and full of rancor. All were convinced—rightly—that the British intended to impose the King on the embattled nation before a plebiscite was held. They also believed—wrongly—that a British invasion was coming soon, and this misconception fooled the Communists into thinking that the time had come to take over the whole resistance movement.

ELAS was strong—it now had about 35,000 frontline guerrillas and part-time reserves—but it lacked the enormous quantities of arms and munitions needed to defeat and incorporate the rival bands. The picture changed after September 8, 1943, when Italy surrendered to the Allies. While most of the 270,000 Italian troops in Greece deserted or turned themselves over to the Germans, the anti-German commander of the Pinerolo Division and other units surrendered to Woodhouse and the guerrillas on condition that his 14,000 men be allowed to fight under British control against the Germans.

A hitch developed at once. The Pinerolo Division was in the ELAS-dominated Thessaly province, and the Communists promptly began commandeering the Italian equipment. In one village a British liaison officer saw an ELAS man "with a dilapidated cowboy hat" and a pot of paint

As a means of discouraging Greek guerrillas from firing on or wrecking trains under their control, the Germans rounded up Greek civilians and jammed them into open cages like this one, which were pushed along in front of the trains. The cages were thus exposed to any rifle fire, bombs and other explosives aimed at the trains by guerrillas.

stopping Italian trucks so that he could stake ELAS' claim to them with daubed Communist slogans. ELAS managed to disperse the Italians into small units, then surrounded them and stripped them of small arms, as well as mortars, machine guns and 20-odd pieces of light mountain artillery.

In mid-October this welcome booty was rushed across the Pindus Mountains to Epirus for use by the fanatic Aris, who had been sent to the area. Fighting between Aris' ELAS guerrillas and Zervas' EDES forces had erupted there a week before, with each side blaming the other for striking first. But, as the British later learned, there was now no question as to who was the aggressor. The message that ELAS headquarters received from the EAM Central Committee in Athens was clear and succinct: "Let Aris loose on Zervas."

The Germans were watching with interest. After letting Aris and Zervas battle it out for a week, they hit both forces in Operation *Panther,* a series of devastating attacks backed by air support, tanks and artillery that killed some 1,400 guerrillas. During the next three months, a vicious three-cornered war was fought: the Germans against the guerrillas and the guerrillas against each other.

By early December Zervas was reeling under the blows of his two adversaries. He had been driven west to Greece's Adriatic coast, and only a last-minute British airdrop of ammunition—plummeting through a low curtain of clouds to the frantic cheers of his guerrillas—saved EDES from annihilation. Further airdrops from the British enabled Zervas to mount a short-lived counterattack against ELAS. Finally, at the end of February 1944, the British persuaded both sides to agree to a formal armistice.

Measured by the fratricidal standards set by the Partisans and Chetniks in Yugoslavia, this four-month first round of civil war in Greece was a minor episode. Rank-and-file Greeks took little pleasure in killing other Greeks and, despite a huge expenditure of munitions, the total casualties probably did not exceed several hundred. "The cost of killing a man was incalculable," Woodhouse commented. "It had taken several thousand rounds at slightly more than extreme range even to frighten one."

Yet the fighting had a profound effect on the Greeks. ELAS' brutal attempt to wipe out EDES alienated many of its moderate supporters. Zervas, the former republican, was driven so far to the right by the Communists' attacks that he permitted his guerrillas to wear the royal insignia on their caps. Increasingly, his EDES movement was held together by what Woodhouse called "a miscellany of negatives, the principal one of which was anti-Communism."

In turn, Zervas' rightist tilt made him ever more susceptible to German overtures and to Communist charges of collaboration. According to the accounts of German commanders, they and EDES did engage in an occasional temporary truce, or a "Balkan gentleman's agreement." Such

cease-fires were mutually beneficial. Indeed, Woodhouse asserted that Zervas' truces with the Germans were a sheer necessity for survival in his struggle against the Communists.

Under guerrilla harassment and the need to replace Italian occupation troops, the Germans had built up their occupation forces on the mainland to a peak of 140,000. From the beginning of the civil war through the summer of 1944, they and their Bulgarian allies launched no fewer than nine major antiguerrilla operations. In these large-scale sweeps over embattled terrain, even second-rate German troops were more than a match for the outgunned guerrillas, who sometimes made the mistake of trying to fight like a conventional army. Their best defense was to disband, throw away their weapons and thus become innocent villagers. The German commanders considered an operation unsuccessful if the casualty rate favored them by only 4 to 1. In two operations the kill ratios were 19 and 22 guerrillas for every one German.

In spite of their successful counterattacks, the Germans lacked the manpower to keep the guerrillas suppressed for long in any area, so they exploited the deep divisions that were pitting Greek against Greek. They persuaded John Rallis, the latest in a succession of puppet Prime Ministers, to establish an armed force called the Greek Security Battalions for exclusive use against ELAS. Rallis, thinking he might also win British gratitude for saving his country from Communist chaos before liberation, enthusiastically raised about a dozen battalions of some 700 men each. Made up in part of former guerrillas whose small bands had been attacked and scattered by ELAS, they were strongest in the battle-torn southern section of the country. There the revulsion against the brutality of the Communists was so strong that many Greeks considered the members of the battalions to be patriots rather than collaborators. When the Security Battalions paraded through Athens, bystanders cheered.

More and more, however, the Germans resorted to the brutal tactic they had employed against the resistance almost from the beginning in Yugoslavia—indiscriminate reprisals against entire villages.

Late in 1943 the reprisals escalated furiously. The village hit the hardest was Kalavryta, a historic town in the Peloponnesus where the 19th Century revolt against the Turks had first been proclaimed from the monastery of Hagia Lavra. Reacting to the reported execution of 78 German prisoners by ELAS forces near Kalavryta, the Germans rang all the church bells at 6 a.m. to assemble the town's 2,500 people. Women and children were taken to the schoolhouse and locked up. Five hundred and eleven men and boys over 15 were taken to a hill where they watched the town burn; then they were cut down by machine guns. The Germans had set fire to the schoolhouse, but the women and children escaped when an officer took pity and opened the doors. They poured out, choking on the smoke, and attempted to bury their men by scratching into the frozen earth with their bare hands.

The atrocities were repeated in village after village. According to a Greek estimate, 21,000 Greeks died in German reprisals, 9,000 in Italian reprisals and 40,000 in reprisals by their old enemies, the Bulgarians.

In defense of the reprisal policy, Germans said that the

Greek guerrillas and members of the German Army's 999th Rehabilitation Battalion are photographed together. The unit, composed of supposedly rehabilitated German political prisoners, was sent to Greece in 1944 as part of the Axis occupation force. But when the men got there, they quickly switched sides and wound up helping the Greek guerrillas fight the army to which they were supposed to belong.

Tough raiders of a small, specially trained Anglo-Greek detachment take up firing positions on Symi, one of the many enemy-held islands in the Aegean Sea. In just two months in 1944, the unit conducted 20 raids in the islands, forcing the Germans to keep garrisons on them and to maintain a supply fleet.

DAREDEVIL PLOT TO KIDNAP A GERMAN GENERAL

In September 1943 at a cocktail party in Cairo, two British officers, 20-year-old Major Patrick Leigh-Fermor and 18-year-old Captain Stanley Moss, coolly concocted a daring scheme to kidnap the German commandant of Crete. British headquarters agreed to the plan, and on February 4, 1944, an RAF bomber bearing Moss, Leigh-Fermor and two Greek agents took off for the island. But the weather was so bad that only Leigh-Fermor managed to parachute out. It took two months and 12 attempts—eight by plane and four by boat—for his companions to join him.

Leigh-Fermor and Moss calmly studied the comings and goings of the German commandant, General Heinrich Kreipe, for two weeks, then decided to seize him at a hairpin bend in a road, where his chauffeur would have to drive slowly.

On the night of the 26th of April, the Greek agents and guerrillas, hidden near the hairpin turn, signaled that the general's car was approaching. Moss and Leigh-Fermor, dressed up as German lance corporals, motioned for the driver to halt. The guerrillas knocked the driver unconscious, while the two Englishmen bound the general, tossed him onto the floor of his Opel and drove off with him. With Leigh-Fermor posing as Kreipe in the back seat, they roared past 22 German sentries before coming to isolated country. There they abandoned the car, leaving a letter inside stating that General Kreipe was on his way to Cairo, with the postscript: "By the way, we are terribly sorry to have to leave this beautiful car behind."

After traveling two and a half weeks—during which Kreipe fractured his shoulder—Moss and Leigh-Fermor received a radio message from British agents in Cairo saying that a motor launch would meet them on the night of May 14 on the southern coast. In spite of the fact that 30,000 German occupation troops were on the lookout for them, Leigh-Fermor and Moss safely conducted their prisoner to the British boat at the appointed time and made the crossing to Egypt.

Kreipe, who was later dispatched to a POW camp in Canada, was quite upset by the journey. "For a whole fortnight," he complained, "I had no clean handkerchief unless I first washed it in water!"

At a dress rehearsal for the kidnapping, Leigh-Fermor and Moss don German uniforms.

His arm in a sling, General Kreipe steps into the custody of British soldiers in Cairo.

Greeks were no less barbaric. They cited frequent examples of guerrilla raids on unarmed Red Cross convoys in which all of the patients were killed. Germans also pointed out that many Greek civilians were actually combatants; if they were not part-time guerrillas themselves, they were spies and suppliers for the bands, and innocent citizens were indistinguishable from the killers. But high German officials clearly were afraid that the reprisal policy would boomerang—and it did.

Each Axis excess fed the ranks of guerrillas with new recruits. By the spring of 1944, ELAS claimed some 30,000 full-time guerrillas. ELAS now controlled more than half of Greece. The major areas outside its rule were Epirus, where the remnants of EDES still held out, and the island of Crete, where independent nationalist guerrillas helped two British officers pull off a fantastic caper—the kidnapping of the German general in command of the island garrison, who was snatched from his automobile, hidden in caves and then taken by boat to North Africa (left).

Just as important as ELAS' military dominance was the burgeoning power of its political parent, EAM, whose myriad front organizations now had the active support of perhaps as many as 700,000 Greeks. The Communists' labor front had staged a series of strikes that prevented the conscription and deportation of many thousands of Greeks to Germany to work in factories there. And the Central Committee of EAM was the dominant political force in areas uncontested by the Germans or Zervas' EDES. However, with EAM's Communist identity unmasked by ELAS' ruthlessness in the civil war, the party leaders felt they needed another disguise. Therefore, they set up the PEEA (Political Committee for National Liberation), and in April 1944 held elections in the areas controlled by ELAS. The Communists' candidates—some of them respected non-Communists—were elected to a 250-man national parliament. They now possessed a provisional government in opposition to the Greek government-in-exile.

News of PEEA's shadow government immediately precipitated a crisis in Egypt, where political discontent was running high among the nearly 20,000 Greek refugees and expatriates who had formed a Greek army and navy in exile.

Many of the men in these units shared PEEA's opposition to the monarchy and staged a mutiny in support of the underground government. Mutinous sailors took over five ships of the Greek Navy, and disorders spread through an Army brigade stationed near Alexandria. The British, hoping to end the mutiny without bloodshed, surrounded and laid siege to the brigade's encampment. After two uneventful weeks, loyal Greek troops boarded and recaptured the rebel ships, and in a few days the British moved in on the rebellious soldiers and disarmed them. Some 10,000 rebels—half of the Greek units that the British were counting on to help the King's triumphant return to Athens—were interned in detention camps.

The results of the mutiny were more serious than the uprising itself: King George's Prime Minister resigned and so did his successor after only two weeks. Arguments for and against recognizing the PEEA continued to wrack the Greek government-in-exile. On April 26 a new Prime Minister emerged from the dissension and confusion. He was George Papandreou, a long-time politician who was both antimonarchist and anti-Communist. Papandreou had recently fled Greece at the behest of the British, who were trying to broaden the appeal of the government-in-exile.

Papandreou proved himself a shrewd manipulator. He invited representatives of 17 political parties and resistance groups, including the Communist Party, PEEA and other Communist fronts, to meet with him in Lebanon in May. There he outmaneuvered the Communist delegates by winning their agreement to take part—in a less than dominant role—in a new Government of National Unity.

Communist leaders back in the mountains of Greece were outraged by the concessions their delegates had made at the Lebanon conference. They repudiated the agreements and then argued with Papandreou at long distance through most of the summer over how many seats they would receive in his government.

Liberation of the homeland was at hand and still the Greeks—Communists, monarchists, socialists and republicans of every hue—went on squabbling. "Why," asked Winston Churchill in exasperation, "cannot the Greeks keep their hatreds for the common enemy?"

INCIDENT AT RICHEA

Secure in the mountain hamlet of Richea, where Germans rarely came, Greek guerrillas and villagers in this Bernard Perlin painting listen to a BBC broadcast.

THE BUOYANT START OF A SECRET MISSION

Guerrilla wars, like those that were fought in Greece and Yugoslavia, involve countless small actions and twists of fate that usually are lost to history. But for those who are involved, these actions may be the most important happenings of the war—or of their lives. One such incident took place in the mountain village of Richea, in southern Greece, where the minutiae of a minor reconnaissance—and the effect of an exploding grenade on well-laid plans—were preserved for posterity because one participant was a painter.

It all began on a June morning in 1944, when a motorized schooner slipped out of a cove on the Turkish coast, bound across the Aegean Sea to the coast of German-occupied Greece. On board were 13 men with a mission: nine British commandos and their captain, a Greek liaison officer and two observers—Alexis Ladas, a young Greek attached to Cairo's Allied Middle East Headquarters, and Bernard Perlin, an American artist commissioned by LIFE to cover the war in the Middle East. The group had orders to spend some 15 days making forays along Greece's southern coast, harrassing the Germans and gathering intelligence.

To avoid German patrols, the ship sailed mostly at night and hid under camouflage netting in island coves during the day. On reaching the mainland, the commandos put in at ports along the coast, and villagers who had not seen visitors from the unoccupied world in three years swarmed aboard the ship (opposite) to drink coffee the men offered them—the first they had tasted since the War began—and wolf down whatever food could be spared. At their last port of call, Plytra, in the Peloponnesus, the commandos were mobbed by locals who hailed them as the English Army, come back as liberators—"all 13 of us," wryly noted Perlin.

There the party met up with Communist ELAS guerrillas and traveled with them in mule carts through farmlands to the foothills of the mountains. On the ensuing ascent of the mountains (left), the ELAS guides insisted on walking, while the commandos rode mules and donkeys up the steep and slippery grades to the village of Richea, where their odyssey was to take a fateful turn.

Jolting in wooden saddles, the travelers endure a long, painful night ride as their cavalcade winds up along hairpin curves, lit only by the moon.

Commandos on their camouflaged ship play host to villagers, one of whom asks Perlin (the bearded man left of the mast) to take a letter out of Greece for him.

A GHASTLY ACCIDENT AND ITS AFTERMATH

Shortly after the commandos' arrival at Richea, while they were busy conferring with ELAS officers, sentries reported that the Germans were planning to encircle the village. The commandos suggested a joint ambush of the German troops, and the ELAS guerrillas readily agreed.

The Englishmen were making ready for the attack when Perlin heard a yell, followed by an explosion. Hurrying back to the commandos' billet, he discovered that the room was splattered with blood and dense with cordite fumes: while the men were preparing their weapons and ammunition, a grenade had slipped from a commando's hand and exploded on top of a sleeping bag on the floor. As the smoke cleared away, it revealed the scene above: shrapnel had slightly wounded four commandos and mangled the leg of a fifth.

Realizing that the joint operation was no longer possible, the ELAS guerrillas quietly slipped away. The commandos and the villagers fashioned a stretcher to transport the crippled grenade victim and began the long trek down to the coastal town of Neapolis, where they would be able to find a surgeon. During the grueling journey, as other Greeks took the place of the Richeans, the commando's wound became gangrenous. At Neapolis a hasty leg amputation was required.

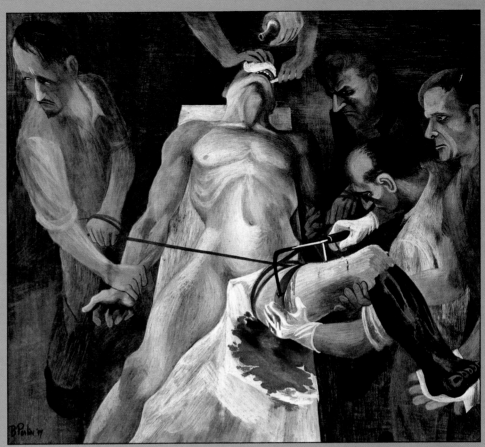

Bleeding commandos stand in shocked silence after the explosion, while another member of their group lies in agony on the ground near ripped-up floor planks. The hand grenade had gone off between the young man's feet.

The young commando's buddies help as his leg, blue with decay, is amputated with a hacksaw.

Women of Neapolis keep vigil while medical personnel confer on the amputee's recovery.

Two doomed German prisoners are paraded up a street, unbound but barefoot—to prevent their escape and also because shoes were valuable booty. The

Since he spoke both English and Greek, Ladas became the unappointed chief of the mission.

The Greek woman who attended the amputee was nicknamed Florence Nightingale by Perlin.

This fellow—although only a teenager—accompanied the ELAS guerrillas on their missions.

bold graffiti "Greece, Russia, America" and clasped hands painted on the wall at right indicate the close ties between the Greek guerrillas and the Allies.

BLOODY REVENGE FOR A GERMAN ATTACK

In spite of his grievous wound and the ordeal of the operation, the young commando survived. His fellow commandos, their mission thwarted, watched from a coffeehouse for the vessel that was supposed to pick them up. Perlin passed the time sketching Alexis Ladas, now the expedition's acknowledged leader, and the local people *(left)*, while Ladas studied re-gional political and guerrilla operations.

One day the sound of an excited crowd attracted the commandos into the main street. There, flanked by jeering townspeople, walked two German soldiers *(above)*, followed by grinning ELAS men. The German prisoners had been captured as they were picking vegetables to carry back to a nearby radar station. Their kidnapping was in retaliation for a recent German raid on an ELAS band, and the guerrillas clamored for their death.

Alarmed, Ladas managed to postpone their sentence by persuading the guerrillas to let him interrogate the prisoners. One, a young Austrian farmer eager for his life, told all he knew about the radar installation, but his companion, who was a former schoolteacher and a fanatic Nazi, refused to speak. Ladas got permission to continue the questioning the next day, but that evening a young member of ELAS swaggered into the coffeehouse brandishing a bayonet still dripping blood. "With this I got them," he boasted. "You should have heard them squeal."

COUNTDOWN TO FAREWELL

The date set for the commandos to be picked up came and went with no sign of a ship. Unable to contact their base in Turkey because their radio transmitter had broken down, fearful of a German raid and worried by the amputee's condition—his stump was not healing, and he needed a skin graft—the men waited an additional week and then made desperate plans. They arranged to borrow a small boat in which four of them would try to take the patient across the Mediterranean to Africa. Then they would return for the others.

When the departure day arrived, they awoke to find in the harbor a British motor launch that had been searching for them. They boarded the launch *(right)* that evening, and the wounded commando was taken to a hospital in the neutral port of Izmir in Turkey. Other members of the group returned to their Turkish base. For all its drama and excitement, the mission was written off officially as merely an unsuccessful reconnaissance.

Perlin sketched this guerrilla coming in from sentry duty with German boots and Italian gun.

In a moving tribute, the people of Neapolis wave goodbye as the commandos head for their ship. "There were unashamed tears on both sides," wrote Perlin.

6

On October 9, 1944, an extraordinary agreement concerning the future of Greece and Yugoslavia was concluded in the Kremlin in Moscow. The decision makers were Winston Churchill, whose government had encouraged and aided the Balkan guerrillas, and Josef Stalin, to whom the Communist ELAS guerrillas of Greece and the Partisans of Yugoslavia owed their ideological allegiance.

As Churchill later recalled in his memoirs, he opened the discussion by saying to Stalin, "Let us settle about our affairs in the Balkans. So far as Britain and Russia are concerned, how would it do for you to have 90 per cent predominance in Rumania, for us to have 90 per cent of the say in Greece, and go 50-50 about Yugoslavia?"

Churchill wrote the percentages on a piece of paper and shoved it across the table to Stalin. The Soviet leader "took his blue pencil and made a large tick upon it. It was all settled in no more time than it takes to set down."

After a long silence Churchill suggested, "Might it not be thought rather cynical if it seemed we had disposed of these issues, so fateful to millions of people, in such an offhand manner? Let us burn the paper."

"No," replied Stalin. "You keep it."

Churchill's deal with Stalin concluded five months of discussion in scattered top-level meetings, and it reflected the decisive turn that the war had taken during 1944. The Western Allies had invaded France in June and were closing in on Germany itself. Meanwhile, Soviet armies were advancing all along the Eastern Front. Even as the two leaders talked in Moscow, Russian armored columns from Rumania were rolling across eastern Yugoslavia, forcing the German troops to pull out of Greece and head for home before their escape route was cut. All of these developments pointed to the end of the war and increased the need for a general political settlement in the Balkans.

But in spite of their Moscow accord, Stalin and Churchill were clearly working at cross-purposes. Stalin had conceded Britain's primacy in Greece and had settled for only 50 per cent influence in Yugoslavia because he attached greater importance to occupying Hungary and Austria. Churchill, worried about the westward spread of Soviet power, was maneuvering vigorously to block the Russian advance and to enlist the United States in various anti-Soviet schemes. But President Roosevelt had repeatedly refused to send

BALKAN SHOWDOWN

U.S. troops on any politically motivated detours. Americans were doing the lion's share of the fighting in the Pacific, and Roosevelt was determined to end the European conflict as expeditiously as possible to free battle-tested divisions for an all-out assault on Japan.

The deal between Stalin and Churchill set the stage for the final wartime showdown in the Balkans. Inevitably, their agreed-upon percentages had a profound effect on the emerging political order there. But the guerrilla leaders of Greece and Yugoslavia were not helpless pawns on the international checkerboard, and they could be counted on to play politics with the big powers for their own advantage at home. As ever, the only thing that was certain in the unpredictable Balkans was that many well-laid plans would somehow go wrong.

In Greece the Communist Party and its ELAS guerrillas knew that their great wartime gains were in jeopardy even before Stalin wrote them off with one big tick of his blue pencil. Back in July 1944 the Soviet Union had sent ELAS its first military mission. The arrival of the Russians had proved to be an eye opener to both sides. According to British intelligence reports, ELAS "expected the Soviet mission to bring manna from heaven," but was told not to plan on Russian arms or supplies. The Soviet officers, expecting to find ELAS a first-rate guerrilla army on the order of the Yugoslav Partisans, instead "found a rabble thinly veiled in an elaborately centralized command." If Stalin had not made up his mind earlier to sacrifice ELAS, the report from his mission clinched the matter.

The failure of the Soviets to come through with supplies prompted the Greek Communist Party to reexamine its two strategic options—to seize power by force or to seek power by political maneuvering. Throughout the Axis occupation, the party had vacillated between the two strategies as its conservative wing, led by the colorless Secretary-General George Siantos, waged a seesaw struggle for control with proponents of violent take-over, personified by the charismatic chieftain Aris Velouchiotis. By September of 1944 the conservatives had regained the upper hand.

Almost overnight, the Communists performed an astonishing about-face. They agreed to join George Papandreou's government-in-exile—the so-called Government of National Unity—on the same unfavorable terms they had been rejecting vociferously all summer, accepting only six seats out of 15 in the Cabinet. ELAS agreed to work in harness with the republican guerrillas of EDES, whom they had been attacking with the same savagery they showed the Germans. The Communists' change in attitude was so sharp and sudden that it surprised even the hard-bitten chief of the Allied military mission in Greece, Chris Woodhouse, now promoted from major to colonel. "As if by a magic wand," he wrote, "the angry, anxious, bewildered obstinacy of the early summer was translated into good will."

True to its word, ELAS cooperated with EDES in harassing the German forces as they withdrew from Greece that autumn. The guerrillas' main target was Greece's only north-south railroad, which the Germans needed desperately to move their remaining 90,000 occupation troops through Belgrade before the advancing Red Army reached there. In their attacks on German troop trains, the guerrillas received expert help from small British and American units that were parachuted in or smuggled ashore by boat. These troops arrived equipped with rocket-launching bazookas, which proved to be marvelously effective as a train-busting weapon. The guerrillas and the Allied teams together did their destructive job so well that Greece had little rolling stock left to aid its postwar recovery.

Many of the 250 American train busters were men of Greek ancestry, and for them the mission had special emotional rewards. Several Greek-Americans experienced fortuitous family reunions. One man parachuted into the mountains near the home of his grandmother. Another man was lying ill in an upland cottage when his father walked in. But there were special risks, too, for Americans with Greek names. Communist guerrillas sought them out, played on their sympathies for Greece and tried to turn their nostalgic patriotism against the British, who had persistently tried to saddle the country with its unpopular exiled King, George II. Some of the Greek-Americans did not have any reason to like the British, but nearly all of them resisted the political overtures of ELAS.

During September, while the Germans were withdrawing steadily under guerrilla harassment, British headquarters in Cairo prepared for the formal liberation of Greece: Operation *Manna*. To avoid unnecessary fighting, the British planners shrewdly decided to bypass the stubborn German garrison in Crete (it eventually held out until May 1945, long after the Germans had evacuated the rest of Greece). The British invading force numbered only 4,000 men. But it seemed to be big enough to show the flag, to discourage any last-minute ELAS ambitions and to help the Greek government-in-exile take over in Athens.

On October 1 the liberation army landed unopposed on the west coast of southern Greece. The British then set out for Athens. The possibility that ELAS might try to take the capital before they arrived worried one officer of the liberation army, Lieut. Colonel Frank Macaskie, who had been dubbed "The Scarlet Pimpernel" for his daring exploits in occupied Greece. Macaskie had been taken prisoner during the short-lived British defense of Greece in 1941 but had escaped and had helped smuggle some 250 runaway POWs out of the country. He had twice been recaptured, but both times he had escaped again, once by bribing his jailers.

Now, deciding to liberate Athens without further delay, Macaskie raced toward the capital with a detachment of 10 British soldiers. They arrived at 4 a.m. on October 12. Macaskie changed into civilian dress and quickly made his way

to the palace of Greece's highest ecclesiastic official, Archbishop Damaskinos of Athens. The archbishop was an old friend who had given Macaskie refuge earlier in the war. Damaskinos, unfazed by the German rear-guard detachments that were still patrolling Athens, persuaded Macaskie to don his uniform and ride with him in his limousine through the streets to "show the people you have come."

As the men drove through Athens, church bells pealed, proclaiming the city's liberation and setting off a tumultuous celebration. That night the last of the Germans pulled out of the city through "streets filled with a sea of humanity so dense that our car could only pick its way through with difficulty," recalled Roland Hampe, a German civilian official. "I have never seen men in the grip of such joy and enthusiasm."

Three days later Athens welcomed the main body of British troops, and the government-in-exile arrived three days later still. The establishment of Papandreou's regime proceeded without serious incident. The Communist politicians abided by their recent agreements. They ordered ELAS units in Athens to place themselves under the authority of Papandreou's government, which had delegated the super-

vision of all the guerrillas to the commander of the British liberation army, Lieut. General Ronald Scobie. ELAS headquarters in central Greece obeyed Scobie's orders to keep organized units out of Athens. ELAS also heeded the party's orders to put a checkrein on the fanatic Aris, who had been riding through southern Greece on a white horse, presiding at mass executions of citizens suspected of collaboration with the Axis. The Communist front organizations in Athens, under orders to behave themselves, did even better. For the delectation of incoming British units, they painted the town red with friendly slogans in slightly askew English—such as "Well Come Brave Allies."

But the euphoria that followed liberation did not last for long. The Greeks began to realize the full extent of their country's suffering, and they were appalled. Famine was widespread. Money had become so worthless that it cost 140 million drachmas to buy a loaf of bread. Greece lay in ruins, with nearly 1,700 villages destroyed. These problems could not be met without the cooperation of all the political parties. But by November the Communist Party was no longer cooperating.

The Communists had a new political grievance. They feared that the Papandreou government, in which they and their sympathizers were a minority, was favoring those who had collaborated with the occupation forces. Athens was largely in the hands of the city police, many of whom had been members of the former puppet government's anti-ELAS Security Battalions. Almost every night, Communists and their sympathizers were assaulted on the streets by members of a right-wing organization called X—after the initial letter in its name—and the police were suspiciously tolerant of those attacks. Moreover, the leader of X, a former army colonel named George Grivas, seemed to have an understanding with the British.

Many Communists saw a vicious pattern in all this: the traitors who had collaborated with the Axis were now collaborating with the British to bring back King George II before a plebiscite could be held to decide the fate of the Greek monarchy. In fact, the British had already agreed that the King would not return to Greece until after the plebiscite. But the Communists did not believe the British.

The Communists' suspicions were greatly intensified on November 10 by the arrival in Athens of the Greek 3rd Mountain Brigade, marching in battle order and led by three bands. This unit of the Greek army-in-exile consisted of 4,000 troops who had refused to join their antimonarchist compatriots in the Alexandria uprising of April 1944; it had later served gallantly with the British in the Italian campaign. Obviously the brigade was promonarchy and anti-Communist. British Colonel Woodhouse, whose Allied military mission to the guerrillas was now in the process of being phased out, had counseled his government against bringing in the Greek brigade. The move, Woodhouse later wrote, was "provocative, even if unintentionally" and constituted "the most important single factor contributing to the loss of faith" by the Communists.

On November 26 the British made another inflammatory move. General Scobie, exasperated by the Communists' ceaseless bickering, decided to pull ELAS' teeth by demobilization; his plan, which was endorsed by the Greek government, called for all of the guerrillas to disband and turn in their weapons between December 10 and 20. Napoleon Zervas immediately agreed to dissolve his EDES force. But the Communists were by this time thoroughly convinced that the Greek brigade would be used against them if they laid down their arms. They declared that ELAS would not surrender its weapons unless the Greek brigade was also disarmed. Papandreou's government, backed up by the British, refused.

The breach rapidly widened. Those Communists who favored taking power by force regained control of the party. They were encouraged by a message from Yugoslavia; Marshal Tito, reacting to what he considered Britain's excessive intervention in Greece's internal affairs, sent his Greek comrades a vague offer of help.

On December 2 the Communists and their sympathizers suddenly resigned from Papandreou's government. They organized a big demonstration for the following morning to protest the demobilization order. ELAS units began moving toward Athens, and ELAS reservists inside the city mobilized for action. In turn the British judged these hostile moves to be a Communist attempt to seize power and prepared to fight fire with fire.

With each side convinced of the other's evil intentions, Greece needed only a chance spark to touch off civil war.

The spark was struck on Sunday morning, December 3, in Athens' historic Constitution Square. At 10:45 several hundred left-wing protesters converged in the square, openly defying the police, who had been given orders to prevent the demonstration.

Shots rang out. The question of who started the trouble was never settled. The rightists claimed that the Communists deliberately provoked the police, and the leftists maintained that the demonstrators were unarmed. In any event, all of the shooting casualties—by various accounts, seven to 28 dead and many more wounded—were civilians. The infuriated demonstrators then proceeded to tear several policemen limb from limb.

Before long the bloodshed in the square had attracted an angry crowd of approximately 60,000. According to William Hardy McNeill, the American assistant military attaché in Athens, many of the people in the crowd viewed the fallen demonstrators as patriotic martyrs: "Around the spots on the pavement where their fellows had been slaughtered, little borders of flowers and twigs were erected, and hundreds of persons bent down to dip their handkerchiefs in the blood which lay fresh on the pavement. These were made into banners, which were paraded through the crowd while their bearers exhorted all around them to touch the bloodstained rags and swear vengeance against the men who had made the slaughter."

That night the battle for Athens began with ELAS attacks on the city's police stations. Next day ELAS was heavily reinforced by units from the suburbs, and by dawn of the third day its men had taken all of the 24 police stations and the road between Athens and the port of Piraeus. The position of the British in Athens was so dangerous that several units had been called in from Italy, where they were also needed desperately. Although 2,000 reinforcements had already arrived, they were not nearly enough. General Scobie had at his disposal only 6,000 British soldiers, the 4,000 troops of the Greek brigade and Grivas' 600-odd right-wing street fighters.

At first Scobie carefully avoided pitched battles with ELAS, which had well over 20,000 guerrillas and reservists in the Athens area. To make his predicament worse, the guerrillas were now better armed than they had been through the whole occupation; the departing Germans had deliberately left many supply dumps intact in the hope of encouraging fighting among the guerrillas in their wake. Yet the guerrillas, too, backed away from open clashes with the British and settled for fighting the Greek brigade. In fact, five days after the fighting began, ELAS men played an amicable soccer game with a British unit of South African sappers at Marathon, some 20 miles from embattled Athens. But by then Scobie had been galvanized by a stern cable from Churchill in London: "Do not hesitate to act as if you were in a conquered city where a local rebellion is in progress. We have to hold and dominate Athens."

Scobie threw his troops into the battle. For the first time in the war, the British faced the frustrating guerrilla tactics that their military mission had helped bring to bear on the Axis occupation troops. The British could not tell who or where their Greek tormentors were. The ELAS men wore civilian clothes or odds and ends of British uniforms that had been air-dropped by the RAF, and they lurked in ambush in alleys and on roofs, prepared to shoot down soldiers on patrol.

Many of the guerrillas were not men at all but young women—versatile veterans of ELAS campaigns. The women fought with rifles and submachine guns, lured lone soldiers into fatal traps and proved to be proficient at heaving homemade fragmentation bombs—nicknamed "Scobie Preserves" after the British commander—which consisted of two sticks of dynamite packed with scrap metal in a tin can. During fighting at RAF headquarters near Athens, several hundred airmen surrendered to 2,000 ELAS guerrillas, and many were shocked to recognize among their captors a bevy of gun-toting young women with whom they had enjoyed friendly dates just a few weeks before.

All through December the fighting raged. Athens, which had survived the Axis occupation unscathed, was battered by British tank cannon, rocket-firing Spitfires, 75mm artillery in the hands of ELAS and, on occasion, exploding tram cars that the guerrillas had filled with dynamite and sent on uncontrolled rides through the streets of the city. The British fought against their former allies, and Greeks mercilessly battled Greeks. Many a Greek family was tragically split apart. While Papandreou worked to put down ELAS, his actress-daughter Miranda made trips behind the ELAS

Sprawled in the gutter, a left-wing demonstrator lies dead in Constitution Square in Athens on the 3rd of December, 1944. The man was one of several Greeks who were killed when police of the British-backed Papandreou government fired into a flag-waving crowd marching toward University Street. The act sparked a civil war that raged for six weeks.

barricades and gave performances for guerrilla audiences.

By mid-December, the ELAS forces appeared to have victory within their grasp. The Greek brigade, which had tried and failed to clear ELAS units out of the capital's suburbs, was now hemmed in on the outskirts of town, virtually cut off from the British. In the center of Athens General Scobie's main force was squeezed into a narrow strip about two miles long and five or six blocks wide. The defenders could be resupplied only by sea, which meant that British details had to fight their way to and from the port of Piraeus through ELAS lines. One embattled stretch on their route became known as "the Mad Mile."

With most of the British pinned down in Athens, ELAS turned its attention to unfinished business with the staunch guerrilla allies of the British, Napoleon Zervas and his EDES men, who were still isolated in their Epirus sanctuary in the northwestern mountains. The attack on EDES was mounted on December 21 by two ELAS veterans, Aris Velouchiotis and Colonel Stephanos Saraphis, who had been charged with consolidating the Communist hold on the interior. The odds against Zervas were not insuperable: 11,500 ELAS to 8,000 EDES. But Zervas was short on supplies and had lost his enthusiasm for combat now that the Germans were gone; he made only a token stand. The British Navy had to come to Zervas' rescue. Three destroyers and nine landing craft ran a ferry service to the island of Corfu, evacuating 7,000 EDES men, an equal number of civilian sympathizers and uncounted cows, turkeys and other livestock.

In the meantime, on the 25th of December, Churchill arrived by plane and joined the battle for Athens. He was not very jolly this Christmas Day. In northern Italy the Allied forces were dug in for the winter below the Po Valley. In Belgium's Ardennes region the Germans had launched an enormous counteroffensive that the Americans called the Battle of the Bulge. And Churchill himself was under fire both at home and in the United States for Britain's role in the increasingly unpopular Greek civil war. The New York Times went so far as to call him "a product of 19th-Century thought fighting a 20th-Century war for 18th-Century aims."

That remark was unkind but not totally unjust: Churchill's tactics in Greece did resemble an old-fashioned imperialistic power play. He was fighting there to make the country politically safe for Britain's postwar aim to resume its dominant role in the Mediterranean. Yet Churchill was also fighting for political freedom in Greece; true democracy, he had stated in the House of Commons, "is no harlot to be picked up in the street by a man with a tommy gun."

In any case, Churchill was much less disturbed by the personal criticism than by President Roosevelt's hands-off policy in Greece. Instead of helping the beleaguered British troops, high-placed Americans were leaning over backward to remain neutral. Lincoln MacVeagh, the U.S. Ambassador in Athens, pushed neutrality to absurd lengths: when the Communists cut off the water supply, he refused to let British soldiers draw water from the well in his garden. Far more serious was the order from the U.S. Chief of Naval Operations, Admiral Ernest J. King, forbidding American

ships to carry supplies to the British. That order, which could be given only by the Allies' joint headquarters, violated the chain of command and was quickly withdrawn.

Sheer frustration had brought Churchill to Athens to try a new tack. He now realized that military muscle alone would not save Greece from the Communists. To be sure, the British reinforcements that were pouring in daily from the Italian front were driving ELAS out of Athens. But not nearly enough troops could be spared from the war on Germany to loosen ELAS' grip on the rest of Greece. So Churchill hoped to implement a political settlement by temporarily establishing a regency. As a formal substitute for the King, an impartial regent might help persuade the antimonarchists that Britain did not intend to return George II without holding a plebiscite as promised.

Churchill had been advised that Archbishop Damaskinos was the ideal man for regent. The 54-year-old prelate, who stood well over six feet tall and still showed the powerful physique of his youthful days as a champion wrestler, had been a tower of strength in the struggle against the Axis occupation. Besides helping escaped British prisoners-of-war flee the country, he had saved the lives of many Jews by baptizing them as Christians, and when the Germans began deporting Greek civilians to work in their factories, his persistent opposition—together with strikes by the Communists' labor front—had stopped the practice. Damaskinos' courage and patriotism had won the admiration of Greeks of every political hue.

Churchill was dubious about the archbishop, fearing him to be too far to the left. But his doubts were dispelled that Christmas Day when he met Damaskimos on board the British cruiser H.M.S. *Ajax*, which lay at anchor near Athens. Churchill was awed by the sheer size of the archbishop, who seemed to be seven feet tall in his ceremonial miter, and he quickly decided that Damaskinos was "the outstanding figure in the Greek turmoil." (Damaskinos also impressed the *Ajax's* crewmen, who saw him arrive while they were watching some of their shipmates present a traditional Christmas pantomime. The sailors assumed that Damaskinos was part of the show and applauded wildly.)

Next day in Athens, Damaskinos presided at a grand conference called by Churchill. Representatives of all the Greek political parties attended, including three Communists who startled Churchill by showing up in British battle dress. Churchill himself had made a startling entrance: he arrived in an armored car, carrying a pistol.

Although the delegates argued bitterly over everything else, they quickly agreed that Damaskinos was acceptable as regent until the plebiscite settled the fate of the monarchy. The plan to establish a regency convinced even the Communists and the antimonarchists that Churchill had abandoned all hope of bringing back the King before a plebiscite was held.

Churchill, armed with the Greeks' approval, flew home to London and instructed King George II to appoint Damaskinos as his regent. George reluctantly did what he was told. At the beginning of the new year, 1945, Damaskinos was officially installed as regent and a new government was formed. This popular change in regime accomplished what Churchill hoped it would, prying moderates away from the Communists, whom they had joined as the best medium for expressing their opposition to the King.

Militarily as well as politically, the tide was now running strongly against the Communists. The British, their ranks swelled to 50,000 men by two divisions that had just arrived from Italy, had built up the manpower edge they needed to handle the ELAS guerrillas in the Athens area. Breaking out of their narrow perimeter in the center of the capital, they had secured the road to Piraeus and captured two guerrilla strongholds, the ancient stadium and the Fix brewery. ELAS had contributed handsomely to its own defeats. It had failed to make use of some 23,000 guerrillas concentrated in central Greece, and it had squandered its best military leader, Aris, in the meaningless campaign against EDES in Epirus. Aris was not called to Athens until January 2, after a month of fighting there, and by then the Communists' tactical position was hopeless.

While fighting rear-guard skirmishes in Athens, ELAS began one last orgy of futile barbarism. Guerrillas siezed thousands of civilian hostages at random and marched them off to the north into the cold and snowy mountains. Many of the hostages perished from exposure or starvation. Others were executed. By rough estimate, 4,000 of 15,000 hostages died—a senseless toll that undercut the sympathy ELAS enjoyed abroad and further reduced its support at home.

British soldiers, taking shelter at the base of a monument painted with the hammer and sickle symbols of the Communists, fire away at ELAS guerrillas during the civil war in Athens in December of 1944. As fighting swept through the capital city, British troops were repeatedly exposed to attacks by Communist snipers, some of them attired in British uniforms.

By January 5 the British had cleared Athens of all organized ELAS units, and the Communists sued for peace. A truce took effect at mid-month. Then, on February 2, a peace conference was convened in a seaside resort villa at Varkiza, 20 miles from Athens.

Following 10 days of bitter argument, an agreement was signed. The government legalized the Greek Communist Party, which eventually settled its internal differences by splitting into two rival wings, one nationalistic and the other following Moscow's party line. The government also granted amnesty for all political crimes committed after the outbreak of fighting on the 3rd of December and promised to hold the plebiscite on the monarchy before the end of 1945. For their part the communists agreed to demobilize ELAS, which still controlled about three quarters of Greece, and to turn over the guerrillas' arms to the government.

ELAS did, in fact, surrender 41,500 rifles and other assorted weapons. But many guerrillas were embittered by the Varkiza agreement and refused to give up their fight. They fled to the mountains of Albania and Yugoslavia, where they were welcomed by their Communist brethren. They would rise again in 1946 with plentiful weapons supplied by both Tito and Stalin.

Though the Communists had effectively been put out of business, the Greek government had yet to track down the dangerous man who symbolized ELAS' strength and violence. Aris had refused to surrender, and he had disappeared along with a hundred diehard followers. Sometime in June, troops of the new Greek National Guard picked up Aris' trail and began tracking him down. At the village of Milia in the Pindus Mountains, Aris paused long enough to give a young student his considered opinion of why ELAS had failed: "It is because we did not kill enough. Revolutions succeed when the rivers redden with blood."

The National Guard caught up with Aris and his band on June 16 and the guerrilla leader's career came to a violent end. Many conflicting stories were later told about how he died. It was said that a six-hour battle took place, that Avis was betrayed by an old comrade, that he committed suicide, that he was killed by a former EDES rival. Whatever the circumstances of his death, hundreds of Greeks later saw his head on display in the main square of the town of Trikkala.

Winston Churchill was vastly relieved by the settlement in Greece. During his Christmas visit to Athens, the situation had seemed so hopeless that he muttered to U.S. Ambassador MacVeagh, "All we want is to get out of this damned place." Having nailed down Britain's 90 per cent predominance in Greece, Churchill was indebted to the man who might well have stopped him but who had not really tried. In February 1945, at the Big Three Conference at Yalta, Churchill thanked Stalin "for not having taken too great an interest in Greek affairs."

A year before the settlement in Greece, at a time when the war was still raging in Italy and Russia, Churchill addressed himself to the problem of Yugoslavia's political future—and Britain's stake in it. He had just decided, for military reasons, to back Tito in spite of his doctrinaire Communism. For all practical purposes, Churchill had to rely on diplomacy to assure Britain of any postwar influence in the country. He was hardly optimistic about his chances for success.

Churchill began his political maneuvering in Yugoslavia early in 1944. He chose as his instrument the exiled King Peter II, prompting a critic to remark in the House of Commons, "The Prime Minister cannot see a king without wanting to shore him up." Churchill did feel a fatherly obligation to bolster Peter, a rather helpless young man who was said to be "happiest when he was talking about motor cars and aeroplanes." He had sent the King to study at Cambridge and arranged for him to train as a pilot with the RAF. When Peter contemplated marriage to a Greek princess, Churchill approved the match against the objections of Peter's ministers-in-exile, who said that it would be damned as frivolity by their suffering countrymen. The ministers were right. In Croatia, where the Serbian King had never been popular, news of the marriage gave rise to a satirical ditty: "Tito took arms, the King took a wife."

Churchill, realizing that Tito would be the dominant force in postwar Yugoslavia, tried to arrange a political alliance between him and the King. The first step was to push Peter into jettisoning Tito's rival, the Chetnik leader Mihailovich, whom Churchill called "a millstone tied around the neck of the little King." A new royal government-in-exile was formed, with Mihailovich conspicuously absent from his former post as minister of the armed forces.

To draw the Communists into this government, the new

Prime Minister, Ivan Shubashich, flew off to Yugoslavia to have a conference with his fellow Croatian, Tito. They met on the island of Vis, where Tito had established his headquarters under British protection in June of 1944. Their talks were encouraging.

Then Churchill himself had a meeting with Tito in Naples. When the two leaders finally came face to face, Churchill nearly wept, saying, "You're the first person from enslaved Europe I have met!"

But the tone was set for their discussions by the sartorial differences between them. Churchill, the confident, long-powerful host, was casually dressed for hot weather in loose white duck trousers and a shirt open at the neck. Tito, a Johnny-come-lately who was eager to legitimize his rise, had dressed himself and his aides in resplendent new uniforms of heavy gray serge decorated with gold lace imported from America. "It was not, perhaps, an ideal costume for the sweltering heat of a Mediterranean August," observed Fitzroy Maclean, who was present. "But then it was not designed for comfort. It was designed to show conclusively

to all concerned that Tito and his staff were not just Communist guerrillas in borrowed battle dress, but members of the high command of a properly constituted national army, come to negotiate on equal terms with an allied high command." Churchill described Tito's attire as a "gold-laced strait jacket."

In his work sessions with Tito, the Prime Minister was generous in offering armaments but firm in setting the price for British recognition. He lectured Tito on how important it was to reach an accommodation with King Peter. He stipulated that recognition would be forthcoming only following the successful conclusion of Tito's negotiations with Shubashich's government-in-exile. Tito made no firm commitments. He said that he had no intention of introducing a communist system in Yugoslavia, but he declined Churchill's request he make a public statement to that effect. Churchill bluntly asked if Tito would permit personal freedom after the war, and Tito blandly said, "That is our basic principle—democracy and the freedom of the individual."

Far from being reassured, Churchill came away from the two-day conference feeling "somewhat disenchanted," according to his foreign secretary, Anthony Eden. Within a month it became obvious that Tito had won his fencing match with Churchill. With the German troops withdrawing from the Balkans and with the Partisans gaining strength every day, it was Tito—not Churchill or even Stalin—who held the trump card in Yugoslavia. Tito's Partisans were now firmly established, both politically as well as militarily, in all of the provinces of Yugoslavia with the significant exception of Serbia.

Tito needed Serbia, the nation's economic heartland, and its chief city, Belgrade, Yugoslavia's capital and main transportation center. Ever since Tito was pushed out of Serbia by the Germans at the end of 1941, the staunchly royalist peasants there had resisted the return of the Partisans, and Tito feared that the British would seize upon this fact to revive an old scheme to partition Yugoslavia into two nations—the western part Communist, the east Chetnik and

royalist. In fact, Churchill briefly considered partition as a fall-back plan.

To eliminate that possibility, Tito in the summer of 1944 had begun pounding away at the last Serbian strongholds of Mihailovich's Chetniks. Mihailovich could no longer maintain even a pretense of fighting the Germans; after the Allies cut off his supplies the previous spring, it was all he could do to fend off the Partisan attacks.

Nevertheless, Mihailovich continued to help the Allied war effort. His Chetniks, like the Partisans, gave shelter to American airmen who were forced to bail out on the massive 1,000-plane bombing raids against the Ploesti oil fields in Rumania. In August 1944 more than 250 downed fliers were hiding in Serbia with the Chetniks.

American plans to evacuate the airmen were organized by Lieutenant George Musulin, a former star tackle for the University of Pittsburgh football team. Musulin, whose parents were Yugoslavian immigrants, was chosen for the job because he had served as a liaison officer with Mihailovich until the Allied mission to the Chetniks had been withdrawn three months before. When he parachuted in to supervise the evacuation, the 250-pound lieutenant landed on a chicken coop and demolished it; he had to pay the farmer 15,000 dinars ($10) in damages.

In six days of superhuman effort, Musulin and a gang of Chetniks prepared for the landing of the big American C-47 transports by lengthening the primitive airstrip on a mountainside 50 miles southwest of Belgrade. Then, on August 10, the American airmen were evacuated by 12 planes that landed and took off at five-minute intervals.

Musulin's rescue mission, together with a visit by a three-man American intelligence-gathering team, raised Mihailovich's hopes that the Allies might yet resume aid to his dwindling forces. In early September, 1944, when the Allies mounted Operation *Ratweek* to harass the German troops then beginning to withdraw from Greece, Mihailovich issued his long-awaited order for a general uprising against the occupation. But he had no weapons to equip the recruits who answered the call to arms. And then his Serbian bastion suddenly collapsed all around him.

Tito, too, had joined Operation *Ratweek,* and the extra Partisan divisions he poured into Serbia attacked the Chetniks as well as the Germans with redoubled fury. As Mihai-

lovich reeled back under a series of defeats, he suffered still another reverse—a devastating broadcast from London by King Peter on September 12. Peter, in an attempt to improve relations with the Partisans for his patron Churchill, urged "all Serbs, Croats and Slovenes to unite and join the National Liberation Army under the leadership of Marshal Tito." The King, whom Mihailovich had served so loyally if sometimes misguidedly, had abandoned him.

The King's speech completed the demoralization of the Chetniks. Mihailovich's army crumbled, with many of his guerrillas going over to the Partisans. His headquarters near the Chetnik airstrip southwest of Belgrade was overrun by the Partisans. Mihailovich and a few loyal men fled west into the mountains of Bosnia. There, under the protection of the Germans, he gathered around him the ragtag remnants of the various puppet armies.

Tito's forces now controlled large parts of Serbia. However, his principal objective, Belgrade, was the main rail hub for the German withdrawal from the Balkans, and it was strongly defended. To liberate Belgrade, Tito knew he needed the tanks and artillery of the Red Army, which was poised at the Danube River on the Rumanian-Yugoslav border, pointing like an arrow into Serbia. And he intended to get that help on his own terms.

On the night of September 18, Tito left for Moscow to negotiate with Stalin. A DC-3 piloted by a Soviet airman whisked him away from a British airfield on the island of Vis in complete secrecy; Tito even put a sack over the head of his well-known wolfhound Tiger to muffle any telltale barking. After a couple of days the British realized that Tito was missing, but they did not learn where he had gone until Churchill himself went to Moscow in October to reach his percentages agreement with Stalin.

The last time Tito had been in Moscow, 1940, he had been the representative of a party so obscure and powerless that he would not have rated an audience with the mighty Stalin. Now he was the marshal of Yugoslavia and, when they met, Stalin embraced his comrade so enthusiastically that Tito was literally lifted off his feet.

Tito soon came down to earth. He found that Stalin was much shorter than he appeared in pictures, "coarse and touchy" in conversation and even more patronizing than

American fliers, shot down over Yugoslavia, catch up on their sleep in a hayloft after being rescued by the Chetniks. During the war some 600 Americans were rescued by the Chetniks at great personal risk. "Our guides told us in all sincerity," said one of the fliers, "that the Germans executed five of their people for failure to disclose our whereabouts."

Churchill had been. Stalin addressed him by his old Moscow code name, Walter, as if Tito were still one of his minor agents. Moreover, the Soviet dictator irritated Tito by advising him that he ought not oppose the return of King Peter to Yugoslavia. When Tito protested, Stalin retorted: "You don't have to take him back forever. Just temporarily, and then at the right moment a knife in the back."

In discussing the liberation of Belgrade, Tito asked for Soviet military support but laid down strict conditions. The Partisans would retain military autonomy, free of interference from the Soviet Army command; all areas liberated would come under Partisan civil administration; and, most important, Russian soldiers would move on to Hungary after their joint operations with the Partisans were completed. Stalin offered Tito a whole Soviet armored corps and agreed to his terms. But Tito's show of independence had jarred Stalin and prompted him to start recruiting Soviet spies among the Partisans.

Returning to Yugoslavia in early October, Tito established a new headquarters on the Rumanian border and took over personal charge of coordinating the movements of the Soviet forces and his Partisan divisions. By that time the Soviet armored columns from conquered Rumania had already crossed into Yugoslavia, and ironically the first guerrillas to greet them had been a band of Chetniks, sent by Mihailovich in a vain effort to win favor with the Russians. The Soviet commander had accepted the Chetniks' offer of joint action against the Germans but later, at Tito's insistence, disarmed them and turned them over to the Partisans.

Together, the Partisans and the Soviet troops drove on Belgrade. For the first time in Yugoslavia, the Germans had to face an enemy whose forces fairly bristled with tanks and artillery. They fought fiercely and skillfully in a week-long battle that cost the Partisans and Russians several thousand casualties. But the Germans lost heavily, too, and they were driven back into Belgrade. On the night of October 19, the Partisans and Russians drew up before Belgrade and prepared to take the city by storm the next day.

At this point, a lone patriot seized an opportunity—rarely granted to individuals—to exert a personal impact on great events. He was an elderly retired schoolteacher. As the old man glanced out of the window of his Belgrade apartment on the night of October 19, he saw German sappers wiring demolition charges on the only bridge across the Sava River, which the Germans were planning to blow up after they had withdrawn across it westward from Belgrade. By a strange coincidence, the schoolteacher had observed an almost identical scene when he was a Serbian soldier in the Balkan War of 1912. He had acted then, removing demolition charges from a bridge that the retreating Turks intended to destroy behind them.

Now, 42 years later, the old man acted again. He hurried downstairs, crossed the street and, in constant danger of discovery by German guards, spent a harrowing half hour disconnecting the charges.

Next day, the Partisans and Russians smashed into Belgrade, with Tito's First Proletarian Division taking the center of the city by storm. The Germans fought their rear-guard action as planned, retreating through the capital and across the bridge over the Sava. But the bridge did not blow up, and the Partisans and Russians streamed across it to ram home their victory.

For saving his first bridge in 1912, the schoolteacher had won a gold medal from the first King Peter; for saving his second bridge in 1944, he received another gold medal—from the Partisan enemies of the crown.

The capture of Belgrade was the ultimate moment for the Partisans. Returning in triumph to the city he had fled three years earlier to build up the Partisans' strength in the mountains, Tito watched with pride as his guerrilla heroes and heroines marched in review. No matter that their lines were somewhat ragged nor that captured German and Italian uniforms had replaced their guerrilla tatters. They had won a war in which all they had once dared to hope for was their own survival.

Thus ended the guerrilla phase of warfare in Yugoslavia. With the Partisans in control of most of the country, the fighting became a conventional war of position, and so it remained through the winter of 1944-1945. The Germans established a stable front in an area known as the Srem. Facing them were the massed armies of the Partisans, whose ranks were fast nearing their wartime peak of 800,000. On Tito's northern flank was the Danube River. Across the Danube in Hungary was the Soviet Army. In mid-November, in accordance with Stalin's pledge to Tito, the Russians had

Under the protective cover of a Russian tank, wounded Partisans are carried to safety through the streets of Belgrade. In the battle to liberate the capital, the Partisans and Russians reportedly killed 16,000 Germans and captured another 8,000 during house-to-house fighting that lasted a week.

withdrawn from Yugoslavia, leaving the Partisans to mop up with their new Bulgarian allies, who had quit the foundering Axis and declared war on Germany.

Politically, too, a new phase was beginning for the Partisans. Negotiations for a unified government went forward with the King's Prime Minister, Shubashich, just as Churchill had intended. But despite Fitzroy Maclean's cordial relations with Tito, there was increasing friction between the Partisans and the Western Allies. Some of the trouble stemmed from thorny political issues, such as the conflicting claims of Yugoslavia and Italy to the Adriatic coastal territories of Trieste and Istria. But much of it grew out of Partisan suspicions about British and American motives, which had been inflamed by the actions Churchill had taken against the Greek Communists in December 1944. These suspicions were being encouraged by Stalin, who saw Britain and the U.S. as postwar rivals rather than as wartime allies. He had already delivered to Tito's aide, Milovan Djilas, a typical warning about the perfidies of Western leaders: "They find nothing sweeter than to trick their allies. Churchill is the kind who, if you don't watch him, will slip a kopeck out of your pocket. Roosevelt is not like that. He dips in his hand only for bigger coins."

The Partisans imposed limits on the travels of American and British liaison officers. They insisted that their own people, rather than representatives of the United Nations Relief and Rehabilitation Administration, should distribute food and other aid to the war-ravaged country. A group of Partisan soldiers even became suspicious when some British officers named their dog "Tito." Resentful of the apparent slur against their leader, the Partisans were plotting to kill the dog when the British assured them that in the West it was a common practice to name pets after popular figures.

The biggest concern of the Partisans was a British regiment of artillery and a British force of 600 Commandos that had landed at Dubrovnik on the Adriatic coast in November of 1944. These troops had come at the Partisans' request and had moved north with them, trying in vain to crush the German forces that were retreating from Greece. But now, with the German defense line well to the north, the Partisans feared that the British were staying on as the vanguard of a much larger British-American invasion force. In fact, though Tito did not know it, Churchill's fertile imagination had conjured up just such a plan; he urged President Roosevelt to send American troops from Italy to join the British in a "right-handed drive to the Adriatic armpit," the object of which was to march due north, seize Vienna and thereby thwart Stalin's obvious intention of establishing Soviet power in central Europe. But Roosevelt said no to the operation, which he considered impractical, unnecessary and politically divisive. In any case, Tito demanded that the British pull their troops back to the Dubrovnik area.

But unfortunately, the British liaison officer assigned to smooth over this troublesome situation was more of a hindrance than a help. He was the eccentric English novelist Evelyn Waugh, who had joined the Allied military mission in Yugoslavia at the request of his friend Randolph Churchill, the Prime Minister's son. Waugh quickly made himself unwelcome by repeating the old rumor that Tito was a woman and always referring to him as "Auntie." Waugh's "Catholic soul," observed a colleague, "was filled with revulsion by the Communists who surrounded us"; and he made himself doubly obnoxious to the Communists by doing research for a report on how the Croatian Catholics would suffer under a Tito regime.

The Partisans thereupon added a demand for the withdrawal of Waugh to their demands for the withdrawal of the British troops. In January 1945 the British acceded to both demands. They removed their troops from Yugoslavia and in the process liquidated Waugh's job.

Flushed with success, the Partisans were impartial in finding fault with their allies. They were even pressing formal charges against their comrades from the Soviet Union, who had behaved abominably before departing for Hungary. Specifically, the Partisans accused the Russians of committing 1,219 rapes, 111 rapes with murder and 248 rapes with attempted murder. Furthermore, a drunken Soviet officer had wounded Tito's son Zharko in a Belgrade nightclub.

But if Russia was losing ground with Tito, Churchill was not winning it; in fact, Britain's hoped-for 50 per cent interest in Yugoslavia kept shrinking steadily. By March 1945, Tito and Prime Minister Shubashich had formed a new government of national unity, and Churchill had to support it, even knowing that Tito was going to swallow it up as soon as it had served his purpose. The character of this new government, which was installed on March 7, prompted Churchill to write resignedly that Britain's role in Yugoslavia "should become one of increasing detachment."

The Cabinet was made up of 25 Communists and fellow travelers, plus three moderates who would be eased out by the end of the year. It named Tito as the Prime Minister and relegated Shubashich to the figurehead role of foreign minister. In addition, three regents were appointed to act for the King—until Tito abolished the monarchy a few months later. For once in the Balkans, politics had followed a predictable course.

Tito's fledgling government was patterned after the authoritarian Stalinist model, and even as it pressed the war against the Germans in the north, it started to settle ac-

Handcuffed and confined to a cell, Chetnik leader Drazha Mihailovich solemnly awaits his fate after being arrested by his Partisan enemies. Accused of treason, murder and numerous atrocities, he was sentenced to be shot. Before his execution, Mihailovich explained: "I was caught in the whirlpool of events . . . a merciless fate threw me into this maelstrom."

counts with its domestic enemies. OZNA, the secret police of the Partisans, methodically tracked down Serbian collaborators, the puppet Ustashi of Croatia and, above all, the Chetniks. Some of the captured fugitives were tried and executed. Others were summarily shot on the spot. No count was kept of these executions, but they contributed thousands upon thousands of dead to Yugoslavia's enormous wartime toll, which was estimated at 1,750,000, or one citizen out of nine. The political executions became so commonplace that Tito cried out in disgust to his party's Central Committee: "Enough of all these death sentences and all this killing! The death sentence no longer has any effect. No one fears death any more!"

On the battlefields the Germans, too, recoiled under the Partisans' lust for revenge. In April 1945 the Partisans broke through the bloody front at Srem and pushed the Germans into the northwest corner of the country. During the final two months of the war in Yugoslavia, the Germans lost—according to Partisan claims—nearly 100,000 men.

Tito did not neglect his last major domestic enemy. Drazha Mihailovich—like his defeated Communist counterpart in Greece, Aris Velouchiotis—refused to abide by the results of the war. In the fighting's final days, Mihailovich headed from Bosnia back to his beloved Serbia with a few hundred Chetniks—all that remained of his Yugoslav Army in the Homeland. He was lured home by a Partisan ruse: the secret police, using a captured Chetnik radio code and posing as a still-effective band of his followers, sent him messages announcing that conditions were ripe for a general uprising against the new Communist regime.

When the secret police caught up with Mihailovich, he was hiding in a foxhole on the Serbia-Bosnia border. He was exhausted, subsisting on herbs and snails. His fate was a foregone conclusion. Tito's government staged an elaborate trial in a former barracks outside Belgrade. Mihailovich's final ordeal summed up the fratricidal guerrilla warfare in the Balkans. It was a tragedy in which all of the guerrillas—patriots and traitors, victors and vanquished alike—were victims of the cataclysmic forces unleashed by the war.

Mihailovich, accused of war crimes and collaboration along with 23 other Yugoslavs, entered the dock neatly attired in his old Army uniform. His defense was presented for six days, and then for six days more he was rigorously cross-examined. Finally, late one night, he made his long summary statement. He told the court of the medals for valor he won in World War I, of his career-long hatred for the Germans, of the many sufferings of his Chetniks. He admitted to meetings with German commanders but denied all charges of collaboration.

Maclean later reported that Mihailovich "showed himself throughout respectful of the court and oblivious of the crowd, who for once forgot to hiss and listened in complete silence. Hitherto he had appeared incoherent and indeterminate. Now his character stood out clearly and for the next four hours he dominated the proceedings. He spoke without oratory, without rancour towards political opponents or private enemies, lucidly and in detail. He was a professional soldier presenting a military report, compelling because of its simplicity."

Mihailovich's eloquence changed nothing. Along with his 23 codefendants he was pronounced guilty. He and 10 others were sentenced to be shot; the rest received various prison terms. "The verdict," said Maclean, "was received with applause by the crowd," and Mihailovich impassively "stood to attention while it was being read out."

Mihailovich appealed his sentence and was turned down. His wife was permitted to visit him in prison; he did not see his son and daughter, who had long since denounced him as a traitor and gone over to the Partisans' side. And then Mihailovich was taken out—to a former golf course, rumor said—and shot.

Mihailovich needed no epitaph; his remains were buried secretly in an unmarked grave to deny any diehard followers a shrine to rally around. But if an epitaph had been needed, Mihailovich had supplied it in his moving last statement to the court: "I wanted much, I began much, but the gale of the world carried away me and my work."

ATHENS UNDER SIEGE

Within range of guerrilla snipers holed up in nearby buildings, civilians sprint across an exposed street in downtown Athens at the height of the civil war in 1944.

AFTER LIBERATION, A RUINOUS CIVIL WAR

When the Germans pulled out of Athens early in October 1944, the streets of the ancient city rang with the sounds of a celebration that proved to be tragically short-lived. Within a matter of weeks, Athens was in the grip of another brutal crisis—this time a civil war that pitted the Greek Communists against the new Greek government under George Papandreou, supported by British troops.

"Hunger, fear and despair enveloped Athens," a resident wrote later of those bitter times, "and the black days of the occupation seemed to have returned." A general strike called by the Communists paralyzed the city. Drivers abandoned their streetcars, shopkeepers locked up their businesses. Government services ceased, and utilities were shut down. With the Communist guerrilla forces in control of the port docks, British relief ships were unable to land their supplies, and food, scarce during the German occupation, became even more precious.

In addition to these hardships—as recorded on these pages by LIFE photographer Dmitri Kessel—came the horrors of the fighting itself. "Corpses lay one on top of the other like carcasses in an abattoir, awaiting a lull in the surrounding battle so that they could be quickly buried in parks and fields," one of the British Army officers recalled later. "Fire engines tore through the streets and the sky was crimson with the reflections from blazing buildings. Everywhere there was fear and suffering. There was not only no food, no water, no light and no warmth; there was no safety or security anywhere."

Athenians caught in this no man's land could only huddle in their homes, hungry, cold and frightened, while snipers' bullets whined down the streets and mortar blasts shook the buildings. Civilians were allowed to be outside for only a few hours each afternoon. Without newspapers or radio broadcasts, they did not know who was winning the bitter contest or when their ordeal might end. "The icy cold nights seemed endless," one young man remembered. "We looked forward to daybreak in the vain hope that the end of the ordeal would come."

Worthless because of inflation, Greek drachmas—100 million of which equaled one U.S. dollar in 1944—lie with other rubbish in an Athens street.

Their legs warmed by a tattered coat, a Greek mother and her daughters await transport from their embattled neighborhood to the safety of a relative's home.

As an Athens policeman looks on, a Greek lad receives some hot bean soup provided by an Anglo-American relief organization. Fellow townsmen wait their turn

Thick pea soup and a bread crust make a meager dinner for Laloula Stangos, a young Athenian teacher.

LIFE AMID SNIPERS, RUBBLE AND FAMINE

As the Greek civil war raged through December 1944, citizens of Athens trapped in the cross fire spent a bleak Christmas season faced with the prospect of starvation. In the British-controlled sectors they waited hours in long lines for a dollop of soup. Elsewhere in the city many subsisted on weak brews made from grasses and herbs. Those with sufficient money roamed the streets, risking death from a sniper's bullet, to seek out sidewalk vendors and pay grossly inflated prices for a piece of fruit or a vegetable.

Along with hunger, the people of Ath-ens were plagued by the cold of a particularly harsh winter. Fuel was as scarce as food, and many were compelled to burn their furniture for warmth.

As the Athenians grew run-down, so did their city. Athens took on a dismal, forlorn appearance, its streets littered with rubbish and the debris of war. Some neighborhoods were blanketed with a vile stench —the odors of clogged sewer drains and decaying corpses left where they fell. At night, with the electricity turned off, Athens was lighted only by the flames of burning buildings, the eerie glow of parachute flares and the blinding flashes of artillery. Sirens screamed, and the city's dogs, perhaps crazed by the strange noises of battle, howled like wolves through the night.

While venturing through the dangerous streets in search of food for her family, Laloula Stangos runs a gauntlet of checkpoints. In the course of her shoppin

expedition, in which she bought some raisins, a few oranges and a cauliflower, she was searched repeatedly by British soldiers and Greek policemen for weapons.

Children in Athens gather scrap lumber for firewood from a house wrecked by artillery shells.

Without any gas or electricity in their apartment, Laloula Stangos' family tries to ward off the chill in front of a tiny stove they are feeding with scraps of paper.

BIBLIOGRAPHY

Adamic, Louis, *The Eagle and the Roots*. Doubleday & Company, Inc., 1952.

Addington, Larry H., *The Blitzkrieg Era and the German General Staff, 1865-1941*. Rutgers University Press, 1971.

Amery, Julian, *Sons of the Eagle*. Macmillan & Co. Ltd., 1948.

Ansel, Walter, *Hitler and the Middle Sea*. Duke University Press, 1972

Argyropoulo, Kaity, *From Peace to Chaos*. Vantage Press, 1975.

Auty, Phyllis:
Tito. Ballantine Books Inc., 1972.
Tito, A Biography. Longman Group Limited, 1970.

Auty, Phyllis, and Richard Clogg, eds., *British Policy towards Wartime Resistance in Yugoslavia and Greece*. The Macmillan Press Ltd., 1975.

Baldwin, Hanson, *Battles Lost and Won*. Harper & Row, 1966.

Barker, Elisabeth, *British Policy in South-East Europe in the Second World War*. The Macmillan Press Ltd., 1976.

Bethell, Nicholas, *The Last Secret*. Basic Books, Inc., 1974.

Bocca, Geoffrey, *Kings without Thrones*. The Dial Press, 1959.

Böhmler, Rudolf, *Fallschirmjäger*. Verlag Hans-Henning Podzun, 1961.

Brajovid-Djuro, Petar V., *Yugoslavia in the Second World War*. Belgrade, 1977.

Buckley, Christopher, *Greece and Crete 1941*. Her Majesty's Stationery Office, 1977.

Byford-Jones, W., *The Greek Trilogy: Resistance-Liberation-Revolution*. Hutchinson & Co. Ltd., 1946.

Campbell, Arthur, *Guerillas: a History and Analysis*. Arthur Barker Limited, 1967.

The Captured World War II Art of Olaf Jordan (exhibit catalogue). The Hewlett Gallery, Carnegie-Mellon University, 1975.

Cervi, Mario, *The Hollow Legions*. Chatto & Windus, 1972.

Churchill, Winston S., *The Grand Alliance*. Bantam Books, 1962.

Clark, Alan, *The Fall of Crete*. William Morrow and Company, 1962.

Clissold, Stephen:
ed., *A Short History of Yugoslavia*. Cambridge University Press, 1968.
Whirlwind. The Cresset Press, 1949.

Condit, D. M., *Case Study in Guerrilla War: Greece during World War II*. Department of the Army, 1961.

Deakin, F. W. D., *The Embattled Mountain*. Oxford University Press, 1971.

Dedijer, Vladimir:
The Beloved Land. MacGibbon & Kee, 1961.
Tito. Simon and Schuster, 1953.
Tito Speaks. Weidenfeld and Nicolson, 1954.
With Tito through the War. Alexander Hamilton Ltd., 1951.

Djilas, Milovan:
Conversations with Stalin. Harcourt, Brace & World, Inc., 1962.
Wartime. Harcourt Brace Jovanovich, Inc., 1977.

Edwards, Roger, *German Airborne Troops 1936-45*. Doubleday & Company, Inc., 1974.

Epstein, Julius, *Operation Keelhaul*. The Devin-Adair Company, 1973.

Esposito, Colonel Vincent J., chief ed., *The West Point Atlas of American Wars*, Vol. II, 1900-1953. The Department of Military Art and Engineering, The United States Military Academy, 1959.

Eudes, Dominique, *The Kapetanios*. Monthly Review Press, 1970.

Farrar-Hockley, Anthony, *Student*. Ballantine Books Inc., 1973.

Fergusson, Bernard, *The Black Watch and the King's Enemies*. Collins, 1950.

Gardner, Hugh H.:
Guerrilla and Counterguerrilla Warfare in Greece, 1941-1945. Office of the Chief of Military History, Department of the Army, 1962.
The German Campaigns in the Balkans (Spring 1941). Department of the Army, 1953.

Graham, Stephen, *Alexander of Yugoslavia*. Yale University Press, 1939.

Gunther, John, *Inside Europe*. Harper & Brothers, 1938.

Half a Century of Revolutionary Struggle of the League of Communists of Yugoslavia (exhibit catalogue). Museum of the Revolution of Yugoslav Peoples, 1970.

Hayden, Sterling, *Wanderer*. Alfred A. Knopf, 1970.

Heckstall-Smith, Anthony, and Vice-Admiral H. T. Baillie-Grohman, *Greek Tragedy 1941*. W. W. Norton & Company, Inc., 1961.

Hoptner, J. B., *Yugoslavia in Crisis 1934-1941*. Columbia University Press, 1962.

Huertley, W. A., H. C. Darby, C. W. Crawley and C. M. Woodhouse, *A Short History of Greece*. Cambridge University Press, 1965.

Huot, Major Louis, *Guns for Tito*. L. B. Fischer, 1945.

Huxley-Blythe, Peter J., *The East Came West*. The Caxton Printers, Ltd., 1964.

Iatrides, John O., *Revolt in Athens*. Princeton University Press, 1972.

Judd, Denis, *Eclipse of Kings*. Stein and Day, 1974.

King, William B., and Frank O'Brien, *The Balkans, Frontier of Two Worlds*. Alfred A. Knopf, 1947.

Kousoulas, Dimitrios G.:
The Price of Freedom. Syracuse University, 1953.
Revolution and Defeat. Oxford University Press, 1965.

Lanz, Hubert, *Partisan Warfare in the Balkans*. Office of the Chief of Military History, Department of the Army, 1950.

Lavra, Stephen, *The Greek Miracle*. Hastings House, 1943.

Lawrence, Christie Norman, *Irregular Adventure*. Faber & Faber Limited, 1947.

Leeper, Sir Reginald, *When Greek Meets Greek*. Chatto and Windus, 1950.

Long, Gavin, *Australia in the War of 1939-1945*, Vol. II, *Greece, Crete and Syria*. Australian War Memorial, 1953.

Macksey, Kenneth:
Panzer Division: The Mailed Fist. Ballantine Books Inc., 1972.
The Partisans of Europe in the Second World War. Stein and Day, 1975.

Maclean, Fitzroy:
Disputed Barricade. Jonathan Cape, 1957.
Eastern Approaches. Jonathan Cape, 1949.

McNeill, William Hardy, *The Greek Dilemma*. J. B. Lippincott Company, 1947.

Martin, David:
Ally Betrayed. Prentice-Hall, Inc. 1946.
Traitor or Patriot? The Case of General Mihailović. Hoover Institution, 1978.

Matthews, Ronald, *Sons of the Eagle*. Methuen & Co. Ltd., 1937.

Milazzo, Matteo J., *The Chetnik Movement & the Yugoslav Resistance*. The Johns Hopkins University Press, no date.

Montagu, Ewen, *The Man Who Never Was*. Bantam Books, 1965.

Moss, W. Stanley, *Ill Met by Moonlight*. The Macmillan Company, 1950.

Mulgan, John, *Report on Experience*. Oxford University Press, 1947.

Murphy, Robert, *Diplomat among Warriors*. Greenwood Press, 1964.

Myers, E. C. W., *Greek Entanglement*. Rupert Hart-Davis, 1955.

O'Ballance, Edgar, *The Greek Civil War 1944-1949*. Frederick A. Praeger, 1972.

Pack, S. W. C., *The Battle for Crete*. Naval Institute Press, 1973.

Papagos, General Alexander, *The Battle of Greece 1940-1941*. The J. M. Scazikis "Alpha" Editions, 1949.

Paris, Edmond, *Genocide in Satellite Croatia, 1941-1945*. The American Institute for Balkan Affairs, 1961.

Pavlowitch, Stevan K., *Yugoslavia*. Praeger Publishers, Inc., 1971.

Peter II, King of Yugoslavia, *A King's Heritage*. G. P. Putnam's Sons, 1954.

Piekalkiewicz, Janusz, *Secret Agents, Spies, and Saboteurs*. William Morrow and Company, 1974.

Playfair, Major-General I. S. O.:
The Mediterranean and Middle East. Her Majesty's Stationery Office.
Volume II, *The Germans Come to the Help of Their Ally*. 1956.
Volume IV, *The Destruction of the Axis Forces in Africa*. 1966.

Powell, Dilys, *Remember Greece*. Hodder and Stoughton, 1941.

Roberts, Walter R., *Tito, Mihailović and the Allies 1941-1945*. Rutgers University Press, 1973.

Rootham, Jasper, *Miss Fire*. Chatto & Windus, 1946.

Sarafis, General Stefanos, *Greek Resistance Army*. Birch Books Limited, 1951.

Singleton, Fred, *Twentieth-Century Yugoslavia*. Columbia University Press, 1976.

Skrigin, George, *War and Stage*. Turisticka Stampa, Belgrade, 1968.

Smith, R. Harris, *OSS: The Secret History of America's First Central Intelligence Agency*. University of California Press, 1972.

Spasić, Zivojin B., *Fourteen Centuries of Struggle for Freedom*. Military Museum, Belgrade, 1968.

Stavrianos, L. S., *Greece: American Dilemma and Opportunity*. Henry Regnery Company, 1952.

Stephanides, Theodore, *Climax in Crete*. Faber & Faber Limited, 1946.

Stevenson, William, *A Man Called Intrepid*. Harcourt Brace Jovanovich, 1976.

Stewart, I. McD. G., *The Struggle for Crete, 20 May—1 June 1941*. Oxford University Press, 1966.

Sweet-Escott, Bickham, *Baker Street Irregular*. Methuen & Co. Ltd., 1965.

Swire, J., *Albania, the Rise of a Kingdom*. Williams & Norgate, Ltd., 1929.

Szinyei-Merse, Antoinette de, *Ten Years, Ten Months, Ten Days*. Hutchinson & Co., Ltd., 1940.

Thomas, David A.:
Crete 1941: The Battle at Sea. New English Library, 1976.
Nazi Victory: Crete 1941. Stein and Day, 1972.

Tomasevich, Jozo, *The Chetniks*. Stanford University Press, 1975.

Tsatsos, Jeanne, *The Sword's Fierce Edge*. Vanderbilt University Press, 1969.

Von der Heydte, Baron, *Daedalus Returned, Crete 1941*. Hutchinson & Co., 1958.

Von Mellenthin, Major General F. W., *Panzer Battles*. University of Oklahoma Press, 1956.

Vucinich, Wayne S., ed., *Contemporary Yugoslavia: Twenty Years of Socialist Experiment*. University of California Press, 1969.

West, Rebecca, *Black Lamb and Grey Falcon*. The Viking Press, 1941.

White, Leigh, *The Long Balkan Night*. Charles Scribner's Sons, 1944.

Whiting, Charles, *Hunters from the Sky*. Leo Cooper, 1974.

Winterbothan, F. W., *The Ultra Secret*. Dell Publishing Co., Inc., 1976.

Winterstein, Ernst Martin, and Hans Jacobs, *General Meindl und seine Fallschirmjäger*. Gesammelt und Neidergeschrieben, no date.

Wolff, Robert Lee, *The Balkans in Our Time*. Harvard University Press, 1956.

Woodhouse, C. M.:
Apple of Discord. Hutchinson & Co., Ltd., 1948.
The Struggle for Greece 1941-1949. Hart-Davis, MacGibbon, 1976.

Wykes, Alan, *SS Leibstandarte*. Ballantine Books Inc., 1974.

Xydis, Stephen G., *Greece and the Great Powers 1944-1947*. Institute for Balkan Studies, 1963.

Zotos, Stephanos, *Greece: The Struggle for Freedom*. Thomas Y. Crowell Company, 1967.

PICTURE CREDITS
Credits from left to right are separated by semicolons, from top to bottom by dashes.

COVER and page 1: George Skrigin, Belgrade.

A ROYAL CAST OF CHARACTERS—6, 7: Ullstein Bilderdienst, Berlin. 8, 9: Wide World. 10: Popperfoto, London; Wide World—Ullstein Bilderdienst, Berlin. 11: H. Roger-Viollet, Paris. 12, 13: United Press International, except top left, Ullstein Bilderdienst, Berlin. 14, 15: National Archives—Bildarchiv Preussischer Kulturbesitz, Berlin; Wide World.

HITLER'S SOUTHERN FLANK—18: United Press International—Istituto Luce, Rome. 20: Map by Elie Sabban. 22: Dimis Argyopoulos, from Archives of Greek Ethnological Museum, Athens. 23: Harissiadis Agency, Athens. 24: Archives of Greek Armed Forces/Navy Headquarters, Athens. 26: Courtesy Federal Committee for Information, Belgrade. 27: Foto-Tanjug, Belgrade. 29: Radio Times Hulton Picture Library, London—Ullstein Bilderdienst, Berlin. 30, 31: Imperial War Museum, London.

THE BUMPIEST BLITZKRIEG—34, 35: Dever from Black Star. 36, 37: Bildarchiv Preussischer Kulturbesitz, Berlin. 38: National Archives. 39: Bundesarchiv, Koblenz—Wide World. 40, 41: Bundesarchiv, Koblenz; Bildarchiv Preussischer Kulturbesitz, Berlin—Dever from Black Star. 42, 43: Bundesarchiv, Koblenz.

HUNTERS FROM THE SKY—46: Map by Elie Sabban. 48: Karlheinz Reisgen, Düsseldorf. 49: Wide World. 51: Karlheinz Reisgen, Düsseldorf. 53: Orbis Publishing Ltd., London. 55: Imperial War Museum, London—Professor Dr. Karl Bringmann, Düsseldorf. 56: Bundesarchiv, Koblenz, courtesy Manolis Karellis, Mayor of Heraklion, Crete.

A COSTLY AIRBORNE CONQUEST—58, 59: Imperial War Museum, London. 60: Archiv Hans-Georg Schnitzer, Cologne. 61: Bundesarchiv, Koblenz—Imperial War Museum, London. 62, 63: Professor Dr. Karl Bringmann, Düsseldorf; insets, Archiv Hans-Georg Schnitzer, Cologne. 64, 65: Bundesarchiv, Koblenz, except bottom right, courtesy Ernst Winterstein, Braunschweig. 66: Professor Dr. Karl Bringmann, Düsseldorf. 67: Courtesy Randolf Kugler, Neuwied—Wide World. 68, 69: Imperial War Museum, London; Hans-Georg Schnitzer, Cologne—Archiv Professor Dr. Karl Bringmann, Düsseldorf. 70, 71: Bundesarchiv, Koblenz, except bottom right, Bildarchiv Preussischer Kulturbesitz, Berlin. 72, 73: Dever from Black Star, except bottom left, Archiv Hans-Georg Schnitzer, Cologne.

CHETNIKS AND PARTISANS—76: Map by Elie Sabban. 78: United Press International. 81: Courtesy W. R. Mansfield. 82: Österreichisches Institut für Zeitgeschichte, Vienna. 83: Ullstein Bilderdienst, Berlin. 85: Yugoslav Press and Cultural Center. 87: Wide World—Publifoto Notizie, Milan. 88: George Skrigin, courtesy Yugoslav Press and Cultural Center.

COMRADES-IN-ARMS—90, 91: John Phillips ©1976. 92: Muzej II Zasjedanja AVNOJ-a, Jajce. 93 through 96: George Skrigin, Belgrade. 97: Military Museum, Belgrade—Ekonomska Politika-Borba, Belgrade. 98: Muzej II Zasjedanja AVNOJ-a, Jajce. 99: Courtesy Yugoslav National Liberation Army Photo Unit—Foto-Tanjug, Belgrade; Wide World. 100, 101: Yugoslav Press and Cultural Center—Wide World; George Skrigin, Belgrade. 102: George Skrigin, Belgrade. 103: Yugoslav Press and Cultural Center.

THE BRUTAL OCCUPATION—104, 105: Foto-Tanjug, Belgrade. 106: Fototeca Storica Nazionale, Milan. 107: Courtesy Sir Fitzroy Maclean. 108, 109: Fototeca Storica Nazionale, Milan. 110: Museum of the Revolution of Yugoslav Peoples, Belgrade; inset, Gerhard Gronefeld, Munich. 111: Courtesy Federal Committee for Information, Belgrade—Fototeca Storica Nazionale, Milan. 112, 113: Courtesy Federal Committee for Information, Belgrade—Ekonomska Politika-Borba, Belgrade; Museum of the Revolution of Yugoslav Peoples, Belgrade.

HELP FROM THE ALLIES—117: Courtesy Sterling Hayden. 118: George Skrigin, Belgrade. 119: Courtesy Sir Fitzroy Maclean. 120: Paintings by Olaf Jordan, courtesy U.S. Army Center of Military History, copied by Henry Beville, except top left, painting by Olaf Jordan, courtesy U.S. Army Center of Military History. 121: Painting by Olaf Jordan, courtesy U.S. Army Center of Military History, copied by Henry Beville. 123: Imperial War Museum, London. 124: Courtesy Federal Committee for Information, Belgrade—George Skrigin, Belgrade. 125: George Skrigin, Belgrade. 127: Imperial War Museum, London, courtesy T. B. L. Churchill. 128: Courtesy T. B. L. Churchill, except center, courtesy Jack Churchill.

HEROES AND ENTERTAINERS—130 through 139: George Skrigin, Belgrade.

YUGOSLAVIA'S MARSHAL TITO—140, 141: John Phillips ©1976. 142: Military Museum, Belgrade. 143: Foto-Tanjug, Belgrade. 144, 145: Foto-Tanjug, Belgrade—George Skrigin, Belgrade; George Skrigin, courtesy Foto-Tanjug, Belgrade. 146: Yugoslav Press and Cultural Center. 147: Imperial War Museum, London. 148, 149: Imperial War Museum, London; Military Museum, Belgrade (2). 150, 151: U.S. Army; John Phillips ©1976.

GREECE'S MOUNTAIN WARRIORS—154: map by Elie Sabban. 156: A. Michalopoulos, Athens. 158: From *With the Guerrillas in the Mountains* by Spyros Meletzis, 1976, Athens. 159: Constantine Megaloconomou, Athens. 160, 161: From *With the Guerrillas in the Mountains* by Spyros Meletzis, 1976, Athens, except top, second from right, Spyros Meletzis, Athens. 163: Constantine Megaloconomou, Athens. 164: From "Der Deutsche Antifaschistische Widerstand 1933-1945," Roderberg-Verlag Frankfurt/Main. 165: Photo-Publicité-Presse, Paris. 166: Janusz Piekalkiewicz, Rösrath-Hoffnungsthal.

INCIDENT AT RICHEA—168, 169: Painting by Bernard Perlin, copied by Henry Groskinsky. 170: Painting by Bernard Perlin, from U.S. Army Center of Military History, copied by Charlie Brown. 171: Painting by Bernard Perlin, courtesy Frank Davis, copied by Charlie Phillips. 172, 173: Paintings by Bernard Perlin, copied by Henry Groskinsky, except top left, painting by Bernard Perlin, from U.S. Army Center of Military History, copied by Charlie Brown. 174 through 177: Paintings and sketches by Bernard Perlin, copied by Henry Groskinsky.

BALKAN SHOWDOWN—180: Imperial War Museum, London. 183: Wide World. 184: United Press International. 187: Dmitri Kessel for LIFE. 188: Courtesy Nick Lalich. 191: Military Museum, Belgrade. 192: Foto-Tanjug, Belgrade.

ATHENS UNDER SIEGE—194 through 203: Dmitri Kessel for LIFE.

ACKNOWLEDGMENTS

The index for this book was prepared by Mel Ingber. For help given in the preparation of this book, the editors thank Alfonso Bartolini, National Secretary, Associazione Nazionale Partigiani Italiani, Rome; Gérard Baschet, Editions de l'Illustration, Paris; Belgrade City Museum, Belgrade, Yugoslavia; Dana Bell, U.S. Air Force Still Photo Depository, Arlington, Va.; Leroy Bellamy, Prints and Photographs Division, Library of Congress, Washington, D.C.; C. A. Bimrose, M.C., North Leeds, Yorkshire, England; Carole Boutte, Senior Researcher, U.S. Army Audio-Visual Activity, Pentagon, Washington, D.C.; Col. Oreste Bovio, Ufficio Storico, Ministero Della Difesa, Rome; Prof. Dr. Karl Bringmann, Dusseldorf; Walter Cate, U.S. Air Force Still Photo Depository, Arlington, Va.; Col. Jack Churchill, Mayford, Nr. Woking, Surrey, England; Major-General T. B. L. Churchill, C.B.E., M.C., Crediton, Devon, England; Patrick Dempsey, Geography and Map Division, Library of Congress, Alexandria, Va.; Department of Photographs, Imperial War Museum, London; V. M. Destefano, Chief of Reference Library, U.S. Army Audio-Visual Activity, Pentagon, Washington, D.C.; Hans Dollinger, Wörthsee, Germany; Maj. Richard L. Felman, Tucson, Ariz.; F. O. Finzel, Oberkirchen, Germany; Rear-Admiral Morgan Giles, D.S.O., O.B.E., M.P., London; Marylou Gjernes, Curator, Center of Military History, Department of the Army, Alexandria, Va.; Dr. Matthias Haupt, Bundesarchiv, Koblenz, Germany; Werner Haupt, Bibliothek für Zeitgeschichte, Stuttgart; Sterling Hayden, Wilton, Conn.; Heinrich Hoffmann, Hamburg; Jerry Kearns, Prints and Photographs Division, Library of Congress, Washington, D.C.; Fay Ball King, Charleston, S.C.; Heidi Klein, Bildarchiv Preussischer Kulturbesitz, Berlin; Dr. Roland Klemig, Bildarchiv Preussischer Kulturbesitz, Berlin; Gene Kubal, The Army Library, Pentagon, Washington, D.C.; Lieut. Colonel Geoffrey Kup, London; Alexis Ladas, N.Y.C.; William H. Leary, National Archives and Records Service, Audio-Visual Division, Washington, D.C.; Sir Fitzroy Maclean, Bart., Argyll, Scotland; Military Museum, Belgrade; Stavis John Milton, West Palm Beach, Fla.; Phaedon Morphis, Director, Foreign Press Division, Ministry to the Prime Minister, Athens; Museum of Revolution of the Peoples and Nationalities of Yugoslavia, Belgrade; Museum of the Second Session of the Anti-Fascist Council of the National Liberation of Yugoslavia, Belgrade; Maj. C. L. D. Newall, O.B.E., Secretary, S.A.S. Association, London; Enzo Nizza, Milan; Bernard Perlin, Ridgefield, Conn.; Alexander Phylactopoulos, Counselor of Embassy, Embassy of Greece, Washington, D.C.; Ruzica Popovitch, Slavic and Central European Division, Library of Congress, Washington, D.C.; Lieut. Colonel Karl Ruef, Innsbruck, Austria; the Rev. Hans-Carl Scherrer, Freiburg, Germany; the Rev. Johann Georg Schmutz, Heitersheim, Germany; Axel Schulz, Ullstein, Berlin; Georgije Skrigin, Belgrade; Foto Tanjug, Belgrade; John E. Taylor, Archivist, Modern Military Branch, National Archives, Washington, D.C.; Burton Thiel, N.Y.C.; Constas Triandafyllides, Athens; Penelope Tsilas, European Law Division, Library of Congress, Washington, D.C.; U.S. Defense Mapping Agency, Washington, D.C.; Paul White, National Archives and Records Service, Audio-Visual Division, Washington, D.C.; Marie Yates, U.S. Army Audio-Visual Activity, Pentagon, Washington, D.C.; Yugoslav Press and Cultural Center, N.Y.C.

treatment of wounded Partisans, 88; withdraws from Athens, 180

Gliders: DFS 230A, *53, 65;* used in invasion of Crete, 47

Göring, Hermann, and Max Schmeling, *49*

Grazzi, Emmanuel, 16

Great Britain: aids opponents of Yugoslavia's pro-German government, 24; and ELAS, 156, 157, 158, 159, 162; and Greek Communists, 157-158; and Greek monarchy, 163, 167, 181; inflames suspicions of Communists after liberation of Greece, 181; and National Bands agreement, 158, 162; offer of aid to Greece, 23; Operation *Animals,* 159; protests U.S. presence in Yugoslavia, 122; reaction to Greek civil war, 183; SOE, 158, 163; support for Chetniks, 75, 78, 80, 86, 114, 116, 126-127; support for EDES, 153, 155, 157, 164; support for Partisans, *99,* 116, 118, 122-123, 129; and Zervas, 153

Great Britain, Air Force of: bases in Greece, 22; on Crete, 46, *51;* strength of, in Greece, 28; supports Tito's retreat, 129

Great Britain, Army of: at Aliakmon Line, 28; in Athens, 182-183, *184,* 185-186; attacks on German troop trains in Greece, 179; bypasses Crete, 180; camouflage system on Crete, 48; commando operation at Richea, *170-173, 175, 176-177;* contact with guerrillas, 155; control of guerrillas after liberation, 181; at Corinth Canal, *29,* 33; on Crete, 44, 46-47, *48,* 49-52, 56-57, 60, 65; evacuates Crete, *56,* 57; forces in Greece, 23, 24, 28; and Greek civil war, 182-183, *184,* 185-186; kidnapping of German general on Crete, *166,* 167; liberation of Greece, *180,* 181; at Maleme, 47-48, 50-51, 52, 54, 56; and Partisans after Germans move north, 192; plan for defense of Greece, 27-28; raid at Asopos, 162; raid at Gorgopotamos, 155-156; and rebellions against Greek government-in-exile, 167; retreat in Greece, 28, *30-31,* 32-33, 41; at Sphakia, 57; at Thermopylae, 32-33; treatment of wounded on Crete, *55;* withdrawal from Yugoslavia, 192

Great Britain, Navy of: and battle of Matapan, 24; evacuates EDES, 183; evacuation of Crete, 57; and evacuation from Greece, 24, 33; intercepts German landing on Crete, 51-52, *67;* losses in battle for Crete, 57; supply of Crete, 46; transports Tito, 129

Great Britain, Special Operations Executive (SOE), 158; reorganized, 163; supports guerrillas, 158, 163

Greece, map *154,* 155; accepts British aid, 23; Athens liberated, *180,* 181; attitudes within government, 32; bridge over Corinth Canal, *29;* British liberation of, *180,* 181; British mission lands in, 155; British withdrawal from, 28, 32-33; civil war, 164, 181-186, *194-203;* collaborators in government, 181; Communist Party legalized, 186; Communists withdraw from government, 181; economic deterioration, 152, 181, 196; famine, *156,* 181; German invasion of, 27, *29,* 32-33, *34-43;* German political prisoners in, *164,* 165; government-in-exile, 163, 167; Government of National Unity, 167, 179, 180-181; Italy intends to occupy, 16; Kalavryta, 165; occupation by Germany, 152, *156,* 159, 164, 165, 167; opposition to monarchy, 163; plan for defense, 27-28; politics between world wars, 8, 10; provisional government, 167; puppet government, 152, 165; Security Battalions, 165; Symi, *165;* Varkiza conference, 186. *See also* Athens; Guerrillas

Greece, Army of: on Crete, 46, 60; defense of Albanian front, 19, 23; and German invasion, 28, 32-33, 36-41; invasion of Albania, 19, 21, *22;* at Metaxas Line, 28, *36-37;* mountain tactics, 19; supply problems, 19; 3rd Mountain Brigade in Athens, 181, 183

Greece, National Guard, and Aris, 186

Greece, Navy of, 14

Greek-Americans, 179

Grivas, George, 181

Guerrillas, aliases, 153. *See also* Chetniks; Partisans

Guerrillas (Greece), *160-161;* airfield, 162; areas of operation, *154,* 155; attacks on German troop trains, 179; British attempt to demobilize, 181; demand political recognition, 162-163; and German political prisoners, *164;* island raids, *165;* kidnapping of German general, *166;* major German offensives against, 165; and National Bands agreement, 158, 162; and Operation *Animals,* 159; and Operations *Panther,* 164; organization of, 152-153; surrender of Italians to, 163. *See also* EDES; EKKA; ELAS

Gypsies, killed by Ustashi, 106

H

Hampe, Roland, 180

Hamson, Denys, 157, 162

Himmler, Heinrich: on Partisans, 95; on Tito, 142, 150

Hitler, Adolf: and airborne invasion of Crete, 44-45; Balkan policy, 17; and bombing of Belgrade, 26; decision to intervene in Greece, 22; directs invasion of Greece, 44; division of Yugoslavia, 74; halts negotiations with Partisans, 127; orders Greek surrender made to Italy, 32; orders invasion of Yugoslavia, 25; on paratroopers, 60; reaction to Italian invasion of Greece, 17; and reprisals against Yugoslav resistance, 78, 106

Hudson, D. T. "Bill," 78, 80, *81,* 114, 116

Hungary, control of part of Yugoslavia, 74; Soviet designs on, 178

Huot, Louis, 119, 122

I

Italy: claims on Trieste and Istria, 191; control of part of Yugoslavia, 74; surrenders to Allies, 118

Italy, Army of: and Chetniks, 86, 115-116; in Greece after Italian surrender, 163-164; high command, 21; invasion of Greece, 17, 19, 21, 22; invasion of Yugoslavia, 26; Julia Division, 19; at Louros valley, 153, 155; in Montenegro, 85; occupation of Albania, 17, *18,* 23; occupation of Greece, 152; occupation of Yugoslavia, *107, 108;* Operation *Weiss,* 115; plan for invasion of Greece, 17, 19; soldiers join Partisans, 119; in Yugoslavia after Italian surrender, 118-119

Italy, Navy of: and battle of Matapan, 24; and invasion of Crete, 52; withdrawn to Italian-controlled waters, 24

J

Jews, killed by Ustashi, 106

Jordan, Olaf, paintings by, *120-121*

K

Kardelj, Edvard, 146

King, Ernest J., forbids U.S. aid to British in Greece, 184-185

Kippenberger, Howard K., 49, 54

Klaras, Athanasios, 153. *See also* Velouchiotis, Aris

Kondylis, George, 10

Korneyev, N. V., 126

Koryzis, Alexander, 32

Kovacich, Ivan Goran, *136*

Kreipe, Heinrich, *166*

Kup, Geoffrey, *127*

L

Ladas, Alexis, 170, *174,* 175

Lanz, Hubert, 153, 155

Leckie, D. F., 48

Leeper, Reginald, 163

Leigh-Fermor, Patrick, *166*

List, Wilhelm, commands German forces in Greece, 36

Löhr, Alexander, commander of operations on Crete, 50

M

Macaskie, Frank, 180

McIntyre, Peter, 57

Maclean, Fitzroy, *119;* and Churchill, 118, 119, 122; and Partisans, 118, 119, 122, 127, 129; on Randolph Churchill, 118; and Tito-Churchill meeting, 187; and trial of Mihailovich, 193

McNeill, William Hardy, 182

MacVeagh, Lincoln, 184

Makiedo, Sergije, *117*

Manna, Operation, 179-180

Marija, 117

Matapan, battle of, 24

Mercury, Operation, 45

Metaxas, John, *10,* 16, 22

Metaxas Line, 28, *36-37*

Mihailovich, Dragoljub (Drazha), *78, 79;* aids U.S. airmen, 189; bounty offered for, 80, 126; British reassess support for, 114, 116; and Chetniks, 74-75; and coup against Prince Paul, 24; disenchantment with British, 116, 126; fame, 86; and government-in-exile, 75, 81, 86, 186; King Peter withdraws support for, 189; loss of influence, 126; meets with Germans, 80; in Montenegro, 86; retreats from Ravna Gora, 80; strategy, 75, 78, 80; and Tito, 78-79; trial and death, 192, 193

Morava, 117

Moss, Stanley, 166

Mussolini, Benito: on cold winter of 1940, 21; and Hitler's Balkan policy, 17; informed of invasion of Yugoslavia, 25; insists Greeks surrender to Italy, 32; intends to invade Yugoslavia, 17; and invasion of Albania, 18, 21-22; and Pavelich, *87;* plans to invade Greece, 17; replaces Badoglio, 21

Musulin, George, 189

Myers, Eddie, 155; and Aris, 155; assigned to work with guerrillas, 156; attempts to form unified non-Communist guerrilla group, 158, 162; and Cairo negotiations, 162-163; and ELAS, 158; and raid at Gorgopotamos, 155-156; sent to London, 163; and Zervas, 155

N

National Bands agreement, 158, 162-163

Nedich, Milan, 81

New Zealand, Army of: on Crete, 46, 47, 48, 50-51, 52, 54, *56,* 57, 65; at Galatas, 54, 56; in Greece, 45; at Maleme, 47-48, 50-51, 52, 54, 56; at Sphakia, 57

Noli, Fan S., *12*

O

Ochi Day, 16

P

Papandreou, George, 167; and civil war, 182; government established, 180-181

Papanicolis, 24

Parachute troops, German: and invasion of Crete, 44-45, 48-49, *58-59,* 60, 62, *63-65, 67,*